GOVERNING GLOBAL DERIVATIVES

Global Finance Series

Edited by
John Kirton, Munk Centre for International Studies, Trinity College, Canada,
Michele Fratianni, Indianna University, USA and
Paolo Savona, LUISS University, Italy

The intensifying globalisation of the twenty-first century has brought a myriad of new managerial and political challenges for governing international finance. The return of synchronous global slowdown, mounting developed country debt, and new economy volatility have overturned established economic certainties. Proliferating financial crises, transnational terrorism, currency consolidation, and increasing demands that international finance should better serve public goods such as social and environmental security have all arisen to compound the problem.

The new public and private international institutions that are emerging to govern global finance have only just begun to comprehend and respond to this new world. Embracing international financial flows and foreign direct investment, in both the private and public sector dimensions, this series focuses on the challenges and opportunities faced by firms, national governments, and international institutions, and their roles in creating a new system of global finance.

Also in the series

Full listing at the back of the book.

Governing Global Derivatives
Challenges and Risks

CHIARA OLDANI
University of Viterbo "La Tuscia", Italy

Routledge
Taylor & Francis Group
LONDON AND NEW YORK

First published 2008 by Ashgate Publishing

Published 2016 by Routledge
2 Park Square, Milton Park, Abingdon, Oxon OX14 4RN
711 Third Avenue, New York, NY 10017, USA

Routledge is an imprint of the Taylor & Francis Group, an informa business

British Library Cataloguing in Publication Data
Oldani, Chiara
  Governing global derivatives : challenges and risks. -
  (Global finance series)
  1. Derivative securities 2. Derivative securities - Law and
  legislation
  I. Title
  332.6'32

Library of Congress Cataloging-in-Publication Data
Oldani, Chiara.
  Governing global derivatives : challenges and risks / by Chiara Oldani.
  p. cm. -- (Global finance)
  Includes bibliographical references and index.
  ISBN 978-0-7546-7464-1 (hardback) 1. Derivative securities. I. Title.

  HG6024.A3O43 2008
  332.64'57--dc22

                                                                2008022322

ISBN 9780754674641 (hbk)

Contents

List of Figures and Graphs

List of Tables

Note on the Author

Chiara Oldani, born in Rome in 1975 and married to Andrea, has a PhD in Economics and Finance (Tor Vergata University, Rome); is currently Assistant Professor at the University of Viterbo "La Tuscia" and is a columnist for a leading Italian economics newsmagazine since 2005. She graduated *magna cum laude* at Luiss G. Carli University (Rome, Italy) and obtained a Master of Science in Economics at Warwick University (Coventry, UK). She spent part of her PhD at the Finance Department of the Wharton School of the University of Pennsylvania (USA), and visited the Cambridge Endowment for Research in Finance (UK) in 2007. She has been an economist at the Italian Institute of Economic Analysis, has won many scholarships and devoted most of her professional effort toward the study of derivatives. She has been teaching economics at undergraduate level at Luiss G. Carli University in Rome since 2002, and published her first book on derivatives in 2004.

Preface and Acknowledgements:
The Role of Derivatives in Governing
Global Finance

Derivatives world markets involve resources that are more than 10 times bigger than world GDP. Despite their size, the literature has devoted very little attention to their global effects, which materialized in a very negative and unexpected way in 2007. Apart from their size, these securities play a special role in the present international financial structure, which is highly deregulated and where there is little compensation for risks. Derivatives, as with other innovative financial securities in the history of economics and finance, deserve our attention because they contribute to modify the world financial system. The dominating finance theory relies on a perfect market hypothesis and considers the free market as the best scheme to design an efficient system; however, the perfect market hypothesis holds when rules and markets players are homogenous, which we will see is unfortunately not our situation.

Derivatives have been traded in the world financial system since the ancient Mesopotamian empire, 1,700 BC, when commodity-related risks were hedged by means of forward-future types of contracts, whose details and working were not very different from those traded today. The amazing dimension and growth of the world derivatives market can be demonstrated in a few figures: according to the BIS Triennial Survey released in December 2007, the average daily turnover of traditional foreign exchange derivatives has grown by an unprecedented 71 percent rate since April 2004, reaching US$4.2 trillion, which corresponds to an annual 20 percent increase; the average daily turnover rose by 65 percent in the same period. This increase was much stronger than the one observed in the previous survey, between 2001 and 2004. What is interesting to emphasise is that the composition of turnover by counterparty changed substantially. Transactions between reporting dealers and non-reporting financial institutions, such as hedge funds, mutual funds, pension funds and insurance companies, more than doubled between April 2004 and April 2007 and contributed more than half of the increase in aggregate turnover.

Table 1 Global derivatives market turnover*

Daily averages in April, in billions of US dollars				
	1998	*2001*	*2004*	*2007*
Foreign exchange turnover	959	853	1,292	2,319
Outright forwards and foreign exchange swaps	862	786	1,152	2,076
Currency swaps	10	7	21	32
Options	87	60	117	212
Other	0	0	2	0
Interest rate turnover**	265	489	1,025	1,686
FRAs	74	129	233	258
Swaps	155	331	621	1,210
Options	36	29	171	215
Other	0	0	0	1
Estimated gap in reporting	39	43	93	193
Total	1,265	1,385	2,410	4,198
Exchange-traded derivatives	1,382	2,198	4,547	6,173
Currency instruments	11	10	22	72
Interest rate instruments	1,371	2,188	4,524	6,101

Note: * Adjusted for local and cross-border double-counting. ** Single currency interest rate contracts only.
Source: BIS triennial survey on derivatives activity, 2007.

The virtues of derivatives justify their amazing growth: exchange-traded contracts are liquid, available at the world level, and traded on a 24-hour basis, with an ever increasing range of maturities and underlying assets; OTC contracts are designed around customers' needs, and then are flexible and non standardized. Derivatives break existing rules on accounting, monitoring and supervision, and this explains the most common perception of them, which is not very positive. Following some losses, Warren Buffett named derivatives "weapons of mass destruction", or "time bombs" in 2003. But, after a certain number of realized gains, he changed his mind, and in the 2007 shareholders' letter of Berkshire Hathaway, admitted the use of derivatives and showed the profits they brought to his fund. Buffett's opinion does not seem very consistent, but I believe that his change of mind is simply the result of deeper knowledge and more aware trading of such complex securities.

I want to contribute to the debate on derivatives by clarifying the role these securities play in the international financial system, which at present has a very unstable structure. Deregulated markets and players, such as hedge funds and subprime mortgages and lending, modify the structure of the system and its equilibrium by attracting resources under opaque rules, and altering the effectiveness of prudential rules (like Basle II) as well as diminishing the ability of international financial institutions to intervene successfully when a shock or crisis occurs. Derivatives have great virtues, but can contribute to exacerbate risks and losses if misused. This book is devoted to a wide range of readers: academics, professionals and civil servants, who are interested in the evolution of finance and should be aware of the potential negative effects of mismanagement and misreporting.

The introduction of the fair value accounting principle as the single measure for all financial securities in the balance sheet of banks, financial and non-financial institutions represents an important turning point, which should lead to a better representation of exposure to risks. At the same time, it can increase the firm's volatility and then affect its valuation by markets' participants. The ever-growing figures related to derivatives transactions pose a number of challenges with respect to financial globalization, which, at present, is highly unregulated. The number of derivatives-related crises are small, but their size is not. The LTCM, probably the best known and worse case ever of bankruptcy, registered some US$3.5 billion losses under the very small capitalization regime allowed for hedge funds. In 2008, the French bank Société Générale reported €4.9 billion losses related to positions taken by the equity derivatives desk. Since the bank does not operate under small capital, it recovered fast, the loss did not eliminate annual profits, but shareholders have been asked to intervene.

The deregulation process of financial markets and players has been the principle applied by US authorities, but, after the 2007 subprime mortgages crisis, doubts and concerns, domestically and at the international level, modified the strong belief that the market automatically comes back to equilibrium. In particular, the deregulation of OTC derivatives has been under scrutiny in the US since 2000, when the Security and Exchange Commission (SEC) testified to Congress to stimulate the development of a better regulatory framework for OTC. At present, since some transactions are not under the control of the Commodity Future Trading Commission (CFTC), nor under the Commodity Exchange Act (CEA) "derivatives products can be tailored to circumvent regulation or tax consequences". The approach of the SEC is that of increased legal certainty, and not of introducing bans or limits, since the SEC itself recognizes the strategic importance for firms of innovations such as OTC transactions. More recently, the SEC, CFTC, and Security Issue Board (SIB) have issued a common statement, based on which they will co-operate to a greater extent with respect to OTC derivatives. At the international level, the International Monetary Fund (IMF) has the duty of financial surveillance, and its mission should consider the evolving role and importance of the financial account of the balance of payments. At present, a crisis is more likely to originate in the financial account, than in the current account, as the first represents far more resources than the second in G10 countries. This evidence should be explicitly embodied in the Fund's mission. Cooperation with the other institution that has superior knowledge in the field of derivatives and banking regulation, the BIS, should increase up to the moment when supervision, surveillance and standard settlements are implemented by the same authority.

Financial markets evolve due, not to rule-based, but to principles-based regulation. By applying principles, rather than rigid rules, which will one day or another be circumvented, it is possible to align regulation to business practices at a reasonable cost.

Derivatives are leaders in the financial globalization process, and special types of contracts, like credit default swaps and currency derivatives, can be of help to achieve special objectives of the monetary authority. Derivatives play a role in the transmission mechanism of monetary policy; they influence the monetary aggregates, the portfolio substitution, the interest rate channel and the expectations setting. The monetary nature of derivatives refers to their influence on money for transactions. Derivatives, especially exchange-traded futures, can provide the central bank with relevant information, although they cannot be considered as policy instruments, nor as substitutes for a more comprehensive monetary analysis. Derivatives are partly responsible for the progressive lack of informative power of wide money aggregates, as in the case of M3 in the USA. However, they can be of help in determining a different informative relationship between money and the underlying economic activity. Monetary policy is an expectation management exercise, aiming at price and financial stability. The Taylor rule is the operational rule adopted by most monetary authorities, and it links the nominal interest rate to deviations of inflation and output from their target (or potential) levels. This rule can be equipped with another relevant piece of information coming from financial markets, which has been the source of concern for a number of monetary authorities over the last decade. The implied volatility of options written on marketable and liquid contracts can signal market instability, providing information to the authority.

Modern governments interact with financial markets in order to raise funds and manage expenses and outstanding public debt. They accept market rules, although, given their relative size and rule-setting ability, they can contribute to changing them. Derivatives can also be used to manage the tax burden of households. This behavior is limited to high-income and skilled taxpayers, but its effect are not negligible. Public debt management does not follow the same rules as those of corporate, or banking debt management. In particular, the accounting of financial instruments is not inspired by the IAS principles. If excessive risk is taken by non-monitored public administrations, the opaque representation of the actions of governments with derivatives and innovative instruments can pose severe stability problems. Moral hazard is due to the lack of accounting, control and monitoring. International financial institutions, like the IMF, face political problems in setting the principles according to which they should monitor how sovereign states invest in financial markets. The proposal by the Government Accounting Standard Board (GASB) has my outmost support, since it is starting to introduce the first, necessary, transparency in this field. Derivatives are widely used for public debt management by US states, developing countries and in Europe. The disclosure of information is not satisfactory, and this issue becomes even more relevant when evaluating the financial stability of highly indebted countries, like Italy. After greater local freedom was introduced, Italy was very active in the derivatives markets, at central and periphery levels, but a comprehensive picture of amounts, rules and future effects is not provided. A small and simplified IS-LM model is shown to describe the adverse effects of a certain amount of risk taking with derivatives for a highly indebted country, in cases where the (autonomous) monetary authority independently sets a preference over the short-run interest rates that is not compatible with the preference of the government (e.g. restrictive monetary policy in the presence of high outstanding debt). The interest rate is the key variable for monetary authority rule (Taylor rule), and we consider how it can be meaningfully implemented with derivatives for the pursuit of stability. The interest rate is also the price of debt, private and public, and I show how opposite (or different) expectations and preferences can lead to an undesirable outcome.

The interest rate is also the price of capital and investments. In the last part of the book we devote our attention to the process that leads to the investment decision, in which expectations play a key role. Since derivatives are able to incorporate expectations, they can be considered as having a role (i.e. signal) in the investment decision and, as a result, in the capital accumulation process. Special derivatives, macroeconomic option contracts, can be useful instruments to hedge on future performance of countries. In the future, I expect the settlement of a market for derivatives on investments: as powerful tools for macroeconomic risks hedging.

The investment decision can be addressed by considering the ability of derivatives to incorporate market expectations; moreover, the market price of assets changes over time, and the Tobin's Q can be modified and applied to derivatives. In perfect financial markets, the difference between investing in underlying and its derivatives should be null. But this is not verified empirically, since market expectation and risk change, modifying the risk premium on the basis of which investments are evaluated. The derivatives modified Q (*Replication Q*) can become an interesting tool to detect when market sentiment is changing; in these cases, any investment decision that relies on past performance is fundamentally mispriced. The hedging ability of derivatives can be employed to specify a stylized model of financial instability. Their contribution to stability is theoretically proved, but the model has non-linear solutions. The variables involved are interconnected in such a way that simple, two-directional relationships cannot be identified.

The interest rate is the price of money, of the public debt, and of a firm's investment. Derivatives, especially futures and options, both exchange traded and OTC, exhibit a relationship with the interest rate and are important in the transmission mechanism of impulses in the global financial system. These linkages are of dramatic importance when considering that financial flows are completely liberalized and deregulated. I support the development and applications of international projects able to clarify risks and accounting rules of such relevant resources, such as the GASB project for derivatives in the financial statement of governments, the IAS principles for corporate accounting, or the improvement of the IMF action. Financial global governance is missing, but global risks have not been eliminated by allowing free access to powerful financial securities to all operators. Financial derivatives are one of the most interesting expressions of animal spirits, but since we are not sure that markets can automatically reach equilibrium, nor that all market players are fully rational, we support a certain degree of monitoring over these securities. Derivatives have been referred to by practitioners in the field as being very similar to hell: easy to enter and almost impossible to get rid of. I hope this book will help in an understanding of both heaven and hell, and possibly light the way to the safest exit.

* * * *

I want to thank those who spent their precious time to improve my work: Rocco Ciciretti, Mardi Dungey, Michele Fratianni, John Kirton, Madeline Koch, Andrea Magrini, Rainer Masera, Sergio Scandizzo, and an anonymous referee. A special thanks to the Scientific Counselor of the "Guido Carli" Association, Paolo Savona, who supported the development of the research project, and to the Faculty of Political Sciences of the University of Viterbo "La Tuscia", which invested in human capital: me. A special thanks to Francesca Camilli, who always provides precious support, and to Maria Chiara Sangiovanni. I also gratefully thank Phillip Arestis, Giovanni Battista Aruta, Rita Arrigoni, Michele Bagella, Emilio Barone, the Cambridge Endowment for Research in Finance (CERF), Antonella De Benedictis, Giorgio Di Giorgio, the Department of Studies at the Faculty of Political Sciences (DISCOM), John Eatwell, Renato Maino, Domenico Nardelli, Fabio Neri, Francesco Nucci, Alan Rugman, Sally Simons, Salvatore Zecchini and Ferdinando Zullo.

A special word of thanks for Kirstin Howgate and her colleagues at Ashgate, for deciding to produce this volume long before derivatives became so popular, and for their efforts to ensure the publication of the manuscript.

Last but not the least, I thank my beloved husband for his never-ending patience, unconditional support and understanding given to my work in this very tough time of our lives.

Chiara Oldani, Viterbo, Italy
April 2008

Series Editor Preface

Derivatives have become a relevant issue in the working of modern economies; there is almost no economic transaction that takes place without some sort of a derivative attached to it. Over a fairly short period of time, derivatives have now reached the notional value of 10 times the value of world nominal GDP. We are living in a new era of capitalism, that of derivatives.

Derivatives have been produced by financial markets to manage risks and hedge, but soon speculation, similarly to what happened for other financial securities in the past, has overcome other functions, further underlying the issue of the stabilizing or destabilizing role played by these securities. Most of the literature has underlined the stabilizing role played by them, but has not distinguished between the transaction and speculative motives. The conclusion has been that derivatives are able to improve the market performance and efficiency, contributing to better manage risks.

The most relevant effort has been put by financial mathematicians to evaluate derivatives value and pricing mechanisms. On the other side, accountants have worked to introduce derivatives in the balance sheets, after years of considering them as off-balance sheet items.

Regardless of the theoretical progress reached by the literature, the pricing formulas of derivatives are based on assumptions which are difficult to verify empirically, and thus inevitably it has led to mistaken choices. From the crash of Long-Term Capital Management to the subprime mortgages crisis we have accumulated a number of events that has should give reason to reflect on the difficult task of evaluating these securities. Moreover, there is a clear risk that the present international architecture of control and supervision by rating agencies, national and international authorities generates moral hazard, if not outright frauds.

This book by Chiara Oldani, however, is not devoted to these relevant operational aspects of derivatives, which are briefly summarized in the first chapter, but focuses on the macroeconomic analysis and implications of derivatives, an issue neglected in the literature. Oldani studies the monetary nature, the effects on central banks operations, the growing use by fiscal authorities, the complex effects on the capital accumulation process, via the interest rate, the linkages of the investment decision and the rate of profit which characterizes an economy, and the effects on income distributions, via the effects on prices. The contribution by Chiara Oldani represents a comprehensive picture and opens a new stream of promising macro-economic analysis.

The recent subprime crisis confirms Warren Buffett's assessment that derivatives are a time bomb, and Alan Greenspan's judgment that monetary policy is no longer the same in the presence of derivatives. The same is true for fiscal policy. Oldani's position is that as a result of the use of derivatives for active public debt management fiscal policy has lost the characteristics described in textbooks.

The lack of awareness of effects of monetary and fiscal policy caused by derivatives prompts for an urgent and deep revision of acquired macroeconomic knowledge, after decades of studies and empirical investigations. This is the main reason to put this issue to the attention of readers, and publish Oldani's volume in the Governing Global Finance Series.

Paolo Savona

List of Abbreviations

ABS	Assets Backed Securities
BIS	Bank of International Settlements
CDO	Collateralized Debt Obligation
CDSO	Credit Default Swap Options
CFTC	Commodity Future Trading Commission
CPI	Consumer Price Index
CSO	Credit Spread Options
DSGE	Dynamic Stochastic General Equilibrium
EMU	European Monetary Union
ET	Exchange Traded
EU	European Union
FAS	Financial Accounting Standard
FASB	Financial Accounting Standards Board
FRS	Financial Report Standard
FSAP	Financial Services Action Plan
GASB	Governmental Accounting Standards Board
GDP	Gross Domestic Product
IAS	International Accounting Standard
IASB	International Accounting Standards Board
IEA	International Energy Agency
IMF	International Monetary Fund
IMFs	Institutional money funds
LTD	Large Time Deposit
MIFID	Market in Financial Instruments Directive
NK	New Keynesian
OI	Open Interest
OTC	Over the Counter
SDR	Special Drawing Right
SPV	Special Purpose Vehicle
TRS	Total Return Swaps

To Andrea and Marceline

Chapter 1

The Macroeconomics of Derivatives: The Issue of Measurement and Accounting

1. Introduction

Financial innovation, which is the process of creating new financial securities, following customers' needs and exploiting temporary faults in regulation, represents the natural evolution of markets, where players are looking for new profitable opportunities and better resource allocation. Innovation exploits the imperfections and inefficiencies of markets, avoids regulation, and gives rise to extra profits, specifically because at the beginning there is no patent protection. Innovation is the way animal spirits emerge on the market, and profits are the premium earned by the innovator.

Imperfections are inevitable ingredients of financial instability and innovation, but while instability usually has disruptive effects, innovation is part of a creative process. "Although difficult to define precisely, financial instability, in my view, connotes the presence of market imperfections or externalities in the financial system that are substantial enough to create significant risks for real aggregate economic performance" (Ferguson 2004). This definition of instability synthesizes its main ingredients, and stresses the main negative drawbacks: financial innovation should not create significant risks if is a positive force in the development process and does not introduce instability.

An important class of innovation is that of derivatives. Derivatives were introduced early in the history of international trade, in the ancient Middle East, to hedge commodity price risks, and today are traded in world stock exchanges, or over the counter (OTC). Exchange-traded (ET) derivatives have a well-established and solid market procedure and settlements system; OTC transactions are un-standardized and opaque, but not necessarily riskier. The Bank of International Settlements (BIS) is the international institution in charge of measuring OTC transactions, and plays a very important role in the disclosure of such opaque transactions.

The economic and financial characteristics of derivatives are fundamental to the understanding of the functions they play in investors' portfolios. The measurement of transactions -ET and OTC- is a necessary methodological premise to their valuation, and their relationship with the market, agents and the economy. The accounting of derivatives, following the introduction and application of the International Accounting Standard (IAS) No. 39 and the Financial Report Standard (FRS) No. 13, is inspired by fair value.

Derivatives are not considered to create new risks, but they can hide existing risks, and the knowledge and awareness of risk is fundamental to maintaining stability. Most cases of derivatives losses are basically due to mismanagement but this does not justify the lack of comprehensive statistics about the phenomenon.

2. A brief history of derivatives

Derivatives contracts are as old as trade. Swan (1999) dates first commodity futures back to ancient Mesopotamia (about 1700 B.C.E.); these contracts were very similar to those traded on stock exchanges nowadays. They were traded in temples, and priests acted as traders or brokers, while trading rules were based on religious principles (i.e. honor, faith, good management). Temples acted like modern exchanges, and the success of the deals was guaranteed by the religious organization, providing the necessary facilities (e.g. grain houses) and insurance against fraud. Ancient Mesopotamian derivatives were basically commodity contracts, since agriculture represented most of the economic activity in these areas. Settlement was possible using precious metals (silver, gold) or farming goods (barley, sesame, spices).

Private transactions were allowed and communities of local or foreign merchants governed by separate laws were a common feature of the Mesopotamian system, still present in the Middle East after the Crusades. Private transactions can be thought of as being non-standardized, similar to OTC contracts nowadays.

As merchants' needs increased, written rules started to be produced, the most famous of which is the Hammurabi Code. The kingdom of Hammurabi lasted between 1792 and 1750 B.C.E, and introduced two important developments for derivatives. The first was the possibility of future delivery, and the second the transferability of rights under a contract of sale. Codes and rules were ancient but not primitive, as Swan observed, and the introduction of written contracts avoided misunderstandings due to different languages and cultures. Mesopotamia was a very modern society, and private property was safeguarded. In a number of cuneiform written texts reporting contractual obligations, there are several sophisticated concepts that are still found in the law of trade. The Mesopotamian policy actively supported the creation of a sound trading system to support the production and trade of commodities and sustain the growth of the region.

A very distinct approach was that of the Egyptians, who did not recognize the strategic importance of private property, and this resulted in very slow development of the market economy. Rather like the Egypt of the Pharaohs, Greek culture was inspired by an undeveloped model of growth, where Greece bartered luxury goods, and conquered to obtain the others. Production models and incentives did not feature in the modern-style Greek democratic system.

The Roman Empire was centralized, and the city of Rome attracted most commodities produced in Europe (grain, clothing, or building materials). Although it was not forbidden, there was little room left for private free trade. The economy was based on agriculture and the army, and trade played a very minor role. The unified coinage and banking system represented a unique example of financial sophistication, unfortunately not supported by real economic development. The contribution of the Romans to derivatives trading, like many other things, lay in the juridical and legal system that governed it; however, the original Roman law system was quite slow and difficult to apply. It improved only after centuries, following the development in commerce and trade throughout the Mediterranean by the Italian cities of Amalfi, Naples, Venice and Bari during the ninth century. The use of derivatives became so common that at that time the municipal public deficit started to be funded through bonds and swaps[1].

The Champagne Fairs during the Middle Ages, and Italy during the Renaissance, were the European centers of private trading, including the development of contracts, payments' systems and commerce. On the other hand, the Church of Rome, "the promoter of the Roman law", was the sole entity allowed to regulate commerce, and was the "largest producer of commodities in Europe", since it was the largest landowner (Swan 1999, 124). After the seventeenth century, Northern Europe (UK and Holland) and North America (USA and Canada) were the most important centers of commodities or financial trade and promissory buying and selling. Derivatives markets were founded in Japan in the seventeenth century, and in Chicago (US) in the nineteenth century. Today, the latter is still the world's most important and biggest derivatives market.

While the trading of commodity derivatives still plays a relevant role in the world market, financial contracts involve more resources: the notional amount of commodity derivates reached US$7 billion, while OTC-only financial derivatives report US$370 billion.

---

1 For example, in 1164 the city of Genoa sold its future revenues to a group of investors called Monte in exchange for present payment (Swan 1999, 104).

Table 1.1 Commodity derivatives by instrument and type*

Notional amounts outstanding at end June 2007 (in millions of US dollars)			
Instrument/ counterparty	Gold	Precious metals	Other commodities (other than gold)
Forwards and swaps	140,927	42,245	3,404,656
Options sold	118,141	30,638	2,023,892
Options bought	230,012	25,121	2,439,400
Total options	284,608	45,581	3,648,655
Total contracts	425,535	87,825	7,053,311
Gross market value			
Total contracts	47,181	6,116	617,112

Note: * While data on total options are shown on a net basis, separate data on options sold and options bought are recorded on a gross basis, i.e. not adjusted for interdealer double counting.
Source: BIS Derivatives Statistics, 2007.

While derivatives, transactions involving uncertainty, are as old as commerce, I will show in this chapter how modern financial markets have exploited their characteristics. This was especially true after the 1970s, when capital controls were removed, fixed exchange rates were abolished and oil shocks were hitting the world economy. Moreover, the pricing theory of derivatives was developed in the 1970s, and the study on Brownian motion and Ito's work on stochastic processes led Black and Scholes to obtain the option's pricing formula.

Today's worldwide regulated markets, based on the year they were founded, are summarized in the following table. However, alliances and mergers, especially over recent years, make this far from straightforward. It is relevant to note, that Europe and the US show very different attitudes toward financial markets. In the US, specialized financial markets are popular and exploit international synergies, like the New York Stock Exchange (NYSE). In Europe, national borders, local interests and different legal rules make a single financial market still a very difficult goal to achieve, and the City of London dominates in terms of trading and liquidity.

Table 1.2 World derivatives exchange traded markets

Country	Market name	Starting year	Main underlying
France-US-UK-DL-NDL-BL-PT-IT	NYSE EuroNext**	2001	All
Germany-Swiss	EUREX	1990	Bonds, Repo, IR*
UK-Italy	LSE	2007	All
Singapore	SGX§-SIMEX°	1999	IR*, StockIndex
USA	CBOT	1849	Shares, StockIndex
USA	CBOE	1973	Shares
USA	CME°	1970s	Commodity

Note: * IR = interest rates. ** EuroNext.liffe is the international derivatives business of EuroNext, comprising the Amsterdam, Brussels, LIFFE, Lisbon and Paris derivatives markets. It was formed following the purchase of LIFFE (the London International Financial Futures and Options Exchange) by EuroNext in 2001. EuroNext.liffe is the world's leading exchange for Euro short-term interest rate derivatives and equity options. It also offers a greater choice of derivatives products than any other exchange: it offers futures and options on short- and long-term interest rate products, on equities, indices, government bonds and commodities. § The SGX is the result of the merger between the SIMEX and SES (Stock Exchange of Singapore) which took place in 1999. Derivates started to be traded in the '80s at SIMEX. ° They form the GLOBEX® Alliance which is the world's first electronic trading network for futures and option contracts. It enables the EuroNext Paris SA, the CME and the Singapore International Monetary Exchange (SIMEX) to trade each others' contracts around the clock.
Source: Markets' own websites.

Since the start of 2006, a merger and takeover wave among stock exchanges has been changing the structures of alliances, in turn widening the opportunities for investors and operators at a cross-border and transatlantic level. Examples of this include the various offers of friendly mergers among NASDAQ, the London Stock Exchange, EuroNext, the New York Stock Exchange (NYSE), Deutsche Borse and the Milan Stock Exchange. This aggregation process also involves exchange-traded futures markets[2].

Since monetary union, the European banking industry has been concentrating on working trans-nationally, and across different sectors (retail, investments, and so on). Aggregation in the financial sector, according to the *HausBank* system (i.e. the German-style financial structure where a bank is a retail, commercial and investment player, and eventually enters the insurance market), is aimed at differentiating risk

---

2 In March 2007 the Atlanta InterContinental Exchange (ICE) launched a hostile takeover on the Chicago Board of Trade (CBOT) and Chicago Mercantile Exchange (CME); the ICE already controls the London and Dublin futures' markets.

and returns. However, the experience provides contrasting results in performance, depending on the business sector, country, and the contingent business cycle. This wave, together with the spread of financial innovation, can modify the allocation of risks, concentrating them in the hands of a few market players, and it might alter the effectiveness of monitoring and supervision. The absence of a homogenous financial regulation is an obstacle toward complete financial integration.

Over recent years, financial institutions which specialize in OTC transactions have attracted the attention of large banks. Acquiring these financial boutiques, has enabled investments banks to conquer new market niches, while highly specialized operators have entered into a large financial group, diversifying their business risk. For example, ICAP Ltd, owned by Michael Spencer, a former London city broker, trades almost 40 percent of the interest-rate swaps on the global market, a half of US public debt OTC transactions and earns US$1.7 billion a year (data refers to 2005).

However, the opacity and scarce disclosure of information, which characterizes OTC derivatives, can increase the risk exposure (i.e. credit, liquidity and, especially, counterpart risks). The nature of derivatives, a powerful risk management instrument and a speculative tool at the same time, reflects the nature of animal spirits, which manifest themselves by pushing for innovation and in risk taking.

Table 1.3a Derivative financial instruments traded on organized exchanges

By instrument and location

Notional principal (in billions of US dollars)

	Futures					Options				
	Dec 2003	Dec 2004	Dec 2005	Dec 2006	Sept 2007	Dec 2003	Dec 2004	Dec 2005	Dec 2006	Sept 2007
All markets	**13,752.9**	**18,903.7**	**21,619.3**	**25,699.8**	**28,638.5**	**23,034.0**	**27,688.8**	**36,197.0**	**44,811.9**	**66,244.8**
Interest rate	13,123.7	18,164.9	20,708.8	24,472.8	27,178.6	20,793.7	24,604.1	31,588.3	38,170.2	56,453.8
Currency	79.9	103.5	107.6	178.4	189.1	37.9	60.7	66.1	78.6	120.9
Equity index	549.3	635.2	802.9	1,048.6	1,270.8	2,202.4	3,024.0	4,542.6	6,563.1	9,670.1
North America	**7,700.0**	**10,465.9**	**12,326.8**	**13,745.0**	**14,711.8**	**11,804.0**	**17,142.6**	**24,067.4**	**28,808.5**	**37,620.9**
Interest rate	7,384.6	10,043.6	11,855.2	13,079.7	13,973.3	10,381.8	15,286.7	21,255.4	24,844.7	32,066.2
Currency	64.9	91.5	90.7	136.4	120	18.5	40.6	28.3	32.6	52.1
Equity index	250.4	330.7	380.8	528.9	618.6	1,403.7	1,815.2	2,783.8	3,931.2	5,502.6
Europe	**4,363.2**	**5,972.3**	**6,284.8**	**8,149.3**	**9,349.2**	**11,043.2**	**10,335.5**	**11,697.7**	**15,120.1**	**27,183.9**
Interest rate	4,200.2	5,756.1	6,050.5	7,800.8	8,921.4	10,357.2	9,282.0	10,235.7	12,756.4	23,377.5
Currency	0.3	0.3	2.4	1.9	5.1	0.3	0.5	0.6	0.7	0.8
Equity index	162.7	215.9	231.9	346.6	422.7	685.8	1,053.0	1,461.4	2,363.0	3,805.6
Asia and Pacific	**1,531.2**	**2,293.8**	**2,695.0**	**3,382.3**	**3,994.1**	**128.7**	**133.1**	**319.0**	**679.6**	**1,098.9**
Interest rate	1,395.4	2,208.0	2,509.8	3,204.0	3,766.5	44.2	13.7	67.4	458.8	803.4
Currency	3.4	3.7	4.3	25.1	39.7	–	–	–	–	–
Equity index	132.5	82.0	180.9	153.1	187.9	84.5	119.4	251.6	220.8	295.4
Other markets	**158.5**	**171.6**	**312.7**	**423.3**	**583.4**	**58.0**	**77.6**	**112.9**	**203.7**	**341.2**
Interest rate	143.4	157.2	293.2	388.3	517.5	10.6	21.7	29.8	110.3	206.6
Currency	11.3	7.9	10.2	15.0	24.4	19.0	19.5	37.2	45.4	68.1
Equity index	3.7	6.6	9.3	19.9	41.6	28.4	36.4	45.8	48.0	66.5

Source: [Tables 1.3a and 1.3b] Table No. 23a of BIS Statisics on Derivatives.

Table 1.3b Derivative financial instruments traded on organized exchanges

By instrument and location

Notional principal (in billions of US dollars)

Turnover

	2005	2006	Q4 2006	Q1 2007	Q2 2007	Q3 2007
Futures						
All markets	1,005,818.6	1,262,958.7	310,485.3	378,225.4	374,721.2	457,698.2
Interest rate	939,590.2	1,169,331.9	285,329.8	346,198.5	339,546.4	413,551.2
Currency	11,126.2	15,276.0	4,354.5	4,701.5	4,704.1	5,592.0
Equity index	55,102.3	78,350.8	20,801.0	27,325.5	30,470.7	38,555.2
North America	564,237.1	713,938.4	175,222.7	209,852.4	201,317.7	253,078.7
Interest rate	529,120.9	667,386.3	162,514.7	195,063.9	185,593.5	232,389.9
Currency	10,258.4	13,685.3	3,901.7	4,175.8	4,063.6	4,855.7
Equity index	24,857.9	32,866.8	8,806.2	10,612.7	11,660.6	15,833.1
Europe	380,613.0	455,731.2	111,469.4	139,779.1	140,768	169,887.4
Interest rate	362,066.3	428,002.8	103,689.0	128,691.4	128,565.2	155,556.5
Currency	37.0	47.0	13.3	17.6	15.4	42.9
Equity index	18,509.7	27,681.4	7,767.2	11,070	12,187.5	14,277.9
Asia and Pacific	53,091.5	82,641.9	20,825.1	24,863.4	27,509.8	29,929
Interest rate	41,666.7	65,714.3	16,864.0	19,730.6	21,569.3	22,229.6
Currency	133.7	282.9	109.3	44.8	46.1	82.4
Equity index	11,291.2	16,644.7	3,851.8	5,088	5,894.4	7,617
Other markets	7,877.0	10,647.2	2,968.1	3,730.6	5,125.8	4,803.2
Interest rate	6,736.3	8,228.5	2,262.1	2,712.5	3,818.4	3,365
Currency	697.1	1,260.8	330.2	463.3	579.1	611
Equity index	443.6	1,157.8	375.8	554.8	728.3	827.2

Table 1.3b continued

By instrument and location

Notional principal (in billions of US dollars)

Turnover

	2005	2006	Q4 2006	Q1 2007	Q2 2007	Q3 2007
Options						
All markets	**402,594.7**	**546,523.3**	**120,630.7**	**153,948**	**161,743.3**	**223,462.3**
Interest rate	328,778.9	446,106.0	95,835.8	120,490.3	123,125.8	180,078.6
Currency	943.7	1,119.9	317.7	376.9	517.9	588.7
Equity index	72,872.1	99,297.4	24,477.1	33,080.8	38,090.6	42,795,1
North America	**254,511.2**	**361,374.9**	**78,502.6**	**94,778.5**	**101,709.1**	**128,430**
Interest rate	229,976.4	326,268.9	69,238.2	83,209.9	88,755,7	114,188.2
Currency	449.0	453.1	120.8	128	140	155
Equity index	24,085.8	34,652.8	9,143.6	11,440	12,813	14,063
Europe	**105,908.1**	**127,098.7**	**29,338.9**	**41,516.3**	**38,804.9**	**70,731**
Interest rate	96,704.2	113,638.3	25,275.7	35,610	32,413	63,635
Currency	7.6	10.4	4.3	1,7	1,5	1,6
Equity index	9,196.2	13,449.9	4,058.9	5,905	6,389	7,093
Asia and Pacific	**40,312.1**	**55,064.2**	**11,973.4**	**16,551**	**19,923**	**22,781**
Interest rate	1,947.8	5,593.7	1,125.6	1,426	1,723	1,948
Currency	–	–	–	–	–	–
Equity index	38,364.4	49,470.5	10,847.9	15,124	18,200	20,832
Other markets	**1,863.2**	**2,985.6**	**815.7**	**1,102**	**1,296**	**1,520**
Interest rate	150.4	605.0	196.3	243	233	306
Currency	487.1	656.4	192.6	247	376	431
Equity index	1,225.7	1,724.2	426.8	611	687	782

3. The Bank for International Settlements

Due to its regulatory and information role with respect to the banking systems of member countries, the most important source of data on OTC derivatives is the Bank for International Settlements (BIS) of Basle. The aim of the BIS is to promote banking regulation and settlement standards. The BIS was founded in 1930. It is one of the oldest financial institutions of the Western world, and is at the center of international cooperation in the economic and banking worlds. The name of the bank comes from its original function, that is, to act as a trust fund for World War I reparations, the Dawes and Young Debt Programs (i.e. international loans for reconstruction) and to promote international banking cooperation. After the payments for reconstruction were abolished, cooperation among central banks became increasingly important for monetary and financial stability. After 1930, cooperative meetings between central banks have regularly been hosted by the BIS. In addition, the BIS has a monetary and financial research department, which contributes substantially to the analysis and implementation of statistics.

Apart from its role in promoting monetary cooperation, the BIS is a traditional bank for the community of central banks (e.g. for gold and currencies transactions), and acts as a trust agency or fund.

The BIS publishes important statistics on banking systems, on government debt issued overseas and at home, on ET and OTC derivatives. While ET data are also available from stock exchanges, the BIS is one of the few sources of OTC data, together with national central banks, the International Monetary Fund and specialized authorities, like the International Swaps and Derivatives Associations. The BIS works also with the Organization for Economic Cooperation and Development (OECD) and the World Bank (WB) on compiling foreign debt statistics.

Banking statistics at the BIS are an important part of the cooperation mission. They were first introduced in response to the Eurodollar, which is an offshore asset for non-US banks, and to the increasing exposure of industrialized countries' banks to emerging countries' debt.

The improvement of banking statistics with respect to the geographical distribution of transactions was originally pushed by the spread of the Eurodollar. Offshore monetary circulation poses problems, in regard to the multiplication of money and the control of liquidity, which influence the transmission mechanism. At the domestic level, money multiplication is controlled by means of supervision on the banks, with compulsory reserves, capital ratios and monitoring. When a foreign currency circulates freely, it is not always possible to apply prudential and quantitative rules, as it is difficult to control the supply. This leads to a problem for the central bank over its sovereignty, which is the basis of its autonomy from the government[3], since monetary control is not granted in the modified environment.

---

3 Fratianni and Savona (1973) give an important monetary analysis of the Eurodollar phenomenon, which is similar to that of derivatives.

The experience of the Eurodollar is similar to the one of derivatives, since statistics and supervision evolve after players have widely exploited the markets.

The BIS provides locational banking statistics and consolidated international banking statistics. The first are quarterly purchases and selling of international bonds by banks and financial institutions resident in a country. The aim of the statistics is to provide information on the role of banks and financial intermediaries in capital flows and intermediation. The present statistical system is made up from 39 countries and considers the headquarters of banks and counterparties. As a separate entry it also considers gross exposure and branches. The statistical methodology is consistent with national accounting, balance of payments and foreign debt.

Consolidated international banking statistics represent the operations of banks outside domestic borders; the need for this information increased during the Mexican crisis (1983) especially with respect to the activity of banks in emerging countries. Data represent the total risk exposure of the headquarters to all branches on a world-consolidated basis, net of internal operations. They can underline who is bearing the credit risk, and provide information on maturities, liquidity and sector risk. Data are available from 1999 onward, and provide a measure of net exposure of instruments to lower credit risk (e.g. collateral).

From the first quarter of 2005, the BIS has provided more refined statistics on the foreign activity of banks, based on risk exposure, information on derivatives, and guarantees issued.

In March 2007, the BIS issued a "Report on New Developments in Clearing and Settlement Arrangements of OTC Derivatives." Major OTC dealers in G10 countries and Hong Kong were interviewed to look at trading arrangements and risk management procedures in order to evaluate potential risks. The Report "focuses on six issues, of which three had already been discussed in the Report issued in 1998 on 'OTC Derivatives: Settlement Procedures and Counterparty Risk', and three others have caught the Group's attention during its discussions with OTC derivatives dealers and service providers: (1) the risks created by delays in documenting and confirming transactions; (2) the implications of the rapidly expanding use of collateral to mitigate counterparty credit risks; (3) the potential for expanding the use of central counterparty (CCP) clearing to reduce counterparty risks; (4) the implications of OTC derivatives prime brokerage; (5) the risks associated with unauthorized novations of contracts; and (6) the potential for significant market disruptions from the closeout of OTC derivatives transactions following the default of a large market participant. The report concludes that, since 1998, the clearing and settlement infrastructure of OTC derivatives markets has been significantly strengthened." There are still some concerns about the relevant size of dealers, and the potential effect of default on market liquidity, and on post-trading procedures. However, it seems that the market has improved to the advantage of transactions.

The BIS plays a strategic knowledge role; it also contributes to the analysis, with its Quarterly Review, and is promoting a more detailed statistics collection on a wide range of securities.

4. Hedge funds

I now turn my attention to hedge funds because they are the most interesting example of deregulated financial players. A hedge fund is a private investment fund that charges a performance fee and is open to only a limited range of qualified investors, and its investment activity is limited only by the contract governing the particular fund. Alfred Winslow Jones is credited with inventing hedge funds in 1949[4]. While there is no legal definition of hedge funds under US securities laws and regulations, they usually include any investment fund that involves more complex and riskier investments, which brokerage firms or investment advisers can invest in because of an exemption from the types of regulation that otherwise apply to mutual funds. Hedge funds have acquired a solid reputation for secrecy in the financial community. Unlike open-to-the-public retail funds (e.g. US mutual funds or European investment funds), which market freely to the public, in most countries, hedge funds are specifically prohibited from marketing to investors who are not professional or are not individuals with sufficient private wealth[5]. To a certain extent, this limits the information hedge funds are compelled to release; it also keeps secret the business interests of the fund. As their name implies, hedge funds often seek to offset potential losses in the principal markets they invest in by employing hedging strategies. However, many of these so-called "hedge funds" do not actually hedge their positions at all, but exhibit a risk-loving attitude in their portfolio.

The 2008 Hedge Fund Asset Flows and Trends Report published by Hedge Fund.net and Institutional Investor News estimates that total industry assets reached US$2.68 trillion in Q3 2007. However, there are no official statistics available. Looking at markets where they invest, we know that hedge fund activity in the public securities markets has grown substantially: it constitutes approximately 30 percent of all US fixed-income security transactions; 55 percent of US activity in derivatives with investment-grade ratings; 55 percent of the trading volume for emerging-market bonds, as well as 30 percent of equity trades (data refer to 2007). Hedge funds play a strategic role in financial markets, since they raise huge amounts of resources from their shareholders, and can invest in the way they prefer. Hedge Funds dominate certain specialty markets, such as trading in derivatives with high-yield ratings, and distressed debt.

---

4   Cf. "Hedge Fund" on Wikipedia, and Black (2004).
5   In Europe the minimum endowment for an investor to enter a hedge fund is €500,000.

The most popular hedge fund in the recent history of finance is probably the Long-Term Capital Management (LTCM), which earned amazing profits in the 90s, and then bankrupted over an incredibly short period (i.e. weeks) after the Russian default (Jorion 1999). While hedge funds are not intermediaries that raise funds from households or non-professional investors, their relatively large size has attracted the attention of regulators. Hedge funds have few disclosure requirements, and no explicit size limits. Moreover, contrary to requirements for banks and other regulated financial institutions, they have no limit of capital ratio type. Because of this freedom, they can operate with almost zero capital, by means of collateralized loans, and circumvent the prudential regulation on soundness and liquidity (such as the Basel II and the IAS rules).

The system of collateralized loans and securities moves risks from the originator of the security to final holders, who can be physically far removed and not completely aware of what has been collateralized. Credit rating is the vehicle through which risks and returns are sold. The US Congress intervened in 2006 to improve the financial environment and try to solve the conflict of interest between credit rating agencies and their customers. This conflict is as old as finance and commerce, since there is a clear incentive to cheat on customers' creditworthiness, if customers pay the agency to be rated. The US Agency Act states that rating agencies cannot sell any other service to their customers, and that the credit rating can be modified, even after the issuance (of any type of security), if conditions change. This rule was introduced in order to avoid, in Professor Coffee of Columbia University's terms, the downgrading that is an "obituary: when credit rating agencies downgrade a firm, investors are left with scratch paper, and no defense." (*The Epoch Times*, 2007) The power of inspectors has been reinforced, in order to avoid any circumvention of the new rules.

As with derivatives, which are the product of financial freedom, hedge funds are the products of deregulation of financial intermediaries. In the next chapter we describe the subprime crisis, where deregulation plays a key role, and explain to a greater extent our position. At present, there is a clear push toward stronger regulation of hedge funds and other non-traditional financial intermediaries or investors, such as sovereign wealth funds, to improve market structures and restore market expectations. In the recent past, the US Federal Reserve and the Security and Exchange Commission actively used moral suasion as a tool to restore markets expectations[6], while the lender of last resort function was used with far more caution. While stronger regulation can achieve the desired stability, it can also act like sand in the wheel, that is, exacerbating the negative effects of the turmoil. The central banker in the globalized financial world has the very difficult job of balancing the pros and cons.

---

6 In the case of the LTCM, the US Fed used its maximum dissuasive power with respect to counterparty banks of the fund, which finally agreed to buy all LTCM stakes and honor its debts. In this way, no market participants suffer any loss, other than counterparties of the fund, which lend the fund under very small capitalization.

5. National statistics on derivatives

Statistical data on derivatives at the domestic level consider transactions among domestic market players and should provide a picture of the flow of funds; statistics have changed over the last decade and details are improving. Three parties are involved in exchange-traded (ET) derivatives transactions: the buyer and the seller and the clearing-house. The clearing-house is the institution that contributes to lower the default risk by imposing margins (opening and maintenance) proportional to the position. To open a position in derivatives (future, option, etc.) long or short, it is necessary to pay a sum, based on the nominal value of the contract, the margin, which guarantees the counterpart in case of default. The margin is the daily loss/revenue and is cash settled. When the price oscillates and the (initial) margin is not enough to cover the risk (i.e. loss), the clearing-house asks for repayment (maintenance margin). The clearing-house finances itself within the system and covers the entire loss in case of default of one part (buyer or seller). Margins' system (or premium for options) lowers the default risk and does not influence the systematic risk of the financial transaction.

The dimension of the contract is standardized with respect to the minimum and maximum size, and stock exchange prudential regulation and risk monitoring systems are applied. Trading on regulated exchanges are reported in the standard financial statistics, also if the nature of these transactions is different, given the presence of a third part, the clearing-house, which guarantees the settlement of transactions, and the mechanism of margins and premium, i.e. the leverage.

Relevant data on derivatives refers to over the counter (OTC) transactions, that is, operations between (big) market players outside regulated markets, not standardized, with no clearing house, and without the payment of margins or premium. OTC transactions are highly tailored to the customers' needs and are less transparent, but involve higher amounts; being less transparent and so more risky, it is more difficult to enter these transactions. Only big players with an important credit standing and a solid reputation can enter this market. This justifies the higher average dimension, on one side, and the lower default rate, on the other. The huge profits these deals provide are the best way to disincentive moral hazard or fraud.

The code of conduct is the voluntary rule of law applied in these markets, and is inspired by best practices' principles[7]. The enforcing power of codes of conduct, typical of the Anglo-Saxon business world, does not rely on laws or rules, but on the reputation of market players. The market does not crash because the incentive is towards efficiency and good faith in transactions. This is also the reason why it is difficult to apply codes of conducts to other markets (i.e. in the Roman law system). Examples are the small financial boutiques that specialize in particular OTC transactions, and earn billions of dollars each year (ICAP Ltd.).

---

7   An example is the International Organization of Securities Commissions (IOSCO) code of conduct for credit rating agencies.

The most comprehensive statistical report on derivatives is the triennial report of the BIS, published in the spring[8]. The BIS Quarterly Review provides the main synthetic statistics (turnover, nominal value by currency, instrument and counterpart), especially for OTC. According to the BIS triennial survey released in December 2007, the average daily turnover of traditional foreign exchange derivatives has grown by an unprecedented 71 percent since April 2004, to US$ 3.2 trillion, and the average daily turnover rose by 65 percent. This increase was much stronger than the one observed between 2001 and 2004. It is interesting to note the substantial change in the composition of turnover by counterparty: transactions between reporting dealers and non-reporting financial institutions, such as hedge funds, mutual funds, pension funds and insurance companies, more than doubled between April 2004 and April 2007 and contributed more than half of the increase in aggregate turnover. The average daily turnover in OTC foreign exchange and interest rate contracts went up by 74 percent relative to the previous survey in 2004, to reach US$4,198 billion in April 2007, which corresponds to an annual 20 percent increase.

Over the last few years, national statistics have improved at a very high speed. For example, the Italian central bank has started computing derivatives in the financial accounts of the economy among other securities owned by the private sector. The domestic trading of derivatives (i.e. among domestic investors) is reported, and with respect to households and firms, the figure is entered as "other financial investments"[9]. Derivatives computed in these (domestic) entries are both ET and OTC, with a value computed according to the IAS No. 39 (i.e. measured at the market value at the end of the period, and not on the basis of the historical cost). Values reported are those given to the BIS on a quarterly basis, and are very volatile. For this reason, the statistical measurement and accounting could be revised in the near future. The figure from the financial account of the national accounting refers to (net) trading and, as a result, can be linked with the attractiveness and growth of the market.

The public sector is an important domestic player in the derivatives market. Sovereign states and local administrations can be active in these types of transactions, on the basis of the financial freedom they have in choosing their investment tools. A more detailed analysis is presented in third chapter, which addresses to fiscal policy, but we can anticipate that states do not play a minor role, especially in the market of interest-rate OTC contracts, employed to hedge outstanding debt and manage related costs.

---

8   The next report, on years 2004–2007, will be released in spring 2008.
9   Trading between non-domestic investor(s) is reported in the balance of payments.

6. International statistics on derivatives

International statistics on derivatives refer to transactions between non-domestic players, and play a relevant role in the presence of international capital mobility. The analysis of international flows is relevant in the presence of integrated and globalized financial markets; the most relevant document that registers financial flows is the balance of payments. The accounting standards are based on the rules issued by the International Monetary Fund in its *Balance of Payments Manual 5* (BPM5), implemented by all member countries since 2000. Before its application, financial securities were not reported in any detail. The present scheme is the response to the need to describe financial flows and wealth movements in more detail in a financially globalized world. As with other financial securities, before the BPM5, derivatives were not taken into consideration in capital flows.

Cross-border derivatives represent a substantial share of whole transactions. As confirmed by the Federal Reserve Bulletin (May, 2007), the omission of these transactions can lead to mistaken inferences on what is driving the international investment position of a country. A number of issues need to be clarified in order for any accounting rule to be really useful. Derivatives positions can, at different times, be either assets or liabilities (e.g. periodical payments associated to a swap contract) and may switch from one to the other many times before they expire. Moreover, periodical payments associated with derivatives contracts can have ambiguous interpretations: payments can be considered as returns on invested capital, which is a current account entry, or as realized gains-losses, which is entered in the financial account. The International Monetary Fund has recommended considering them in the financial account. According to the US Federal Reserve Bulletin, the inclusion of derivatives net settlements in the US balance of payments (and the rest of the world) would have lowered the statistical discrepancy of roughly 20 percent observed today, providing a final picture for the year 2006 where net world transactions in derivatives approach zero (as expected) and effective risk exposure emerges clearly.

Table 1.4 Aggregate cross border derivatives claims and liabilities, and net positions in derivatives for selected foreign countries, the US and the world 2000–2005

Year/Country	Australia	Denmark	France	Hong Kong	Italy	Japan	Netherlands	United Kingdom	USA	World excl. USA	World
Claims											
2000	13	14	95	17	4	3	29	669	n.a.	876	876
2001	15	11	110	18	4	3	45	858	n.a.	1,101	1,101
2002	20	31	108	23	11	3	72	1,245	n.a.	1,562	1,562
2003	33	24	136	20	23	5	87	1,393	n.a.	1,803	1,803
2004	38	37	169	22	28	6	86	1,594	n.a.	2,087	2,087
2005	27	9	226	17	30	26	70	1,761	1,190	2,626	3,452
Liabilities											
2000	13	13	98	13	3	3	24	674	n.a.	869	869
2001	13	11	105	12	5	4	49	861	n.a.	1,088	1,088
2002	21	28	112	21	9	4	87	1,259	n.a.	1,579	1,579
2003	37	20	148	20	16	7	95	1,424	n.a.	1,848	1,848
2004	38	33	175	21	26	11	99	1,624	n.a.	2,132	2,132
2005	28	0	243	17	38	33	87	1,780	1,132	2,317	3,449

Table 1.4 continued

Year/Country	Australia	Denmark	France	Hong Kong	Italy	Japan	Netherlands	United Kingdom	USA	World excl. USA	World
Net position (Claims less Liabilities)											
2000	-1	1	-3	4	1	0	5	-5	n.a.	7	7
2001	2	0	5	5	0	-1	-5	-3	n.a.	13	13
2002	-1	2	-4	1	2	0	-15	-14	n.a.	-17	-17
2003	-3	3	-11	0	7	-2	-8	-32	n.a.	-45	-45
2004	0	4	-6	1	2	-5	-13	-30	n.a.	-45	-45
2005	-1	9	-17	0	-8	-7	-17	-19	58	-55	3

Note: [Billions of US dollars, yearly]. Components may not sum to total because of rounding. World totals include positions of countries not shown. US claims are aggregated gross positive fair values, and US liabilities are aggregated gross negative fair values. The claims and liabilities positions of some countries include values reported on a net basis. For countries other than the US, data on cross-border claims liabilities, and net positions for years-end were not available as of the publication date.
Source: Federal Reserve Bulletin May 2007, A14.

The homogenous international accounting of financial flows is necessary to monitor effective financial flows among countries, to make inferences about the attractiveness of markets and securities, and to consider risk aversion and international portfolio diversification or diversion. In order to draw any policy implication, the statistics of balance of payments should have a single, unambiguous interpretation.

Non-domestic exchange-traded derivatives transactions are reported in the balance of payments of each country, in the financial account. Since there are no margins or standardization for OTC transactions, these are not reported in the balance of payments, thus omitting a huge part of cross-border flows.

The financial account reports capital flows on the basis of the type of securities that are purchased: stocks, bonds and similar securities are reported on the basis of their market values at the end of the period as credit or debt, and indirectly reflect the country's attractiveness. A net credit in stocks, like the one exhibited by the US, is the mirror of the ability to raise funds abroad, and attract foreign savings. The interpretation of the net figure in the financial account is quite straightforward, once it is corrected for the exchange rates variation observed in the period, which can affect the overall investment decision[10].

On the other hand, the method of measurement of derivatives in the financial account is completely different. As testified by the US government, there is an objective difficulty in "measuring" the contribution of a security, which can be considered as an asset or a liability at the same time[11]. This difficulty is translated into the way derivatives contribution is computed, which is unlike that of any other "traditional" financial security.

Derivatives are measured as the net sum of margins and premiums for cross-borders trading; margins and premiums represent the effective liquidity invested, and are usually a low proportion of nominal value of the contracts (one to two percent). A credit of margins means that derivatives transactions produce an inflow of margins or premiums, which can be due to the fact that they are sold by domestic intermediaries, or that they refer to gains in margins or premiums[12]. Nevertheless, nothing can be inferred about the "underlying" derivative transactions. A net credit of margin means that foreign investors bought domestic derivatives (i.e. traded in the country), but nothing is known about the nature of the purchases (long or short) or about the nature of the underlying asset of the derivative, which can be foreign currency denominated or not.

---

10   The return of the investment abroad is the result of the effective rate of return of the security (dividend and/or price increase), and on the exchange rate; the decision to invest abroad is influenced by a number of variables, some of which are linked to the limited rationality of agents (e.g. the home bias).

11   See, among others, De Santis (2007), who describes the dynamics of the US imbalance and devotes a paragraph on the way derivatives are accounted.

12   An example is the premium earned by the option seller, in case the option is not exercised.

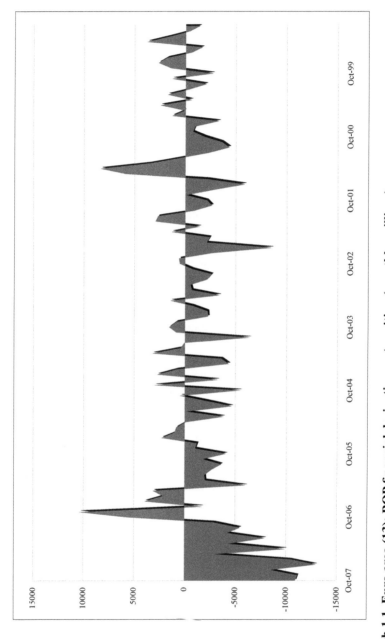

Graph 1.1 Euro area (13): BOP financial derivatives net position (monthly, millions)
Source: ECB statistical warehouse.

A positive number in the financial account of the balance of payments means that credits of margins are higher than debts, but we can infer nothing about the effective flows of derivatives, nor about market expectations, or investor preferences.

Information from other financial accounts' entries describes the effective exposure of the country: a net credit of the financial account means that foreign investors prefer our assets, and that domestic investors prefer home assets. However, how can we interpret a net flow of margin? As it is very unlikely that a credit of margin would correspond entirely to long positions on derivatives written on domestic underlying, then any comment on this entry is necessarily brief and not very deep. More important for an understanding of actual international trading would be the effective exposure: gross market value for OTC and turnover for ET derivatives should be broken down on the basis of flows of funds, as it is for other securities. This information would be interesting and, in all probability, would change the international equilibrium analysis.

7. Measurement methods

In order to understand the economic analysis, the premise of the measurement method is necessary. The BIS reports statistics on OTC derivatives transactions on the basis of:

1. the nominal value, the sum of positions (short or long) corrected for double counting[13];
2. the gross market value, the gross value of positions open in the market;
3. the turnover, number of contracts bought or sold on the market.

The geographical distribution of counterparties is useful to link financial flows with market performance, risks, expectations, and interest and exchange rates variations. The BIS looks at the nature of counterparty, and in particular at: dealers, other financial institutions, and non-financial institutions. This detail is very important for economic analysis. Banks and financial intermediaries have a natural interest in financial trading, whereas a non-financial firm or the government can pursue different goals by means of these instruments, especially if they are opaque.

Measurement methods of exposure are principally of three types: at nominal value, gross market value, and turnover. The nominal value is the measure of market dimension and potential price risk of the transfer of derivatives. The nominal value is the equivalent of spot market dimension for traditional securities (e.g. shares and bonds), and its growth rate and relative weight, with respect to the underlying are useful signs. Gross market value is the sum of the gross position

---

13   Double counting is due to the presence of traders and brokers, who can operate in their own name or that of the client.

opened with positive or negative value, evaluated at market price at the moment of measurement. It represents the transfer of price risk, which takes place on the market and is probably the best measure of derivatives market dimension. The turnover measures the market activity and liquidity; it is the gross absolute value of transactions settled, but not closed in the month. The location of the transaction is reported as the base of the operation, regardless of the headquarters of the parties involved. Each trader should report separately how many operations are involved with its branches and affiliates, to avoid double counting. For OTC transactions, there are no margins or premium, since they are traded on the basis of the collateralization agreements.

8. The accounting of derivatives in the balance sheet

As with other financial securities, derivatives should be represented in the balance sheet and the representation should be reliable, truthful and transparent. The accounting of derivatives transactions is a very controversial issue; the political economy debate focuses on the adoption of a unique measurement principle, which can reflect market size and growth. The choice, reflected in the international regulation, has been in favor of the fair value, instead of the historical costs, widely applied in the recent past. The mark to market accounting of derivatives, and other financial securities, is fundamental to represent clearly and transparently the effective exposures. In the recent past, financial markets experienced sustained growth rates, both in terms of price and volume, but this increase was not reflected in the financial accounts of firms, when the historical costs principle was applied. The fair value valuations have also increased because of recent corporate scandals, which altered investors' confidence. The International Accounting Standard Board (IASB) and other international accounting institutions[14] support the fair value measurement for derivatives.

The American Financial Accounting Standards Board (FASB) introduced Financial Report Standard (FRS) 13 in 1998 to meet the demand for information on derivatives usage (Dunne, Helliar and Power 2003). This standard, applied in the US and the UK, did not address the issue of the evaluation of derivatives securities. The International Accounting Standards Board (IASB) issues common standards, which aim at increasing the transparency of markets, while, as mentioned earlier, the BIS is in charge of the pursuit of banking stability, hosts the Financial Stability Forum and promotes the issuance of standards which guarantee ordered market conditions. The coherence between the goals set out by the IASB and that of the BIS is guaranteed by Pillar 3 (Market Discipline) of the Basle II Capital Accord. Nevertheless, some cases

---

14   As explained in greater detail in the chapter on fiscal policy, the Governmental Accounting Standards Board (GASB) supports the fair value valuation of derivatives' transactions by sovereign states.

Table 1.5a Amounts outstanding of over-the-counter (OTC) derivatives

By risk category and instrument (in billions of US dollars)

Notional amounts outstanding

Risk Category / Instrument	Jun 2004	Dec 2004	Jun 2005	Dec 2005	Jun 2006	Dec 2006	Jun 2007
Total contracts	**220,058**	**257,894**	**281,493**	**297,67**	**369,906**	**414,290**	**516,407**
Foreign exchange contracts	**26,997**	**29,289**	**31,081**	**31,364**	**38,111**	**40,239**	**48,610**
Forwards and forex swaps	13,926	14,951	15,801	15,873	19,415	19,870	24,526
Currency swaps	7,033	8,223	8,236	8,504	9,669	10,767	12,291
Options	6,038	6,115	7,045	6,987	9,027	9,602	11,804
Interest rate contracts	164,626	190,502	204,795	211,97	262,296	291,115	346,937
Forward rate agreements	13,144	12,789	13,973	14,269	18,117	18,668	22,089
Interest rate swaps	127,57	150,631	163,749	169,106	207,323	229,241	271,853
Options	23,912	27,082	27,072	28,596	36,856	43,206	52,275
Equity-linked contracts	**4,521**	**4,385**	**4,551**	**5,793**	**6,783**	**7,488**	**9,202**
Forwards and swaps	691	756	1,086	1,177	1,423	1,767	2,599
Options	3,829	3,629	3,464	4,617	5,361	5,720	6,603
Commodity contracts	**1,27**	**1,443**	**2,94**	**5,434**	**6,394**	**7,115**	**7,567**
Gold	318	369	288	334	456	640	426
Other commodities	952	1,074	2,652	5,1	5,938	6,475	7,141
Forwards and swaps	503	558	1,748	1,909	2,186	2,813	3,447
Options	449	516	904	3,191	3,752	3,663	3,694
Credit default swaps	–	**6,396**	**10,211**	**13,908**	**20,352**	**28,650**	**42,580**
Single-name instruments	–	5,117	7,31	10,432	13,873	17,879	24,239
Multi-name instruments	–	1,279	2,901	3,476	6,479	10,771	18,341
Unallocated	22,644	25,879	27,915	29,199	35,969	39,682	61,501

Source: Table No. 19 BIS Statistics on Derivatives, 2006.

Table 1.5b Amounts outstanding of over-the-counter (OTC) derivatives

By risk category and instrument (in billions of US dollars)

Gross market values

Risk Category / Instrument	Jun 2004	Dec 2004	Jun 2005	Dec 2005	Jun 2006	Dec 2006	Jun 2007
Total contracts	**6,395**	**9,377**	**10,605**	**9,749**	**9,936**	**9,682**	**11,140**
Foreign exchange contracts	**867**	**1,546**	**1,141**	**997**	**1,134**	**1,264**	**1,343**
Forwards and forex swaps	308	643	464	406	435	468	492
Currency swaps	442	745	549	453	533	599	617
Options	116	158	129	138	166	196	235
Interest rate contracts	**3,951**	**5,417**	**6,699**	**5,397**	**5,535**	**4,820**	**6,057**
Forward rate agreements	29	22	31	22	25	32	43
Interest rate swaps	3,562	4,903	6,077	4,778	4,831	4,157	5,315
Options	360	492	592	597	579	631	700
Equity-linked contracts	**294**	**498**	**382**	**582**	**671**	**853**	**1,116**
Forwards and swaps	63	76	88	112	147	166	240
Options	231	422	294	470	523	686	876
Commodity contracts	**166**	**169**	**376**	**871**	**718**	**667**	**670**
Gold	45	32	24	51	77	56	47
Other commodities	121	137	351	820	641	611	623
Forwards and swaps							
Options							
Credit default swaps	–	**133**	**188**	**243**	**294**	**470**	**721**
Single-name instruments	–	112	136	171	186	278	406
Multi-name instruments		22	52	71	109	192	315
Unallocated	1,116	1,613	1,818	1,659	1,707	1,608	1,233

Source: Table No. 19 BIS statistics on derivatives, 2007.

of conflict between the two can arise. For example, the provisional introduction of expected losses is supported by the BIS, but explicitly prohibited by the IASB.

The IASB was founded in 1973 with an agreement between national accounting institutes of Australia, Canada, France, Germany, Japan, Mexico, Holland, USA, UK and Ireland. It is an independent, private, non-political organization based in London charged with issuing a unified set of accounting rules in the public interest, with the aim of providing quality, transparency and the maximum information available. Moreover, it cooperates with national accounting institutes to insure convergence, which includes non-member countries.

The European Union was the first to set the deadline of 2005 for all listed companies to adopt the standards issued by the IASB, including No. 39 on the evaluation of derivatives in the balance sheets of firms[15]. Apart from the numerical measurement at the fair value, IAS 39 and FRS 13 also include the training, information and support to employees provided by the company management on these innovative financial products. The internal information is a very positive feature, since it increases the overall soundness of the reporting. Before these standards were issued, the accounting office was separated in its working practices from the trading floor, even though both deal with the same securities. Now the distance between them must be shortened.

These standards apply to all firms, whether banks, financial or non-financial firms. Banks and insurance companies have questioned certain aspects of the reform for certain portfolios from the very beginning (i.e. the issuance of FSAS 133). Arguments in favor of the fair value measurement are that the more accurate measurement of assets and liabilities would better describe the firm's exposition. In this way, risk management is better handled, and shareholders and stakeholders have a more comprehensive picture of the firm, and the risks taken. This argument holds in perfect financial markets, where prices, which are the basis for the fair value measurement, fully reflect information on the assets and therefore their risks, but if this is not the case, the fair value is not the best solution. Opponents of IAS 39 affirm that for the fair value to be applied successfully, it is necessary to have deep and liquid secondary markets for all securities. Where this is not the case, prices do not reflect the value, and the historical cost is a better measurement. There are also concerns over the adherence on the risk management practices. For example, deposits at banks, which are considered to be redeemable on demand, in practice remain at the bank for months or years, but this is not reflected in the fair value or hedge accounting rules. Banks have a long-time horizon in their lending activity, and short-time variations can reflect other factors, which are not relevant for the loan. The effect of fair accounting is that the planning-time horizon of banks shortens. Moreover, short-term fluctuations can add an extra volatility into the balance sheet, which is not related to the firm's business, but solely to the turbulence of the financial markets[16]. This strong argument against the adoption of

---

15 Details in this paragraph are taken from Shin (2004).
16 This position is shared by Warren Buffett (2008).

fair value accounting is also a general feature of accounting standards, which try to measure the effects on the value of the firm of certain events over a short-time horizon, while the firm is potentially an infinitely living economic organization.

IAS 39 requires securities to be classified in four categories in the balance sheet:

1. originated loans;
2. held to maturity (HTM) investments;
3. financial assets available for sales (AFS);
4. trading assets and other items measured at fair value.

HTM and originated loans are valued at their original cost, while AFS are marked to market, and valuation changes are added to the shareholders' equity, not in the profit and loss. Securities classified as being trading assets are marked to market and valuation changes are accounted in the profit and loss. If more than a negligible part of an HTM is sold before maturity, then the entire investment should be considered as a trading asset. Once the HTM is revalued because of this change, the HTM designation cannot be used for the following two years. This very restrictive rule aims at avoiding any elusion of the application of the fair value, and attributes the original cost only to a very small share of overall financial trading.

All derivatives, according to IAS 39, are then marked to market. Any gain-loss should be put in the profit and loss, unless derivatives are purchased to hedge cash flows, and very strict hedge accounting rules are satisfied. Hedge accounting should be based on a rigid hedging relationship, which has to be documented, measurable, and effective.

An example of this is the interest rate swap, which hedges loans or deposits of a bank. Before IAS 39 came into application, the swap would not be marked to market, but measured though the interests' flow it generated. After the introduction of IAS 39, and of hedge accounting, the swap became mark to market; the value of the entry is very likely to be modified.

The gap between corporate valuation and market price can widen because of accounting rules, and the narrative information firms provide to shareholders should explicitly consider this gap. A sudden decrease in profit can be entirely due to the negative impact of fair value, and not to bad business results, and can affect the equity as a result. Another important gap is that among accounting, tax principles, and market prices. This issue is of incredible relevance, especially in currency and economic unions like the USA or the EU, where accounting rules are homogenous, but tax rules are not, and so a certain amount of arbitrage is likely to take place[17]. If capitals are perfectly mobile and accounting rules are homogenous, the investor would consider the tax burden related to the choice of a

---

17   This is more evident for corporation; see the analysis of the Fondazione La Malfa (2002) on the effects of different tax systems among European countries.

country. For example, the EU corporate tax rate is lower in Ireland, which attracts consultancy and high-tech corporations, while Luxembourg has favorable taxation on investment funds, which attracts savings from other EU countries.

The fair value is considered to be the best way to capture the dimension of transactions. The application of the European directive (MIFID) was the first step toward including derivatives among financial transactions. The Italian civil code does not explicitly refer to them, either for accounting, or for valuation (Cornaggia and Villa 2005). The first step for the accounting of derivatives by Italian firms is law number 366, October 3, 2001 (*Delega al Governo per la riforma del diritto societario*) which at article 6c states that the revision of accounting rules should be inspired to "provide a discipline for the treatment of foreign exchange operations, derivatives, repos, and other financial operations". In the Italian accounting and tax system, derivatives are measured in a non-intuitive way because the basic condition that applies is that the conditions of the securities to be taxed should be specified *ex ante*; in this way, if just one of the conditions is violated, then the tax does not apply at all. This rigidity is solved with the application of IAS 39, as derivatives emerge in the balance sheet at their market value. Core business-related derivatives (assets or liabilities) are valued at their fair value, and the variation is reported in the income statement (profit and loss).

Special attention will be paid in the third chapter to the very particular accounting rules applied by the public sector for the evaluation of financial instruments and reporting. The debate on the use (and misuse) of financial innovation by the public sector is hot, and well grounded.

9. The functions of derivatives

Economic and financial functions of derivatives are important characteristics; financial functions come from their technical characteristics, and are hedging, speculation and arbitrage. These functions describe the main type of investors present on markets. Hedging initially drives derivatives investments; the (core business) risk management procedure, implemented through a diversified portfolio and huge liquidity of exchange-traded contracts, supports the market. High flexibility of OTC derivatives helps to satisfy customers' needs. Risk management is a strategic part of corporate and public finance that provides stability. Speculation is not related to the core business; it is implemented for gain, and corresponds to a risk-loving attitude. Arbitrage is the possibility of buying and selling the same security at different prices on different markets, gaining a positive profit without any risk; this is possible if short-selling is permitted, i.e. selling without the property of the security.

Economic functions are substitution and leverage. Substitution (or liquidity) is the economic function that replicates traditional asset-liability. Derivatives amplify this function and can finally crowd out the demand for traditional (underlying) assets, thanks to their extreme flexibility (OTC) and liquidity (ET). The degree of substitution between assets is the main characteristic, which derivatives increase. Portfolio shifts and adjustments are faster, for example after an exchange or interest rate variation. Leverage is the ability to amplify the exposure by means of the margins-premium system.

Banks and financial institutions enter these markets to exploit their financial and economic functions; they innovate in the market, looking for profits and new market niches. Surprise effects in financial markets are very important, and can help to finance research and development costs; innovation is in the DNA of market operators. Herrera and Schroth (2002) show that the absence of patent protections for financial innovation, especially derivatives, does not negatively influence their emergence. Extra profits coming from innovations introduced in the market, to satisfy customer needs or to avoid stringent traditional regulation, are high enough to cover direct and indirect costs, due to the absence of patent protection (copyright). This is true for banks, financial and non-financial institutions, and feeds the process of market evolution.

The non-financial operators in OTC trading are non-financial firms and the public sector, which can be interested in entering the market to diversify their portfolio and hedge. Traditional assets offered by banks can be insufficiently efficient for their purposes, and different tax rules can provide a further incentive. OTC derivatives are less transparent and not open to small investors, and the lack of common standards implies a strict selection over investors, but there is evidence that non-financial firms widely employ derivatives (Fan et al. 2007).

According to BIS data, the turnover in transactions between non-financial institutions (e.g. pension funds) grew at 132 percent over 2001–2004, reaching US$871 billion. According to 2007 data, non-financial customers are involved in more foreign exchange transactions than in other type of derivatives. The financial centers that trade most derivatives, both ET and OTC, based on 2007 data, are New York and London. A similar, vastly increasing trend is observed for transactions between financial firms and banks. Whereas banks and financial institutions should be buyers and sellers of these financial products, the state and non-financial firms should be net buyers, if they primarily hedge. The increasing details provided by the BIS help to link the finance with the economics of investment; not only how much, but more importantly, explaining why.

10. The use of financial innovation by agents

Financial innovation emerges to satisfy special needs of customers; animal spirits move agents toward new profitable opportunities. In our analysis we observe how economic agents interact and exploit financial innovation, paying attention to the macroeconomic goal of financial stability. In a closed economy, players involved are (private) banks, the central bank, the government and the private sector (households and firms). Investors usually justify derivatives use, regardless of the type of contract, based on their hedging properties; the private sector and the government are undoubtedly attracted by this function, but the market dimension leads us to think that speculation (i.e. derivatives traded not to hedge core business related risks) plays a role in the investment decision. Arbitrage should be absent on markets, since information on prices flows continuously, washing out temporarily misalignments. Arbitrage can appear on non-liquid or opaque markets, violating the perfect market hypothesis, as shown by Nicolò and Pelizzon (2006) on credit derivatives, or as observed in the oil market on Brent crude futures (Tabak 2003).

Innovation is the process of evolution of financial markets, fuelled by frictions, asymmetries and imperfections, which banks and their customers can exploit in order to make gains. Financial innovation is the reaction to imperfection and contributes to create new opportunities. Derivatives are mostly "tailored to the client" contracts, since almost two-thirds of world transactions take place outside stock exchanges: OTC. At the microeconomic level (i.e. at a market or instrument level) derivatives complete the investment opportunities, increase market liquidity and attractiveness, and are usually welcomed[18]. At a macroeconomic level the story is a little bit more complex, since the aggregation principle (i.e. the characteristics of the individual is paramount) cannot always be employed. Market improvements, like the huge liquidity or the lower bid-ask spread, can have little direct impact on macroeconomic variables; moreover, there is increasing evidence that financial markets are far from being perfect and rational. If the microeconomic advantages reflect at a macro level, as hypothesized by neoclassical models, derivatives represent an improvement. But if micro-virtues distribute asymmetrically in the macro economy, because of frictions, irrationality or hazard, it is worth investigating where risks are accumulating.

The world economy is characterized by integrated financial markets, high-speed information and high capital mobility. We know that markets face some rigidity, which comes from asymmetries in legislation and local supply and can temporarily influence the preference of investors, but these can be overcome by innovation.

10.1 Banks and financial institutions

Banks and financial institutions use financial innovation, exploiting economic and financial characteristics, to satisfy customers' needs, and they are the promoters of innovation on the market. Banks gain from innovation in terms of excess-profits and are pushed by Keynesian animal spirits. Banks can use derivatives for hedging and speculation; Gorton and Rosen (1996) observe that commercial banks use swaps extensively, but that derivatives add few interest rate risks to that of the banking system. Hirtle (1996) adds that there is a positive relationship between derivatives usage (swaps) and interest rate risk exposure, but this relationship changes across

---

18 See, among others, Conrad (1998).

banks of different size. The positive correlation could be interpreted in two different ways: first, it basically enhances the leverage effects, or can be used to hedge risks coming from unobserved portfolio characteristics. Results are heavily affected by the accounting system used at the time of estimation, and cannot be considered to be entirely valid today. A very similar causal relationship has been underlined by the Federal Reserve Chairman Alan Greenspan in his last Jackson Hole speech as a Governor of the Federal Reserve System (August 2005).

The application, from 2005, of the IAS 39 fair value could have the effect of pushing toward "new" innovation, to avoid regulation and accounting, both of which limit the actions of banks and customers. The debate is hot on both sides of the Atlantic and the Pacific. Banks use derivatives and there are few cases of crashes, e.g. LTCM (Swan 1999), Barings, Société Générale, which were primarily the results of bad management, and were not caused by the instrument. The events taking place in 2007 and not yet ended when still ongoing at the time of writing, pose a general question about whether financial and non-financial firms are aware of and confident about the risks embedded in their portfolios composed of structured products, and Assets Backed Securities, which represent subprime loans with an increasing default rate. The effective exposure of the financial system in the crisis is estimated by the International Monetary Fund to be worth US$300 billion, depending on banks' effective write-off dimension, which will be known only in late 2008.

Rating agencies are starting to consider OTC derivatives in the valuation of the credit rating of banks and firms, confirming the prominent role these investments can play in corporate finance. Complete and transparent accounting is necessary to understand the size of the phenomenon.

Special attention has been paid recently to credit derivatives, which modify the risk exposure of banks, firms and governments. The intensive use of credit derivatives over a fairly short period and for ever-growing amounts, which reached the value of 7.7 percent with respect to corporate bonds (data refer to the year 2002), and of loans to the non-financial sector, can pose financial stability problems[19]. Moreover, according to available surveys, the insurance industry is a net buyer of credit derivatives, and as a part of the financial sector can be exposed to adverse effects (Rules 2001), especially after market turmoil like that experienced at the end of 2007.

The lack of transparency and information relative to volumes and risks can induce a lack of confidence on the market. International cooperation on accounting and control is to be welcomed and should be improved in the coming years.

---

19   This out-of-date data is the only data available at the time of writing.

Table 1.6 Amounts outstanding of OTC single-currency interest rate derivatives

	By instrument and Financial Institution counterparty						
	Notional amounts outstanding (in billions of US dollars)						
	Jun 2004	Dec 2004	June 2005	Dec 2005	Jun 2006	Dec 2006	Jun 2007
Total contracts	**164,626**	**190,502**	**204,795**	**211,97**	**262,296**	**291,115**	**346,937**
Reporting dealers	72,55	82,258	87,049	91,541	114,474	127,140	148,318
Other financial institutions	70,219	85,729	92,092	95,32	115,089	125,654	153,328
Forward rate agreements	**13,144**	**12,789**	**13,973**	**14,269**	**18,117**	**18,668**	**22,809**
Reporting dealers	6,851	6,502	7,15	7,561	9,653	10,024	10,754
Other financial institutions	5,36	5,478	5,993	6,187	7,692	7,394	11,035
Swaps	**127,57**	**150,631**	**163,749**	**169,106**	**207,323**	**229,241**	**271,853**
Reporting dealers	56,422	64,669	67,994	70,801	87,323	95,995	111,095
Other financial institutions	54,87	68,888	75,378	77,247	92,982	102,758	123,875
Options	**23,912**	**27,082**	**27,072**	**28,596**	**36,856**	**43,206**	**52,275**
Reporting dealers	9,277	11,086	11,905	13,180	17,490	21,121	26,470
Other financial institutions	9,99	11,363	10,721	11,887	14,415	15,501	18,418

Table 1.6 continued

	Gross market values						
	Jun 2004	**Dec 2004**	**June 2005**	**Dec 2005**	**Jun 2006**	**Dec 2006**	**Jun 2007**
Total contracts	**3,951**	**5,417**	**6,699**	**5,397**	**5,549**	**4,820**	**6,057**
Reporting dealers	1,606	2,155	2,598	2,096	2,219	1,969	2,371
Other financial institutions	1,707	2,631	3,265	2,625	2,613	2,223	2,946
Forward rate agreements	**29**	**22**	**31**	**22**	**25**	**32**	**43**
Reporting dealers	10	7	9	6	8	9	12
Other financial institutions	13	12	18	13	15	18	27
Swaps	**3,562**	**4,903**	**6,077**	**4,778**	**4,944**	**4,157**	**5,315**
Reporting dealers	1,435	1,898	2,29	1,781	1,912	1,623	1,978
Other financial institutions	1,57	2,435	3,022	2,378	2,372	1,974	2,662
Options	**360**	**492**	**592**	**597**	**579**	**560**	**675**
Reporting dealers	161	249	298	308	299	337	380
Other financial institutions	124	184	224	233	226	231	258

Source: Table No. 21a of BIS derivatives statistics.

10.2 Central banks

Central banks are the institutions that govern monetary policy according to the mandate of the government or the treasury. They face financial innovation emerging on the market and change their behavior and reaction function accordingly. On the one hand, central banks face financial innovation by operators and need to reconsider their tools and operational scheme. On the other hand, if the domestic market is small, as in Switzerland, or absent, as in Mexico or Brazil, which issue foreign currency denominated bonds and hedge with swaps in order to control the costs of debt and stabilize the exchange rate risk, the central banks can decide to use financial innovation actively for the pursuit of price and financial stability.

Financial stability and orderly market conditions are main goals of modern monetary policy, together with specific economic targets (on inflation, output, unemployment or growth). Financial innovation can be used to implement the policies or to influence the market directly. The latter is, however, very rare in practice and less likely to be successful, because the resources available to financial markets are far bigger than that of any central bank, taken singularly or together. Supervision, monitoring and regulation of banking and financial systems in order to achieve or maintain stability are the main duties of central banks. Accounting and prudential rules should explicitly consider trading activities using non-traditional instruments.

The use of derivatives by central banks has been heavily criticized because of their opacity, which can introduce new risks that are not properly reported or handled (Blejer and Schumacher 2000). A trade-off between orderly market conditions and sufficient space for innovation should be considered by central banks.

Financial innovation can be used by the policy authority to achieve certain targets (such as the hedging of the cost of debt) over short periods and in accordance with markets' expectations. If the bank wants to fight against the wind, and tries to exploit the surprise effect, for instance abruptly changing its policy stance, the effect may not be the one desired, since financial systems are liquid and derivatives can affect the price of many events (von Hagen and Fender 1998).

The traditional instruments used by central banks—monetary aggregates—progressively lose importance in mature financial systems (Savona 2002), because the property of their constituents—their liquidity, risk and diffusion—can be easily replicated with non-traditional securities. An example of this is the monetary aggregate M3 in the Euro area, which was originally part of the ECB monetary strategy, and in 2005 was partly abandoned, remaining as an indicator of the system's liquidity in the monetary analysis (and no longer a pillar of the strategy)[20]. In March 2006 the US Federal Reserve ceased to measure and disclose M3.

---

20   The analysis of monetary aggregates is presented in Chapter 2.

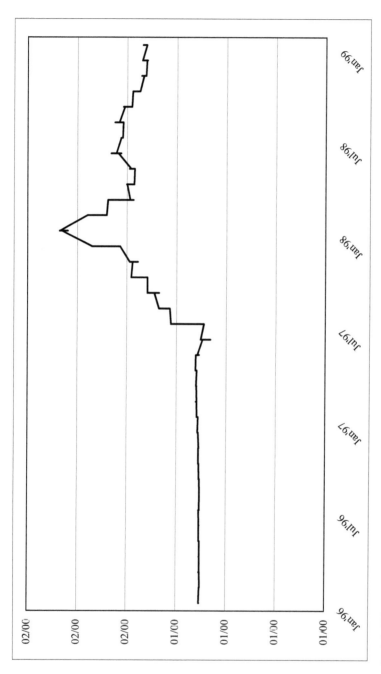

Graph. 1.2 Weekly exchange rate: Thai Baht—US Dollar (1996–1999)
Source: Thomson Financial Datastream.

The experience of the Thai central bank is of interest in this respect. In 1998, following the Asian crisis, which was spreading out the continent, it tried to save the pegged exchange rate regime and avoid devaluation by using exchange rate futures contracts with two weeks maturity. It succeeded in its strategy for the first two weeks, but when the market realized that it was the only central bank to sustain the rate, the speculative attack took place and the rate collapsed.

10.3 The government

Stability of the public sector is a complex theme of great interest in modern finance. It is influenced by financial innovation together with other external forces, such as terrorism, globalization, climate events, ageing population and immigration. Financial innovation can alter the public sector stability by influencing revenues, costs and debt management. Since a government enters the market to finance its expenses and deficit, it accepts its rules and can act like other investors with respect to risk management, hedging and speculation. The theme of public sector use of derivatives is very challenging, and there are no comprehensive data.

Central and local governments use innovation to hedge and achieve targets, but it is not clear what the effective burden of risks and costs, which are shifted toward future budget years, will be, or whether the temptation to raise cash using innovation (e.g. by means of up-front) is properly addressed and carefully limited.

Developed and developing countries (such as Brazil) use derivatives and provide some data which allow us to understand the function they can play in their portfolio[21]. Data on Italy are not helpful in clarifying the picture as there is no disclosure of data on the type of contracts bought or sold, of underlying assets, counterparts involved, costs, and the time horizon over which these contracts will work. The opacity of trading activity, the scarcity of information, and the few accounting requirements do not help our analysis, and do not ensure hazard-free behavior by authorities.

10.4 Firms and households

Firms can use derivatives to speculate and to manage assets and liabilities. The choice of using derivatives is affected by external financing costs (Fan et al. 2007). Hedging is probably the most important function of derivatives, and can contribute to lower the firms' risk (Guay 1999).

Guay and Kothari (2003) studied the use of derivatives, and found out that they are not greatly linked with firms' risk. Using balance sheet data of 234 non-financial firms active in derivatives, they found that derivatives represented only a small part of the risk profile. The median firm uses derivatives to hedge 3–6 percent of interest and exchange rate risks, which is a very small figure. Their results are heavily influenced by accounting methods, which are not very transparent, rather

---

21   Chapter 3 is devoted to a more comprehensive discussion of this theme.

than by the effective benefits derivatives can provide. This figure, moreover, does not match with the ever-increasing market dimension[22].

On the contrary, BIS data (2005) on OTC derivatives by non-financial firms (Table 1.5) show that their use has grown exponentially over the last years for all contracts (commodity, interest and exchange rates) and for all countries compounding the BIS base. Empirical evidence underlining their scarce use might be the result of poor accounting reports, and not the result of market data, confirming the need for more comprehensive accounting standards, allowing OTC transactions to emerge in the balance sheet.

Households also use derivatives, other than hedging and speculating, for tax purposes: it is possible to postpone revenue and anticipate costs, lowering income taxes, that is, tax timing (Zeng 2003). Tax timing can be implemented by skilled taxpayers, and is documented in the US. Tax payers using derivatives show a very high risk attitude and are usually high-income households. This issue will be described in greater detail and discussed in greater depth in the third chapter devoted to fiscal policy.

Another important issue is whether investors exhibit an efficient investment behavior in this type of market. Spyrou (2006) observed that investors in certain commodity derivatives contracts (i.e. Brent crude, coffee and gold) over the 1990–2005 period tended to over (under) react to positive (negative) shocks to prices, leading on average to inefficiencies, which left room for substantial arbitrage in the market. This result is valid for commodity derivatives, but we cannot rule out this irrationality *a priori* because of the lack of comprehensive statistics on financial OTC.

11. The risk

The risk can be defined as the variability of the expected value of the financial security; it is the characteristic of each financial instrument, and influences its demand and supply. Any risk can be managed, but needs to be understood first. Risk is natural in financial markets, and its manifestations can change after innovation emerges on the market. The spread in the use of derivatives carries with it the need for tools to know and manage the risks associated with them.

Derivatives are used to hedge and manage risks, regardless of the physical ownership of the financial or real asset-liability. Risks that can be insured and hedged are limited only by the imagination of market operators; there are derivatives on climate events (tornados, earthquakes), on the weather in Rome and LA, or on junk bonds. Risks managed with derivatives are all linked to the underlying (counterparty risk, default risk, price risk, etc.), but other risks can be present and actively working (i.e. structured or exotic products). Knowledge

---

22   On the other hand, the credit crunch of 2007–2008 will show to what extent firms are actually involved.

advantage in this market is strategic and can have a proportional effect on the probability of gain and on the magnitude of error (and loss).

Knowledge of derivatives, other than the most efficient pricing rules, means that it should be possible to picture these markets reliably for further inference and for supervisors and monitoring authorities. The microeconomic virtues of derivatives are reflected in the interpretation of the risks they bring; the lack of awareness of the unclear macroeconomic effects and interactions, and then of the asymmetric risks they can exhibit, alters the reliability of any analysis.

In 1993, the Group of Thirty at the BIS analysed the risks created by these new financial products. Its president, Paul Volcker, in the official speech to present the 'Report on Practices and Principles', stated:

> The general attitude of the Study towards regulation is plain: derivatives by their nature do not introduce risks of a fundamentally different kind or of a greater scale than those already present in the financial markets. Hence, systemic risks are not appreciably aggravated, and supervisory concerns can be addressed within present regulatory structures and approaches.

The general attitude of the report toward regulation is clear: derivatives do not add new or different risks in financial markets. Systemic risk is not badly influenced and the worries of regulators and supervisors can be solved by applying the current set of rules.

The lack of understanding of the adverse effects of the instrument, rather the instrument itself, is a source of potential risk. The Group of Thirty guided by Volcker proposed 24 guidelines to market operators. Cases of (huge) losses, with or without effective bankruptcy, were the proof of what can happen if these simple guidelines are not followed. These guidelines are very similar to those issued after the LTCM crisis (Basel Committee on Banking Supervision 1999).

My position on the effective risk that derivatives bring to the market is a little bit more uncertain, since if it is true that a derivative in itself does not add new risk, we have to admit that its opacity can, in practice, hide the existing risk. The problem is to what extent regulation and accounting are able to represent the effective market risks and dimension[23]. A direct consequence of that issue is whether risks are compensated.

Since the 1970s, an increasing effort has been put into the pricing and valuation of derivatives. In a world characterized by flexible prices and rates, the tools to evaluate the exposure become very important. In modern finance models, the system of postulates and data becomes an integral part of the security. However, perfect models do not exist. The bounded rationality of human beings, the adverse

---

23 This happened with the subprime crisis. Subprime loans involve less than 10 percent of US mortgage credit, but the crisis due to increased default rate spread out the mortgage industry by means of uncollateralized OTC derivatives, causing an estimated global loss of US$300 billion.

effects of exogenous shocks, the small predictive ability of historical data can, altogether, contribute to alter the ability of the model to fit with reality; this is model risk (Derman 1996). The Basel Committee analysed this issue in 2007.

   Number of parameters need to be fixed *ex ante* to obtain the price of a derivative. For example, in option pricing, the most important parameter is the volatility of the underlying asset, which is estimated from historical data. Volatility can be estimated using backward methods or simulation, but the error is never zero, generating a systematic "model risk".

   A remarkable example of mispricing of options, which led to huge losses, is that of NatWest Bank in 1996–1997. The trader at the interest rate options and swap-options desk had mispriced most of the contracts written between March 1995 and December 1996, but no supervisor realized the losses before they emerged at the end of 1996 and over 1997. The mispricing was due to the bad computation of the implied volatility of contracts, which is the key variable for pricing the structure of a portfolio and the hedging strategy. The complete lack of supervision lasted for a year, as the trader left NatWest Bank in December 1996, and losses emerged clearly only after March 1997. The lack of control and supervision led to an overall loss of £90.5 million, plus a fine of £420,000 by the FSA to NatWest Bank, the supervisor and the trader.

   A very influential investor who explicitly criticized the excessive resources invested in the derivatives markets since their spread in the nineties is Warren Buffett, the chairman of Berkshire Hathaway Inc. In his annual letter to shareholders (2003), he famously described derivatives as financial weapons of mass destruction. "Unless derivatives contracts are collateralized or guaranteed, their ultimate value also depends on the creditworthiness of the counterparties to them. In the meantime, though, before a contract is set, the counterparties record profits and losses—often huge in amount—in their current earnings statements without so much as a penny changing hands. The range of derivatives contracts is limited only by the imagination of man (or sometimes, so it seems, madmen)." Moreover, Buffett maintains that, "Derivatives generate reported earnings that are often wildly overstated and based on estimates whose inaccuracy may not be exposed for many years... Large amounts of risk have become concentrated in the hands of relatively few derivatives dealers ... which can trigger serious systemic problems." His viewpoint is a practical one, and his financial *fiuto* justifies his nickname, the sage of Omaha (headquarters of Berkshire Hathaway). Buffett compares the derivatives business to "hell ... easy to enter and almost impossible to exit". Incidentally, Buffett's investment strategy is one of the few not suffering because of the hi-tech stock exchange bubble that burst after the year 2000.

   In March 2007, according to his shareholders' letter, Buffett changed his attitude toward derivatives and adopted a more opportunistic approach.

   I should mention that all of the direct currency profits we have realized have come from forward contracts, which are derivatives, and that we have entered into other types of derivatives contracts as well. That may seem odd, since you know of our expensive experience in unwinding the derivatives book at Gen-Re and also have heard me talk of the systemic problems that could result from the enormous growth in the use of derivatives. Why, you may wonder, are we fooling around with such potentially toxic material? The answer is that derivatives, just like stocks and bonds, are sometimes wildly mispriced. We currently have 62 contracts outstanding. I manage them personally, and they are free of counterparty credit risk. So far, these derivative contracts have worked out well for us, producing pre-tax profits in the hundreds of millions of dollars. Though we will experience losses from time to time, we are likely to continue to earn – overall – significant profits from mispriced derivatives (Buffett 2007, 17).

This attitude is confirmed in the 2008 shareholders' letter.

The positions of Volcker and Buffett are the result of different perspectives and beliefs in the efficiency and soundness of financial markets. Volcker believes in the power of the free market and its ability to find the best solution. Buffett, who is one of the richest men in the world, thanks to luck and to his ability to speculate successfully, knows that investors are far from being rational, and that the market is not able to balance risks automatically and reach equilibrium. However, both men underline the importance of the regulatory structure in avoiding excessive (and unexpected) risks, and stress the advantages of derivatives.

What we add to these far-sighted positions is that the present international financial structure does not help compensating risks; the international financial system is populated with regulated operators (banks and financial intermediaries) and deregulated ones (hedge and sovereign wealth funds), which can purchase regulated securities (shares, bonds) or OTC. The intersection between them leaves room for herding behavior and hazard, which has no compensation system. In the following chapter we will briefly describe the 2007 subprime crisis, which is a concrete example of how deregulated securities employed by deregulated operators can be employed as vehicles to spread out risks on the basis of asymmetric and insufficient information provided to (regulated) market participants.

12. Derivatives' hangover

Wine and alcohol can be pleasant during a meal, but drinking too much makes you sick; that's exactly what can happen with derivatives[24]. Looking at the leverage effect they can provide and at potential profits, losses can be perceived as "less probable", according to the wrong perception of risk by investors, known as overconfidence[25]. Some firms or banks can be attracted by derivatives and not pay enough attention to potential losses, which should be known and managed.

---

24 Actually this can happen with money, bonds, or equities as well, since the problem is the excessive quantity, and not the security itself.

25 Overconfidence is the excessive confidence investors have in their own judgement, which influences investment decisions, regardless of market signals on the security (Shiller 2000). The similarity with the hangover is clear.

The risk model does not have a clear position in corporate risk management. Moreover, if derivatives are off balance sheet, the representation of the financial exposure becomes difficult, even if all other risks are properly handled. From 2006, the balance sheet and the income statement will better represent the financial exposure of firm. In the recent past there have been some examples of derivatives' hangover, which need to be known in order to understand properly the relevant contribution of accounting information.

There are a number of well-known examples of derivatives turbulence in the recent past: of banks—Barings and the Société Générale; of hedge funds—the LTCM; of firms—the MetallGesellSchaft; and of public administration—the Orange County. Most of these losses come after large financial volatility appearing on the markets due to economic or currency crisis, or simply market turbulence. The pricing of most derivatives, if not all, is implemented on the basis of historical volatility, and when markets experience a structural change in their level, most aggressive portfolios go deep out of the money. At that moment it becomes hard to hedge or restructure the portfolio, and the losses emerge.

We shall describe the most famous examples: the Orange County, the Société Générale and the LTCM, and mention the case of Poste Italiane, which was small in dimension and effects, but further testifies to the importance of proper accounting and internal risk management procedures.

Table 1.7 Derivatives losses

Year	Company	Probably because of	Estimated amount
2007	Société Générale	Subprime crisis	€4.9 billion
1998	LTCM	Russian default	US$ 3.5 billion
1996	Sumitomo	Asian crisis	US$ 2.6 billion
1995	Barings	Asian crisis	US$ 1.4 billion
1994	Orange County	Fed interest rate cut	US$ 1.6 billion
1993	MetallGesellSchaft	Pricing error	US$ 1.3 billion

The Orange County in December 1994 announced that it had suffered a loss of US$1.6 billion. As explained by Marthinsen (2003), the loss was due to mismanagement of funds by the County. The poor control and monitoring systems were unable to look after what the County treasurer, Bob Citron[26], was doing. The total portfolio of the County accounted to US$7.6 billion, all excess funds of the County and another 200 municipal entities (schools, hospitals and others). The investment strategy was based on derivatives with a high leverage; the final exposure was estimated at US$20.5 billion, with a portfolio strategy which

---

26   It is worth noting that treasurer is an elective duty in California.

supposed the interest rates to stay low in 1994. The portfolio was composed of structural notes, fixed income securities and inverse floating rates notes, all interest rate sensitive assets (Jorion 2005).

However, in February 1994 the US Federal Reserve decided to raise interest rates to avoid the US economy overheating[27]. The treasurer believed in the soundness of the strategy and, after the first unexpected interest rate increase, doubled all positions. In December the County decided to lock in the loss, declared itself bankrupt, asked for chapter IV creditor protection and liquidated the entire portfolio.

The total derivatives-related losses were around US$700 million, mainly due to reverse repo, and inverse floating rate notes. Marthinsen (2003), by confronting different replication strategies, concludes that the derivatives' role in the bankruptcy can be considered much smaller (about US$330 million), and poses some doubts over the effective liquidity crisis of the County.

The general lesson to be learned from the Orange County crash is that it is not possible to have safety, liquidity and high yield at the same time. An opaque and complicated investing strategy can create more risk than the costs it saves, or profits it makes. The complete lack of internal monitoring caused much of the distress, since it is not efficient to leave one person in charge without an appropriate system of control.

The Société Générale is a French investment bank with €357 billion worth of assets in 2007. In January 2008 it declared €4.9 billion losses, due to un-hedged long positions taken by the equity derivatives desk corresponding to positions worth €60 billion. The strategy was the following: the desk bet on a upswing of stock exchanges, after the financial turmoil of late 2007 which forced the Federal Reserve to cut interest rates twice in eight days, and the ECB to inject liquidity in the monetary and financial system. These maneuvers sustained a kind of soft landing of stock exchanges, which, however, have not fully recovered. The equity derivatives desk was free to settle its own investments strategy, and the internal control system did not investigate the composition and risks of the portfolio; it is worth noting that on December 31, 2007, the same desk registered a profit of €1.5 billion. The Basel II system, which is not applied by US banks, forced the Société Générale to explain immediately the reasons and origin of the losses, since it failed to satisfy the capital requirements and ratio[28].

The LTCM was a highly leveraged hedge fund, established in 1994, with worth US$1 billion capital. As clearly described by the President's Working Group on Financial Markets (1999), the distinguishing features of the LTCM Fund were the scale of its activities, the large size of its positions in certain markets, and the extent of its leverage, both in terms of balance-sheet measures and on the basis of more meaningful measures of risk exposure in relation to capital. The fund

---

27   Treasury Bill rate moved from 3.54 percent to 7.14 percent over 1994.
28   When writing the French court is still investigating.

reportedly had over 60,000 trades on its books, including long securities positions of over US$50 billion and short positions of an equivalent magnitude.

In 1997, capital reached US$7 billion, due to the incredible profits the fund could realize. As a result of these profits, banks and other financial intermediaries lent money to LTCM with very small collateralization. In 1998, its equity was worth US$5 billion, while total assets were US$125 billion. Out of the balance sheet, there were US$1 trillion OTC derivatives. Volatility influenced the strategy and caused the bankruptcy of the fund. The basic strategy of the fund was called "convergence arbitrage", that is, they exploited the small discrepancies among similar bonds on different markets and maturities (Jorion 1999). At the end of 1997, the convergence process of European countries started to shrink differentials in the bonds markets, lowering the return of the LTCM strategy, and then increasing the leverage it had.

In 1998, the Russian bonds default negatively affected financial markets, and turbulence spread out. At the end of August 1998, the gross notional amount of the fund's contracts on futures transactions exceeded US$500 billion, swaps contracts more than US$750 billion, and options and other OTC derivatives over US$150 billion. Approximately 80 percent of the fund's balance-sheet positions were in government bonds of the G7 countries (United States, Canada, France, Germany, Italy, Japan and United Kingdom). Nevertheless, the fund was active in many other markets, including securities markets, exchange-traded futures and OTC derivatives.

With regard to leverage, the fund's balance sheet on August 31, 1998 included over US$125 billion in assets. Even using the January 1, 1998 equity capital figure of US$4.8 billion, this level of assets still implies a balance-sheet leverage ratio of more than 25-to-1. The extent of this leverage implies a great deal of risk. Although exact comparisons are difficult, it is likely that the LTCM exposure to certain market risks was several times greater than that of the trading portfolios typically held by major dealer firms. The fund's size and leverage, as well as the trading strategies that it utilized, made it vulnerable to the extraordinary financial market conditions that emerged following Russia's devaluation of the rouble and declaration of a debt moratorium on August 17, 1998. Russia's actions sparked a "flight to quality" in which investors avoided risk and sought out liquidity. As a result, risk spreads and liquidity premiums rose sharply in markets around the world.

The size, persistence and pervasiveness of the widening of risk spreads confounded the risk management models employed by LTCM and other participants. Both LTCM and other market participants suffered losses in individual markets that greatly exceeded what conventional risk models, estimated during more stable periods, suggested were probable. Moreover, the simultaneous two shocks to many markets confounded expectations of relatively low correlations between market prices and revealed that global trading portfolios like LTCMs were less well diversified than assumed.

On Tuesday, September 22, a core group of four of the most concerned counterparties began seriously exploring the possibility of mutually beneficial alternatives to default. The main alternative the core group focused on came to be known as the consortium approach. This involved the recapitalization of the LTCM through mutual investments by its major counterparties in a recently set up feeder fund and a relatively small investment in a newly set up limited liability company, which became a new general partner of the fund. Under this approach, the stake of the original owners would be written down to ten percent and the consortium would acquire the remaining 90 percent ownership share, as well as operational control of LTCM. Finally, 14 firms agreed to participate in the consortium. The Federal Reserve Bank of New York provided the facilities for these discussions and "encouraged" the firms involved to seek the least disruptive solution that they believed was in their own collective self-interest. The agreement was reached only after the firms involved became convinced that no other alternative to default was possible. The banks participating in the consortium invested about US$3.6 billion in new equity in the fund, and in return received a 90 percent equity stake in LTCM's portfolio along with operational control. What is relevant is that the responsibility and burden of resolving LTCM's difficulties remained with the counterparties that had allowed the hedge fund to build up its highly leveraged positions in the first place. The principals and investors in LTCM suffered very substantial losses on their equity stakes in the fund when their claim was reduced to ten percent. The LCTM crash is usually described as an event which could have pushed the market to collapse; proper responsibility procedures and the direct intervention of the New York Federal Reserves in the exercise of its most difficult duty, moral suasion, avoided the worst outcome, and stopped the domino effect that would have resulted following the fund's crisis.

The Poste Italiane, a state-owned firm privatized in the 1990s, is one of the biggest European postal and financial firms. Poste Italiane is the public financial intermediary for Italian central and local authority's payment system and raises funds to finance part of the government infrastructures expenditure. Its operating banking unit, the Bancoposta, over the past seven years has been particularly aggressive on the financial market, actively competing with commercial banks, with its 13,000 branches. Bancoposta has three million customers (i.e. households and small firms), and €211,550 million funds, roughly equal to one quarter of the entire Italian banking system[29]. Poste Italiane and its banking unit Bancoposta are not considered as banks according to Italian law, and are not monitored by the Bank of Italy or the European Central Bank, but by the treasury. Bancoposta raises external funds but does not manage them[30]; the management of the funds has been given to private banks, such as Deutsche Bank and JP Morgan. Given the mismatching maturities, for instance raising funds with sight deposits, and lending to local administrations with 20 or more years' maturity, Poste Italiane decided to

---

29   Data available refers to 2002.
30   This because of the different monitoring and vigilance due on Bancoposta.

manage the mismatching, together with the interest rate risk, using derivatives, advised by JP Morgan (Risk Italia 2004). It is likely that the derivatives in the portfolio were designed on the basis of the hypothesis that interest rates could increase in the Euro area over the period 2002–2003. Unfortunately, that did not happen, and the economic performance was poor in that period. Some derivatives went out of the money and generated net losses in 2004 causing the hangover. According to a different analysis, the derivatives strategy was coherent with the firms' structure and strategy, and the losses that Poste would have suffered if interest rates had increased would have been far bigger if derivatives had not been used. The soundness of the hedging strategy can be evaluated by considering what would have happened if the (negative) event took place (i.e. higher interest rates) and no hedging was provided, and not looking at net losses *ex post*. The credit rating of Poste Italiane in the absence of derivatives hedging would have deteriorated, if the (negative) event took place. The Italian press has been very unpleasant with respect to this loss, but this negative attitude is more probably the result of lack of knowledge of derivatives' use, and due to the absence of monitoring of a state-owned financial intermediary that raises savings from the elderly and households, rather than to the loss, which was not large[31].

These are just a few examples, but they clarify that security in itself was not the source of crisis or hangover. The general lesson to be learned after these sad examples of losses and bankruptcy is that aggressive financial investing can provide amazing returns, but since parameters are tied to historical values, when an abrupt change happens, there may be little room left for avoiding losses.

I support the principle that the use of non-standardized derivatives by unskilled investors should be avoided. The MIFID directive tries to clarify the requisites to be considered professional and skilled, but it is very complicated to apply this effectively and difficult to export at the world level. The knowledge advantage of financial intermediaries in deregulated markets can translate into asymmetric transactions, and then the access by non-professional operators should be limited as much as possible.

13. European financial integration

Globalization in Europe has come together with the single market. The introduction of the Euro in 2002 contributed to speed up the process of financial integration and to decrease financial costs for European firms and banks. As well as the exchange rate risk, which has been entirely eliminated in Europe and lowered for accessing countries, legal risk[32] is going to disappear.

---

31 The exact amount is known only to the shareholder (the Italian treasury).

32 The legal risk is associated with the presence of a common financial market, but different local laws and regulation can leave a hole or room for asymmetries and then profits or arbitrage.

The Financial Services Action Plan (FSAP) is the implementation of financial services harmonization by the EU in order to create a unique financial market, after the effective introduction of the Euro. The relevant directives, which aim at implementing the plan, are the Market Abuse Directive, the Prospectus Directive, the Markets in Financial Instruments Directive (MIFID), and the Transparency Directive. The issuance of directives follows the Lamfalussy process, which is a four-step procedure; it has recently been extended to the insurance, banking and investment funds sectors. The principles followed by the FSAP are cooperation and integration, and are coherent with the targets set in the Lisbon agenda: increasing integration and competition in the service sector to create a knowledge-based economic area.

The regulation looks at the service provided and not at the players involved in the transaction, so that different national systems can co-exist, keeping their original differences. The Bolkenstein directive follows these principles and allows for a further evolution of (financial) integration, by imposing the regulation of the place where the service is provided, and not that of the country of origin. From a different point of view, the Lisbon agenda, which underlines the importance of the service sector for the future development of the European economy, also encourages the financial integration process. However, governments manage the process of local implementation of rules and laws, and their slowness can leave room for asymmetries.

The great advantage of the FSAP is that, moving away from the definitions of instruments and players, it easily includes the OTC transactions. Financial innovation is a driving force of European regulation and derivatives are not an exception.

Financial integration in Europe is not yet complete although relevant stock exchanges are already integrated, either with business agreements or *via* mergers and acquisitions. Further integration will come when all countries have fully applied the FSAP principles in their domestic regulation, and a single European financial market will turn into reality.

Europe enjoys a very peculiar financial structure. The biggest European financial center is located outside the Union, in the UK, and attracts increasing portions of European wealth. The City of London speaks all European languages and provides impressive facilities for small- and medium-sized private investors and firms. This strength would probably increase if the UK enters the EMU; the European financial market would then become unified under the Euro. The integration of financial markets is already in place thanks to alliances and mergers, but most OTC transactions involve non-European intermediaries. The leader in this field is American, but this could be changed by further facilitating alliances and developing the finance industry.

14. The role of the International Monetary Fund

The International Monetary Fund (IMF) is the international financial institution in charge of looking after financial stability.

> The IMF is responsible for ensuring the stability of the international monetary and financial system – the system of international payments and exchange rates among national currencies that enables trade to take place between countries. The Fund seeks to promote economic stability and prevent crises; to help resolve crises when they do occur; and to promote growth and alleviate poverty. It employs three main functions – surveillance, technical assistance, and lending—to meet these objectives"[33].

In more detail, the Fund:

1. promotes international monetary cooperation;
2. facilitates the expansion and balanced growth of international trade;
3. promotes stability;
4. assists in the establishment of a multilateral system of payments;
5. makes its resources available (under adequate safeguards) to members experiencing balance of payments difficulties.

The Fund was established in 1945 in accordance with the Bretton Woods agreements and there were fewer than 50 original member states. Today, there are 185 member states, and their quota in the Fund is proportional to their GDP. It is a US-centered institution, since the US is the greatest stakeholder in the fund (17.14 percent), and its headquarters is in Washington DC. The directors are generally American, British, German, Japanese or French, since these countries own around 39 percent of the Fund, and the chairman is chosen from them.

From a practical point of view, the Fund visits all its 185 member countries every year, and verifies their situation (Article IV). Technical assistance to design and implement effective policies is provided free of charge. Other than periodic surveillance, the Fund helps countries in crisis, or close to crisis, to solve the situation and it can act as lender of last resort, up to an amount which is proportional to the quota of the country at the Fund. The Fund can lend to member countries, and interest receipts are used to cover annual expenses.

In the very recent past, the Fund has restated its long-term goals and mission, in order to deal with the changing environment at the global level. The Fund wants to move away from the five goals stated in Article I, which are basically focused on trade[34]. Crises are no longer trade balance-driven, but more often linked to the financial account. The financial account reports all financial transactions (on bonds, equity, derivatives and so on) and it is influenced only to a small extent

---

33   See the Fund's mission at www.imf.org.
34   Cf. the International Monetary Fund in the New Millennium.

by the tools available to the Fund (Special Drawing Rights (SDRs) or quota). Financial globalization, flexible exchange rates and the information technology revolution contribute to increase capital mobility, making it harder to pursue stability following rules designed in the 1940s. Since the Asian crisis, the moral hazard of financial markets has been the main issue for international regulators, including the IMF. Excessive risk taking in the presence of a lender of last resort induces a further increase in risk-seeking behavior, therefore a high degree of transparency is necessary for the market to be safeguarded. The subprime crisis of 2007 and the enormous liquidity injected by central banks have restated the hazard problem in financial markets, as confirmed by the cautious speeches of chairman Bernanke.

We believe that the new IMF should promote economic and financial stability, and orderly market conditions by means of surveillance, technical assistance and standard settlements. The main objectives should be restated as being to:

- promote international monetary and financial cooperation;
- promote and implement ordered market conditions;
- assist in the establishment of a multilateral system of payments;
- coordinate its acting with other international financial institutions avoiding any duplications.

The lending activity should be abolished for those countries that enjoy significant private funds. In no circumstances should the Fund lend to countries, except those which are emerging and poor according to the World Bank definition and analysis.

The opacity of accounting rules for some types of instruments (e.g. OTC derivatives involved in the subprime mortgages market) and the asymmetry among investors in the financial market (i.e. strong regulation on banks and financial firms, and weak or absent on governments and hedge funds) decreases the global awareness of risks effectively run and the final ability to compensate them and manage adverse shocks. In this environment, lending activity fuels hazardous positions. The role of the IMF in the future will be more tailored to the needs of member countries. Its approach should become more active toward international financial coordination and cooperation, including by means of standard settlements and promoting fair regulation, which does not always translate into liberalization.

The mission of the Fund to promote stability cannot be pursued with SDRs or quota. For the sake of all market players, it is necessary to ensure proper market and risk management procedures. However, the Fund has no competence in these fields, which are led by the BIS and the IAS. The implementation of this mission should be updated following the changing environment. The fund's global role would be that of a facilitator, of promoting greater transparency and better disclosure. Because of the awareness of a progressive lack of importance of current-account-driven events[35],

---

35 With the exception of emerging countries.

the Fund is focusing on enhancing fiscal transparency and ordered fiscal policies. In order to handle this issue successfully, the Fund should lead the way in the disclosure of governments' activities, especially in their OTC operations.

As Caballero (2006) explains, the world is affected by a global assets shortage, which pushes up risk-taking behavior and needs policy interventions. Intervention can affect the excessive risk taking, and/or the shortage, so it is more efficient for the government to act in the following way, but this is not without its own price. Governments create a large amount of assets, but need sound credibility, and the existence of derivatives markets, which need collaterals, could introduce a circularity problem. We know that derivatives may or may not be fully collateralized, and the circularity, explained by Caballero and Krishnamurthy (2005), can be broken. Derivatives can help in completing financial markets, speeding up financial development and satisfying the need for assets. The question is whether this solution is efficient or not, considering the partial absence of underling assets. The circularity of assets shortage, derivatives and (de)collateralization can be solved in a world where all financial transactions are collateralized, otherwise excessive exposure, together with excessive risk seeking, cannot be ruled out. This is, however, achievable if OTC transactions take place in a different environment. Today, following the Washington Consensus, the world financial system is highly (or wildly) unregulated, but this structure has failed to guarantee stability. The future structure should be characterized by stronger accountability and transparency. As we have mentioned, the BIS pursues stability similarly to the Fund, but from a different perspective (regulation and standard settlements); it is a traditional bank for the community of central banks, and acts as a fund. If the IMF acts as a global facilitator, its mission can be managed more effectively with higher coordination with the BIS. Financial crises spread out very fast, and the knowledge advantage is necessary for the global institution to operate in a changing world. The incredible growth of financial markets, which is mirrored in the financial account of the balance of payments, is the first and simplest justification for the institutional merger. Banks and non-financial institutions are key financial operators, and the BIS knows better than the IMF how they act. The statistical disclosure implemented at the BIS is a key ingredient of the recipe for an effective surveillance by the IMF. In particular, OTC transactions, which pose more problems in the present financial structure, are monitored at the BIS. The integration of the two international financial institutions would go in the direction of improved market soundness, and stability by means of comprehensive regulation, standard settlements, statistical disclosure and effective supervision/ surveillance.

A political push toward a strong change is needed by the European Union, following its greater internal integration. It should decide to vote with one foot in the IMF, becoming the second or even the first sharcholder. This would change the global financial equilibrium, and move the Fund headquarters to Europe. This would modify the so-called Washington Consensus, and the final outcome would be that of integrated institutions looking after stability and working to restore market credibility.

15. From the traffic light to the roundabout

Control over traffic and transport is a dynamic study of various forces, which could eventually lead to a crash; the way to minimize the probability of accidents in populated areas is the use traffic lights. Traffic lights can be used for 24 hours or less, depending on the benefits, but the violation of traffic lights is a violation of the code of conduct. Traffic lights, however, are severe and inflexible ways of regulating traffic. Suppose you are in the middle of nowhere, nobody is coming, it's three o'clock in the morning and you can safely evaluate whether the violation of the red light would be an actual source of danger. But a violation is a violation. Recently, in most of continental Europe, traffic lights have been substituted by roundabouts. There are rules governing their use, in order to avoid crashes, but they have proven to be far more flexible than traffic lights. The substitution of traffic lights with roundabouts is justified by the diminishing number of accidents, a more responsible style of driving by the population, and a cost reduction (e.g. electricity). Moreover, the circulation of cars becomes more fluid, and traffic jams decrease. Moving from traffic lights to roundabouts means that rigid, over-imposed rules lose to self-regulating agents.

The European integration process is inspired by flexible principles, as explained by Ralph Darhendorf (2003), who supports the project of a European Constitution where principles are stated, and national rules apply these principles and translate them according to domestic peculiarities and special features.

What about finance? It's exactly the same story! Derivatives, innovation, trans-national transactions, globalization are all expressions of the actions of self-regulating agents. Codes of conduct of market players are effective tools in regulating transactions, since the violation is too costly (i.e. the loss of all present and future profits). No fine would be so high.

Derivatives are the result of animal spirits, but are also the result of the impossibility of strict rules working in financial markets. The struggle is essentially between principle-based (or market-based) regulation and rules-based regulation. As described by John Timer (2006), CEO of the British Financial Services Authority,

> "the principles-based regulation is essentially about outcomes or ends while rules-based regulation is about means. Principles-based regulation allows firms to decide how best to achieve required outcomes and, as such, it allows a much greater alignment of regulation with good business practice. Firms should be able to operate a single set of controls, which allows them simultaneously to meet their business objectives and the Financial Services Authority supervisory requirements, rather than being forced to operate controls that have no purpose other than to satisfy the rigid rules. Firms'

managements—not their regulators—are responsible for identifying and controlling risks. A more principles-based approach allows them increased scope to choose how they go about this. In short, the use of principles is a more grown-up approach to regulation than one that relies on rules. There are also practical reasons for shifting the balance towards principles-based regulation. Regulators could set themselves the task of creating a rule for every conceivable source of risk or detriment. But they would never succeed. The complexity of the financial system means that the number of ways in which firms can damage markets, investors or themselves is increasing exponentially. But we need to clarify that a move to a more principles-based approach also poses challenges for supervisors. The task that we are asking supervisors to undertake is much more complex than that of a few years ago. Firms also need to recognize that greater freedom implied by a more principles-based approach also entails responsibilities. Where senior managements fail to exercise effective control the Financial Services Authority will have strong enforcement tools available."

This very general statement fits perfectly with derivatives, which cannot be controlled by rigid rules.

The change from traffic lights (rules-based regulation, standardization) to roundabouts (principles-based regulation, codes of conduct) is a continuous process, and can neither be avoided nor stopped. Professor Alan Rugman has argued, once we presented this viewpoint at the Berlin G8 Forum organized by the G8 Research Group in June 2007, that roundabouts work only in G7 countries, since the people in them are familiar with codes and rules and have a sense of the state or of authority. The introduction of market-based regulation in emerging countries, where this sense is largely absent, would generate chaos. Financial markets and operators, however, are basically G7 centered, so principle-based regulation can be reasonably considered. Usually, the process of becoming a developed country involves improving institutions and regulation, together with the confidence of the population in the institutions.

16. Conclusion

This chapter is a general introduction to derivatives: the history of the innovation process; the role played by the BIS with respect to OTC derivatives; the role of non-standardized financial operators (hedge funds); the statistical measurement and accounting disclosure of data on derivatives, both at national and international level and in the balance sheet; the function and use of derivatives by agents; the risks involved; and the evolving role of international financial institutions in a globalized world where resources invested in the financial markets exceed those invested in other sectors.

The most significant problems posed by derivatives are the lack of homogeneous rules and standards in the presence of common purposes by investors (i.e. profit seeking). Derivatives are as old as commerce and finance, but their strength lies partially in the ability to circumvent (rule-based) regulation from national or international bodies. The market measurement of derivatives cannot rely on notional amounts outstanding, since they are never exchanged between the parties. The fair value of contracts, which is the base for accounting derivatives in the balance sheet of investors, is a very different measure with respect to the notional amounts. There is a problem of intelligibility of data coming from different sources but presumed to be describing the same transactions. Market statistics should be based on the turnover, market value, open interest and margins, and with a higher frequency, especially for OTC transactions, whose disclosure is completely unsatisfactory.

The circumvention of rules has been recently diminished with the introduction of the Basel II Capital Accord, which affects the behavior of banks, and with IAS 39 accounting standard, which also influences the non-financial sector. The public sector is still very opaque since it is not compelled to apply accounting and prudential rules, or respect any capital requirements. The accounting of derivatives is a controversial issue, which involves the need for more transparent and comprehensive information on the risks taken by banks, firms and other operators. However, the fair value measurement can introduce an extra volatility, and have adverse effects, which are more severe where the financial market is far from being perfect or efficient.

Principles-based regulation is a way to prevent circumvention and can be a solution at a reasonable cost. The process of moving from rules-based to principals-based regulation, which feeds OTC transactions, has various explanations: it is very similar to other human processes, and has solid economic justifications. The process of financial integration in Europe has to speed up in response to increasing investment possibilities and protection of investors, and also for non-standardized or deregulated markets, such as OTC transactions, and players, such as hedge funds.

Moral hazard can emerge where the government or a non-financial firm goes into crisis, and the leverage effect of derivatives multiplies the exposure and losses. Episodes of stress in the derivatives markets have not been frequent in recent years, but this doesn't mean that they have not or will not take place. Since the market turmoil in 2007, our negative judgment on poor derivatives disclosure has become no longer a theoretical, but a practical issue. Financial deregulation should not go further, since it proved to be unable to guarantee stability. The IMF should restate its mission entirely in order to pursue stability effectively. The new Fund should be able to facilitate and supervise; its tools will be a more comprehensive (market-based) regulation, more effective standard settlements and deep statistical disclosure.

Chapter 2
Derivatives and Monetary Policy: Global Stability

1. Introduction

This chapter focuses on the monetary analysis of financial derivatives. The literature considers financial derivatives virtuous securities, able to increase market liquidity and completeness on the basis of their microeconomic virtues. However, at the macroeconomic level their virtues might vanish or be dramatically darkened for numerous reasons: the adverse effects of their opaqueness; the moral hazard arising from the application of asymmetric rules; and the reduced ability of institutions to control and monitor these markets and transactions. The monetary literature has explicitly considered the role of expectations management (Galì and Gertler 2007) using both the new Keynesian and real business cycle models, but has ignored the effects and relevance that innovative financial tools, which can incorporate expectations, have on the transmission mechanism of impulses. If this special type of financial innovation is ignored, it is easy to ignore its disruptive effects as well; the subprime mortgage crisis has been an expensive wake-up call about the dangers of ignorance for institutions, policy makers and analysts. This lack of awareness is testified in the absence of comprehensive statistical data depicting the market, transaction types and conditions, and the risks involved.

I believe that ignoring derivatives means ignoring a highly relevant share of financial transactions (and wealth): it is not just an oversight, it is a moral mistake.

Recent experiences of crisis and turmoil testify that the hypothesis of rationality in real financial markets does not hold up: where there is limited rationality, opaque and not-so-liquid derivatives can have negative monetary effects (i.e. they can increase volatility, diminish transparency, modify risk exposure, and modify moral and market hazard).

The pursuit of price and financial stability is the aim of monetary management in a world where the importance of traditional paper money has been lowered and electronic trading and banking are expanding. Monetary aggregates are measures of money in circulation, that it, available for the purchase of goods or the payment of debt. Narrow monetary aggregates (M1 and M2) include very liquid monetary assets, such as money, coins and bank deposits; wide monetary aggregates (M3 and L) include no-so-liquid assets, with a higher return and the ability to be converted quickly into money (i.e. savings deposits, repos, expiring Treasury Bills, time deposits). Nevertheless, most of these securities can be efficiently replicated, in terms of risk, return and liquidity, by derivatives contracts. The substitution of monetary assets by derivatives (or other innovative financial securities) can also work the other way round, since the liquidity available to investors fuels the purchase of innovative securities, and the availability of liquid securities sustains the demand for monetary assets[1]. Derivatives have a monetary nature, close to the Keynesian speculative motive for money (L2), which has been ignored by the literature.

Derivatives play a role in the transmission mechanism of monetary policy from several different points of view: monetary aggregates, portfolio substitution, interest rate channel, and expectations setting.

2. Institutional rules

Before further examining the economic and monetary analysis of derivatives, we should consider the institutional rules that govern financial and monetary markets nowadays. The evolution of institutional rules follows changes in the financial system, and the speed at which changes take place also depends on the adjustment process of investors and market players. This circle cannot be broken but it can be exploited to improve the allocation of resources and to enhance wealth.

Monetary authorities manage and supervise the payment systems and monetary markets in industrialized countries, acting autonomously and independently of the Treasury and the government. This institutional independence can be justified by historical experience and economic theory. The excessive use of money as a way to finance public deficit has been the source of hyperinflation. Monetary authorities are given an explicit behavioral function, which identifies their target and the instruments at their disposal. At the moment, most authorities pursue either price stability or growth, and should guarantee order in domestic market conditions.

Over the nineteenth and twentieth centuries the public sector assumed an increasingly important role in the economy, not only for regulation and control, but also as a significant player in markets. Public interference came with increasing costs, which fed huge public debt.

The stock of debt (B) grows, based on new expenses for interest paid on existing bonds (I), and the current deficit (DEF).

$$B_t = B_{t-1} + I_t + DEF_t \tag{1}$$

The increase in the debt outstanding ($\Delta B = B_t - B_{t-1}$) can be financed by means of issuing new bonds (NIB) or money (M).

$$\Delta B = B_t - B_{t-1} = M_t + NIB_t \tag{2}$$

---

1   This is quite straightforward if considering standardized, liquid and marketable derivatives contracts (e.g. written on Treasury Bills, Bonds or stock indices).

The excessive use of money (*M*) as a way of financing public deficit was the source of hyperinflation in Germany between the two World Wars. To make reparation to the victorious countries of World War I, Germany was forced to issue greater and greater quantities of Deutsche Marks, reaching two- to three-digit inflation rates and complete economic chaos, good grounds for autarky. In the economic theory, inflation is considered an unfair tax, since it hits creditors rather than debtors and reduces the purchasing power of contractual wages.

John Maynard Keynes's economic and institutional analysis of the German experience is an illuminating piece of economic and historic writing. World War I damaged Germany badly; the labor force had been partly destroyed, there were no industries left and no resources available to pay back the punitive reparation demanded by the victorious parties. Keynes tried to explain that forcing Germany to the compensation ordered would negatively influence the return to civil life of an entire country, with effects that would spill over in the European Continent. Unable to convince other countries, Keynes resigned and wrote one of the most far-sighted international economic analyses ever published (1931). The consequences of ignoring the effects of certain choices will sooner or later materialize and come home to roost.

The economic arguments that favor the institutional separation of monetary and fiscal policies and their mutual independence lie in the temptation to inflate, which can reduce the effectiveness of monetary policy, and induce the choice of second-best solutions, which radically decrease wealth and development (Barro and Gordon 1983). Inflation lowers the real value of outstanding debt (*B*) and then induces the government to spend more, running into new debt.

The ways in which institutions favor either inflation or unemployment have been formalized in the economic literature and help explain the reasons to separating the two authorities that issue either debt (*B*) or money (*M*). The authority that pursuits price stability (inflation) should consider the effect its maneuvers have on the unemployment rate. The tradeoff between inflation and unemployment rates, known as the Phillips curve, is mostly empirical, but explains the behavior of these two variables in the UK in the nineteenth century. The tradeoff implies that if preference of one variable (e.g. unemployment) is higher, an increasing quantity of the other variable (e.g. inflation) should be tolerated to obtain a substantial decrease of its rate.

The basic ingredient of the inflation–unemployment tradeoff is money illusion; if they hold more money, agents demand more goods, pushing up employment. In turn, inflation generated by the increasing money supply pushes down demand for goods. To increase employment, an additional dose of inflation is necessary. Barro and Gordon (1983) formalized this preference set, considering the temptation to inflate and the punishment when agents realize that addictive inflation lowers the real value of purchases. The slope of the preference curve of the monetary authority identifies the degree of tolerance between inflation and unemployment. "Hardnosed" authorities like low inflation, while "wet" governments prefer low unemployment.

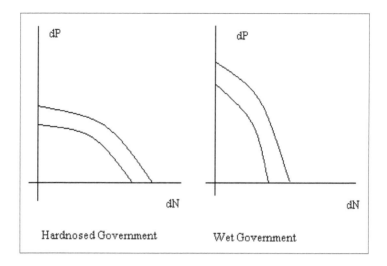

Figure 2.1 Hardnosed and wet governments
Source: Barro and Gordon 1983.

The tangency between the indifference curve of monetary authority (downward sloped) and the short-run Phillips curve (upward sloped) determines the equilibrium. In the long-run, however, monetary and fiscal policies are unbiased and the equilibrium lies on the long-run Phillips curve, vertical at the natural rate of unemployment.

The separation justifies the independence of the monetary authority from the Treasury. Nevertheless this independence can be undermined if the monetary authority does not consider relevant phenomena that may radically modify the environment and the effectiveness of its own maneuvers—like financial innovation. In the following paragraphs I will try to clarify some of the most relevant effects of derivatives. I am aware that the environment in which we live is far more complex than the one described in the Phillips curve, represented by only two variables, but I will start from simple relationships in order to understand the main modifications the environment can experience. The ability of the central banks to control inflation is a relevant part of monetary authorities' mission, so we should consider to what extent it is still possible for the bank to pursue stability effectively. The pursuit of price stability (financial and/or real) is difficult and has to be done in the presence of unknown relationships that modify the effectiveness of a policy based on up-to-date relationships.

Gurkaynak and Wolfers (2005) show that derivatives can be employed to forecast relevant macro variables, like inflation, following Shiller's (1993) idea of the creation of macro-markets. The possibility of buying and selling on different expiration dates allowed investors to bet on relevant macroeconomic variables, diminishing the distance among expectations, and enhancing liquidity in otherwise thin markets.

Financial innovation modifies endogenously the instruments set and target variables, leaving the authorities in much the same position as Wile E. Coyote, always running after the Road Runner but never catching it.

3. Financial globalization

Financial globalization is the process of the growth and diffusion of financial securities, regulated and not, at diminishing costs, and with ever increasing information at investors' disposal. This process is changing the way wealth is allocated worldwide, rendering it more democratic and less policy driven (Rajan and Zingales 2003). Economic globalization, i.e. increase in trade together with lowering tariffs, and the reduction of prices on worldwide markets, is a phenomenon that involves labor forces and generates divergent analysis and opinions[2]. Historically, the economic development of all countries started with the exploitation of labor forces, and as a result strong social and economic benefits have been introduced to guarantee fair production standards. The difference today lies in the amount of information available, which can help to build awareness of consumption and production. Enormous asymmetries in working and production conditions can negatively affect revenues, if a (multinational) firm neglects social responsibility. Financial globalization is far more symmetric than economic globalization since the information available and increased competition have lowered costs and improved investment opportunities. Free capital mobility spreads innovation, satisfying customer needs at lower costs. Financial globalization is a reality, and the ratio between world financial assets and GDP has grown at an incredible rate over the last few years; in 2005 it reached 3.2 (measured in US dollars, based on KPMG data).

Finance is not only a vehicle for moving wealth, but is a tool for creating it. The problem becomes to create wealth in a stable way, limiting the probability of shocks and crisis that will influence the real economy and hit the poor harder. Some authors have criticized derivatives and the freedom they bring to financial markets (LiPuma and Lee 2004). This criticism comes from some very strong assumptions, in particular continuous mispricing, and the complete absence of value of derivatives' contracts, which are very difficult to share and support after decades of continuous growth in terms of volumes, and value. Like other securities, derivatives might have created turbulence and volatility but are not considered directly responsible for any crisis (Marthinsen 2006)[3].

---

2 The work of Pelanda and Savona (2002), Stiglitz (2002) and Fukuyama (2002) is relevant here.

3 The 2007 subprime crisis might modify this belief.

In my view, financial derivatives, which were introduced to manage and mitigate risks, are not the source of new different and new risks. This view is shared by, among others, the Volcker group on derivatives (1993). Of course, if derivatives are misused or misreported, they can exacerbate existing risks, and complicate processes, rendering intervention very difficult or even inappropriate. Financial markets are very integrated, and some are more liquid than others; exchange traded (ET) derivatives contribute substantially to enhancing liquidity, while opaque OTC derivatives can stress the market in turbulent times. At the global level, derivatives contribute substantially to financial globalization. The global financial system lacks an anchor, a role played in the past by gold or silver, and this has allowed investors to look for other instruments to provide continuity in capital value (Bryan and Rafferty 2006). Financial derivatives can play this role, but in the macroeconomic system their effects could be different from achieving price stability, which is one of their microeconomic virtues.

3.1 Scandals, crisis and derivatives

To clarify the role of derivatives in financial development, we need to know to what extent they contribute to financial distress and crisis, as other innovations and crises have done in the past. Derivatives are contracts with deferred effects, fuelled by market expectations and risk-loving attitudes, and their opaque accounting rules can hide risks. The international environment is very volatile, with rapid and enormous portfolio shifts. Corporate bankruptcies on both sides of the Atlantic in 2001–2003, both before and after 9/11, have had a negative influence on investor confidence, while the irrational exuberance turned into a teddy bear. Moreover, a huge portfolio shift from the financial to the real estate market, fuelled by very low interest rates (Graph 2.1), hit the bond market hard. Financial investors have used derivatives, instead of traditional securities like bonds, to speculate and gain, thanks to the advantages they bring with them, e.g. the leverage effect.

Enron was an American energy company, with revenues worth US$111 billion in 2000. The following year the company revealed that its financial condition was sustained by fraudulent accounting, with the possible connivance of its accounting firm, Arthur Andersen, which disappeared soon after. Enron shares dropped from US$90 to a few cents after directors confessed that its effective losses had not been reported in the financial statement, but had been attributed to empty special purpose financial vehicles. Enron owned a certain number of derivatives contracts (on energy and other underlying) that exacerbated the financial disaster through the leverage effect. Derivatives were not responsible for Enron's failure, but they did speed it up.

A similar story is that of the eighteenth-century English South Sea Company[4], which bet on not-yet-issued commercial licenses for South America to be granted by the Spanish government. When it became obvious that the licenses were not

---

4   For the Italian reader, see the description by Augias (2003).

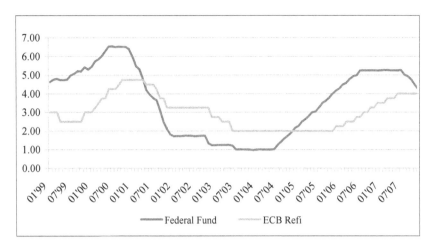

Graph 2.1 US and European central bank rates (monthly, percent)
Source: St. Louis FRED and ECB Statistical Warehouse.

going to be granted, the company's shares plummeted to almost zero. Shares in the company were accepted as collateral to obtain credit (i.e. a forward type contract) to buy other shares, and this leverage effect contributed to the crash. In both cases, Enron and the South Sea Company, managers anticipating the crisis tried to run away with what was left, and as a result were judged severely by the courts.

An indicator of the risk of crisis is the Ponzi rule, taken from the name of an infamous swindler most finance undergraduates learn about.

$$g>r \tag{3}$$

The growth rate of income (g) should be greater than the rate paid on loans (r) for the debt to be sustainable. Income growth rate can be measured in different ways. Corporate indices are very useful and easy to apply, like *return on investment* (ROI), given by the ratio of profit on investments, or *return on equity* (ROE), given by the ratio between profit and shares. Which profit to use depends on what we want to know: before or after taxes profit, core business or non-core business profit provide very different pictures.

Enron, like the South Sea Company, looked at future (wished-for) profits, and the expectation was so high that shareholders bought other shares using Enron shares as collateral. The expected rate of growth of income (g^e) was higher than the interest rate paid to banks ($g^e>r$), but when the Enron share values dropped, the actual income growth rate was insufficient to pay interests and loans ($g<r$). The use of derivatives sped up the loss, thanks to the leverage effect, but it was financial mismanagement that destroyed the value created by both firms. At the time of

both crashes, neither the energy industry (Enron) nor international commerce (the South Sea Company) was in crisis.

Corporate scandals influenced the confidence of investors, who received highly asymmetric information, and bore excessive risks. Monetary policy in the US and the EU lowered interest rates in 2002–2004 and contributed to pushing down short-term returns. This should had induced a preference toward medium- to long-term investments, stimulating growth, but this did not happen because investors still lacked confidence, especially in the bond market.

Financial markets are economic institutions and are constructed on the basis of conflict of interest between all agents: buyers, sellers and regulators[5]. The conflict lies in profit seeking, which leads to the solution of opposite needs in setting rules. The conflict can be solved to build a market structure, which satisfies most of the agents' needs. This is not the most efficient way to create a place where demand and supply can be satisfied, but it is the best in democratic and capitalistic systems. Interest groups and lobbies can distort the allocation of resources, and for this reason some countries have chosen technical authorities to provide autonomous supervision, rather than the government or any political body.

Today financial markets are integrated and highly technological, and transaction costs have diminished, allowing small investors to enter easily and allowing arbitrage to reduce price differences between markets. Information is still the strategic source of extra profits, and recent modifications to safeguard small investors and minority shareholders, and to strengthen market surveillance and monitoring (e.g. Agency Act 2006 in USA, and the MIFID directive in Europe) aim straight at this target. The evolutionary path of financial markets drives the system toward more flexibility, but regulators act to introduce rules and limits for the sake of stability. Derivatives are an important expression of flexibility, and financial globalization sustains their growth.

Globalization looks at asymmetries and punishes countries that are slow to correct their faults. The Sarbanes-Oxley Act, which modified the US financial system after corporate scandals in 2001, has given confidence to financial markets, and contributed to the restoration of investor expectations. The debate around the Sarbanes-Oxley Act has not yet ended since the constraints it imposes are very costly. Zhang (2005) estimates that the loss in market value around the most significant rule-making events amounts to US$1.4 trillion, due to direct, indirect and expected costs of future anti-business regulation. The Sarbanes-Oxley Act will be probably revised in the future, thanks to pressure from various lobbies. In 2006 the US Congress issued the Agency Act to diminish the conflict between credit rating agencies and their customers. The credit rating is a monitoring service, provided by independent agencies, but in practice most customers bought further services from the agencies, whether they needed them or not. Under the Agency Act this is no longer possible. The Act has improved the control and responsibility of agencies, allowing for rating modifications after the issuance of bonds and

---

5   See North (1990).

securities, if conditions change. It restricts potential conflicts of interest between agencies and customers, and strengthens powers of investigation.

The Financial Services Authority in the UK has always had strong investigative powers, attracting many (scared) European investors. After the most dramatic European corporate scandal of recent times, the collapse of the Italian giant Parmalat in 2003–2004, most EU countries introduced significant modifications to their national savings and financial systems. Italy, however, has made no modifications at all, and the likelihood of another corporate fraud there has not been diminished[6]. This can explain the strong tendency toward transnational takeovers of Italian utilities (e.g. Electricité de France taking over Enel, ABN Amro taking over Banca AntonVeneta) observed after 2004. Moreover, the conflict of interests with rating agencies is complicated by the fact that the Italian public sector actively uses financial innovation, like derivatives, to manage costs and risks, while regulation does not impose any supervision or monitoring.

3.2 Incentives for financial markets

Before going further it is important to clarify the incentives designed to guarantee stability and to enhance liquidity in financial markets. The first is (efficient) pricing ability, which should reflect the entire information set; the second is the competitive framework among operators (i.e. best practice); the third is regulation, which should eliminate asymmetries at national and cross-border levels.

Derivatives contracts (standardized or not) are priced on the basis of different rules and methods. The difficulty in pricing contracts, which cannot be very liquid and are intrinsically very difficult to parameterize[7], is discussed as a source of risk in chapter one. Although it is possible to buy and sell derivatives on very special risks, like weather conditions, which are priced in a non-continuous framework, it is not possible to eliminate the business risk associated, while the pricing error can be high if the market is shown to be non-liquid[8]. Together with prices, investors determine which risk to hedge. It is the duty of financial institutions to provide complete information on the structure of contracts to all market players: this is fundamental if crises and crashes are to be avoided. Corporate governance provides a set of rules to be followed (on bankruptcy, fraud, etc.) and insider trading or false communication can be prosecuted. The recent subprime crisis is an example of incomplete information about which assets had been secured having been provided to final holders of assets backed securities (ABS). The crisis hit the credit rating

---

6 After the Parmalat scandal the Italian government issued a law to fill some of the holes exploited by the firm, but did not strengthen the entire financial system.

7 One example is the recent debate on inflation derivatives. Their pricing is based on survey-based forecasts of inflation, and each contract-maturity has a time-variable underlying price index.

8 This is more likely to happen for OTC transactions.

system since the exposure of banking institutions on ABS incorporating subprime is unknown[9], and is not considered in their credit rating.

The perfect competition scheme is very difficult to implement in financial markets, since stability can act in the opposite way. One example is the liquidity stress experienced in September 2007 by the UK bank Northern Rock, which has been fuelled by market panic originating in the subprime mortgage crisis, but which could have been resolved with far smaller losses "behind closed doors," similarly to what happened to the LTCM[10]. Generally speaking, financial wealth moves where profits are higher and rules are better and clearly defined, and the competition scheme is inspiring for most rule-makers.

OTC derivatives, which represent almost two-thirds of the world market, are traded on the basis of codes of conduct and not on rigid rules. They successfully manage settlement, counterparty, model risks and various (exogenous) shocks without crashing. Safe and sound financial regulation cannot be rigid, but it must be inspired by good business practice, proper risk management and sound monitoring principles. Cooperation between markets players is, broadly speaking, the strategic part of regulation that completes the globalization process and can further reduce frictions and temporary asymmetries. This evolving process can lead to a global liquid financial market, with little noise.

As I remarked earlier, finance is not only a way to move wealth; it is also a way to multiply it on the basis of risk and return. If rules are correctly implemented, the finance leverage effect works like the turbo in a car engine, supporting growth and contributing to stability. Where there is crisis or lack of confidence, finance is like a huge rock on which a boat—growth—strands itself: it cannot leave the harbor, but it doesn't sink, either.

4. A special class of contract: Credit derivatives

Credit derivatives are OTC contracts that price, isolate and sell credit risk. They are basically credit default (CD) contracts, and can be swaps (CDS) or obligations (CDO). These contracts aim at hedging the default risk of the counterparty in a loan; they refer to firms, banks and governments, and are priced on the basis of the credit rating, issued by the agency, which is not involved in the contract. Credit derivatives transactions have increased following the abundance of credit that has been observed since 2002 (Tables 2.1 and 2.2). Credit derivatives can be divided into two groups: funded and unfunded. Unfunded credit derivatives are contracts between two parties, which are both responsible for the payment, while funded credit derivatives embed bonds and the final bondholder pays. Unfunded credit derivatives are total return swaps (TRS), credit spread options (CSO), and credit

---

9   The IMF estimates global net losses around US$300–400 billion.
10   This is the position of the EU Internal Market Commissioner, Charles McCreevy.

Table 2.1 Ratio between Domestic Credit and GDP (Domestic Currency)

	USA	France	Germany	Italy	Japan	UK
2003	0.935	1.048	1.408	1.025	1.565	1.737
2004	0.943	1.060	1.380	1.037	1.560	1.857
2005	0.963	1.097	1.361	1.088	1.578	1.949

Source: Own elaboration on Thomson Financial Datastream data.

default swap options (CDSO). Funded contracts are synthetic collateralized debt obligation (CDO) and many others[11].

Their amazing growth rates pose a number of problems of risk monitoring, since they are mostly traded OTC, and as a result are not particularly transparent. The BIS reports that credit derivatives (especially CDS) have reached a notional volume of US$10 trillion (December 2005) and gross market value of US$345 billion[12]. According to available data, the insurance industry is a net buyer of credit risk by means of credit derivatives (IMF 2004), meaning that they invest increasing shares of their portfolios in credit-linked instruments. The insurance industry can benefit from derivatives hedging, since risks can be shared over a larger number of insurers, without issuing new contracts, but the fact that the industry buys risks can complicate the links between the global banking and insurance industries. The insurance sector should be a net buyer of hedging securities, not directly of risks, at a global level, but this cannot be confirmed with available data.

The IMF devotes almost half of its Global Financial Stability Report (2006) to credit derivatives and their influence on financial stability. Their growth has occurred over a very short period of time. This is consistent with the spread of the new instrument (the derivative) with respect to the traditional underlying (banking credit), where the ability to tailor derivatives to customers' needs fuelled demand. Short- and long-term interest rates in the G7 countries have been low during the period 2001–2006, following expansionary monetary policies that alimented liquidity and credit. In the US and Europe credit, has financed consumption (at domestic level and abroad), while in Japan the zero cost of money caused by deflation has been used as a tool to restore monetary policy (Krugman 1992). Regardless of the reasons behind this expansionary monetary policy, the final effect is that credit and credit-related instruments have grown very fast: the growth of the underlying has furthermore alimented derivatives transactions.

The incredible growth of CD, the lack of statistics, and the difficulties in their pricing rules contribute to weaken monetary conduct. The effectiveness of monetary policy can be doubted if a good substitute to banking credit emerges and circumvents regulation and monitoring. Except the BIS quarterly statistics

---

11 ABS involved in the sub-prime crisis are funded contracts.

12 Data released in June 2006, OTC semi-annual statistics.

Table 2.2 Credit default swaps market

	Notional amounts outstanding bought	Notional amounts outstanding sold	Total
In millions of US dollars			
Total CDS contracts	**32,978,816**	**32,917,150**	**42,580,424**
Reporting dealers	23,285,488	23,345,600	23,315,544
Other financial institution	9,231,797	9,151,527	18,383,324
Banks and security firm	4,854,748	4,737,297	9,592,045
Insurance and financial	243,638	87,821	331,459
Other	4,133,411	4,326,409	8,459,820
Non-financial institutions	461,534	420,020	881,554
Maturity of one year or less	2,338,445	2,244,259	2,866,737
Maturity over 1 and 5 years	18,953,490	19,110,672	24,353,126
Maturity over 5 years	11,686,880	11,562,215	15,360,558
Single-name instruments	18,542,936	18,020,326	24,239,476
Multi-name instruments	14,435,880	14,896,824	18,340,948
Total gross market value			
Total CDS contracts	**720,725**		
Reporting dealers	357,959		
Other financial institution	336,146		
Banks and security firm	148,446		
Insurance and financial	2,636		
Other	185,064		
Non-financial institutions	26,621		
Single-name instruments	405,777		
Multi-name instruments	314,949		

Source: BIS Derivatives Statistics.

and IMF global analysis, there is no public disclosure of data; exposure by single investors can be excessive (i.e. with respect to assets or shares), but opacity hides potential risks (counterparty risk). Moreover, in case of credit crunch, the leverage effect of credit default derivatives exacerbates the restrictions.

Nicolò and Pelizzon (2006) use a stylized signaling model to show that the existence of an opaque credit derivative market, together with capital requirements for credit risk like those that characterize the present Basel II system, induces an adverse selection problem, because banks with low-quality risks may cover their exposure with (opaque) credit derivatives contracts. In this way the availability of credit derivatives does not benefit the economic system, but, on the contrary, can exacerbate excessive risk-taking behavior, and negatively affect wealth and stability.

The tension observed in the banking industry after the summer of 2007 posed the same policy problem of credit rationing; some banks experienced severe difficulties (e.g. Northern Rock in the UK, and Société Générale in France), and this contributed to lower growth expectations and aggregate demand. This very recent empirical evidence, together with the theoretical results synthesized above, should be a warning to regulators and monitoring authorities about the global stability of the credit derivatives system, and the spillover effects it can have on the entire banking and financial industry.

5. The subprime crisis of 2007 and the role of derivatives[13]

The year 2007 started under the star of prosperous growth, both for developed and emerging countries[14], and ended in turmoil in the money and financial markets, which anticipated a global slowdown in 2008. But we need to step back to understand the roots of the crisis.

In the US the mortgage industry has been sustained by both the Treasury and the Federal Reserve as a strategic sector to help the economy recover after the stock exchange bubble burst in 2001. The confidence of investors has been reduced, following the collapse of dot.com shares, and of a series of crises in large corporations (e.g. Enron and WorldCom). The real estate sector and the credit system sustained the soft landing of the US economy, and help it recover faster. Mortgage loans are subprime if given to lenders with a credit score lower than 620. The growth in subprime lending represents a natural evolution of credit markets, according to the US Federal Reserve (Gramlich 2004), and has been possible thanks to deregulation of the banking sector by Congress and a liberal approach to lending activity. Subprime lending allows a larger share of households to purchase a home, but it introduces a higher dose of risk in the credit system. Compared with prime loans, subprime loans typically have higher loan-to-value ratios, reflecting the greater difficulty that subprime borrowers have in making down-payments and the propensity of these borrowers to extract equity during refinancing. The deregulation of the credit system allowed by the US Federal Reserve gave another nine million homeowners the chance to finance their purchase; subprime mortgage loans rose by a whopping 25 percent per year over the period 1994–2003 and prime mortgage lending grew by a strong annual rate of 17 percent, reflecting the same trends. However, prime loans increased at a slower rate than subprime

---

13   I would like to thank Rainer Masera, Renato Maino and Paolo Savona for useful insights and brainstorming on this issue. Any errors are solely mine.
14   Source: the IMF World Economic Outlook, September 2006.

over the same period. In 2006 subprime loans represented less than 10 percent of the entire American mortgage activity.

According to 2003 data, delinquency rates in subprime loans, although far higher than that of prime credits, were acceptable to the banking and financial system, thanks to the sustained supply of credit, and good profits of intermediaries. The real estate industry has been enjoying amazing growth rates (Graph 2.2) and the low interest rates over the period 2003–2007 fed demand further. In the last quarter of 2006 house prices started to decline in the US, which pushed the delinquency rate of subprime up to 12.2 percent. Since there is an inverse relationship between house prices and delinquency rates, as testified by the US Federal Reserve statistics and analysis (Gramlich 2004), this is not very surprising.

After economic forecasts were revised downward for the years 2007 and 2008, the credit standing of the US banking and financial system deteriorated, stressing the yield curve in its short-term segment. The credit market is highly integrated, and the negative effects due to increased delinquency spread outside the American market, infecting the global interbank market. Credit derivatives, issued after ABS incorporating subprime credit and sold in the international market as funded credit default contracts, have been the vehicles for the diffusion. In the subprime case, the final holder of the ABS (CSO or other type of credit derivative) has been compelled to pay as a result of the default of the (underlying) subprime mortgage credit. Securitization is not a new financial tool to separate risk from credit, but what has changed abruptly has been the default rate (i.e. delinquency rates), which forced final (unaware) holders to pay.

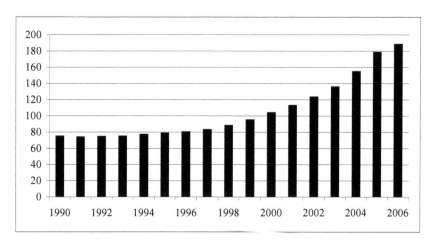

Graph 2.2 Case-Shiller home price index
Source: Thomson Financial Datastream.

The possibility of separating risk from credit, and selling it funded or not, modifies the effective allocation of risk for the entire financial system. The fact that credit derivatives markets are opaque fuels concern for the ease with which they can undermine stability. It has been demonstrated in the literature that the opaqueness of OTC credit derivatives can affect the stability of an entire financial system (Nicolò and Pelizzon 2006). The complete separation between the originator of the subprime credit, usually a monitored and regulated bank, the distributor of the security deriving from the subprime, usually a special purpose vehicle (SPV) subject to little regulation and monitoring, and the last holder, who finally pays the default price attached to the OTC (unregulated) derivatives contract, underlines the adverse effects of asymmetric regulation and opaque transactions. Global uncertainty is reflected in the fact that the figure for overall losses is unknown; the IMF estimates, on the basis of its world econometric model, a global US\$300–400 billion. The world GDP, measured in US\$, was worth \$48,244 billion in 2006, at which point the subprime crisis involved around eight percent of world resources. This figure, which is impressive in absolute terms, is not that frightening if considered in relative terms; bankruptcies in the Italian banking system experienced in the 1980s involved around 10–20 percent of domestic resources, and similar figures are found in other European countries. The uncertainty refers also to the market where these losses will be more concentrated. Many analysts believe that emerging and deregulated markets will suffer the most, because of their higher structural risks, and because of the absence of tools and policies to counterbalance the slowdown and keep capital inside the country or market, in case of "flight to quality".

Paul Krugman (2007) is severe on the Federal Reserve for authorizing the financial system to undertake excessive risks: "money still talks in Washington, and the mortgage industry is a huge source of campaign finance. But maybe the subprime catastrophe will be enough to remind us why financial regulation was introduced in the first place". He singles out two things in particular that led the least sophisticated borrowers to run high risks deriving from very sophisticated securities: asymmetric information and excessive deregulation. Krugman's position is tough, but not illiberal. The turmoil in financial markets in 2007 has further underlined the issue of the liquidity of opaque markets and players. The lack of confidence in the inter-bank market has stressed the shorter segment of the yield curve, where liquidity is priced; the European and American central banks pumped liquidity to restored the market confidence and lower the bid-ask spread on the very short segment of the curve.

When the risk structure of a bank is unknown to outsiders (e.g. regulators), risk management and monitoring become very difficult. An important further element is the distinction between inside and outside liquidity. The first is provided through the market, and the latter through open market operations by the authority (Holmstrom and Tirole 1996). The turmoil has stressed the inside liquidity and dried it up.

The impressive growth of unregulated financial securities over the recent past can be interpreted using a modified version of the Keynesian liquidity paradox, where everybody feels liquid because of very low nominal monetary rates fueling banking credit, low inflation rates, and increasing demand for deregulated synthetic securities, characterized by high leverage. But when an exogenous shock happens and modifies the risk return path, volatility increases, prices exhibit a higher variance, and it can happen that synthetic securities cannot continue to insure the desired risk-return profile. This means that portfolios need to be restructured fast, squeezing liquidity. The leverage effect of derivatives amplifies losses, and the underlying credit system is put under further pressure. This paradox has dangerous consequences, since it can be worsened by hazard and herding behavior.

6. Exchange rate management with derivatives

Like other risks, the exchange rate can be managed by means of derivatives. The type of contracts and the most appropriate strategy depends on the exchange rate regime adopted by the country, the cooperation with the fiscal policy authority, and credibility.

Following the collapse of the Bretton Woods system, global exchange rates regimes are floating, priced on the basis of demand and supply. Fixed exchange rates or dirty floating regimes were used in the recent past by small countries wanting access to world trade; they were adopted in order to acquire credibility and maintain stability[15].

Trading of US$-denominated derivatives dominates the world market, followed by the Euro. This is confirmed for forwards, options and swaps, when measured either with notional amount or at gross market value. After 1972 the leading currency, the US dollar, has floated over other main currencies, but in fact the US authorities believe in some form of exchange rate management to achieve specific targets. After 2003 the US dollar devalued with respect to the Euro, lowering the real value of American external debt, created by the persistent deficit of the current account, which reached six percent of GDP in 2006. The Euro area has no explicit exchange rate management, since the European Central Bank (ECB) does not have the power to enforce a price, although it owns the foreign exchange reserves. While the ministers of finance or economics in EU countries have the power to manage price, they do not have the reserves to implement any currency policy at all.

Less industrialized countries, like Latin America and the emerging Asian economies, use currency boards or other pegs to stabilize the current account and attract foreign direct investments, which are welcomed to sustain the development process. The pegged regime pushes for an increase in foreign exchange reserves, which are employed to maintain the peg; the accumulation of reserves is very costly, since it subtracts resources to domestic development, and binds the monetary policy

---

15   Among others, see Krugman (1992).

to the external target of the rate. After a certain credibility is achieved, the exchange rate can be allowed to float, foreign reserves can be sold, and resources allocated domestically (ECB 2006).

In the case of pegged exchange rates, derivatives can help to stabilize the rate and manage the (low yield) reserves; they can be tools that both reduce and enhance market risks associated with given net flows. Garber (1998, 2) maintained that derivatives can play a very important role in capital flows. They can be useful to "evade risk-control or prudential regulation, circumvent capital controls, drive the dynamics of currency instabilities, and obscure true risk positions and thereby undermine the usefulness of balance of payments capital account categories." Garber has been one of the harshest to criticize the lack of information the balance of payments provides with respect to financial flows, and has contributed substantially to the international debate which finally lead to its modification.

The Balance of Payments Manual 5 (BPM5), applied from 2000 onward, filled part of the information gap, introducing greater details on securities and enhancing transparency. BPM5 recognized the role of cross-border derivatives, and explicitly considered them, separately from other securities[16].

Derivatives, especially OTC swaps or forwards, are used by sovereign states to manage exchange rate risk. This procedure is useful when the state issues foreign currency denominated bonds, or when the country has a high degree of openness[17], other than when there is an explicit currency peg to manage. Examples are Brazil and Mexico, which issue bonds denominated in US$ (OECD, 2002) or Italy[18], which sells part of its outstanding debt overseas and the hedges the associated risk. Most countries prefer OTC contracts because the size of their purchase is large, and because contracts are flexible enough to satisfy complex hedging needs. However, countries can hedge and manage but cannot fight against the market when a speculative attack takes place. In 1998, Thailand experienced a tough speculative attack on its currency, and tried to use futures to fight against back, but was brought to its knees by the market within a few weeks, since the central bank was the only buyer, while all market players were selling.

The cooperation between monetary and fiscal policy is necessary to achieve debt targets and exchange rate simultaneously. The role played by the information coming from the balance of payments and BIS statistics in that respect is fundamental, since it gives a wider picture of cross-border derivatives and of cross-border issued sovereign debt.

---

16 See Chapter 1 for further details.

17 The degree of openness is given by the sum of exports and imports over GDP. It is considered a measure of integration (or dependence) in international markets.

18 For further details see the Italian Treasury report on public debt management procedure, issued on a yearly basis.

Table 2.3a Amounts outstanding of OTC foreign exchanges derivatives

Notional amount outstanding at end June 2007, in millions of US dollars				
Instrument/ counterparty	Total	US dollar	Euro	Japanese Yen	Pound Sterling
Outright forwards and foreign exchange swaps	**24,525,828**	**21,244,032**	**8,648,254**	**4,142,517**	**3,873,248**
with reporting dealers	8,796,014	8,217,974	2,582,598	1,762,330	1,365,059
with other financial institutions	10,010,044	8,687,038	3,512,399	1,471,334	1,454,745
with non-financial institutions	5,719,775	4,339,020	2,553,260	908,852	1,053,447
Total including gold	**24,666,752**				
Currency Swaps	**12,290,774**	**10,308,388**	**5,426,230**	**1,852,125**	**2,823,987**
with reporting dealers	4,897,903	4,490,125	1,987,507	776,882	1,147,912
with other financial institutions	5,259,662	4,245,206	2,302,969	715,192	1,125,162
with non-financial institutions	2,133,213	1,573,057	1,135,753	360,050	550,912
Options sold	**8,607,448**	**6,592,249**	**3,081,453**	**3,393,783**	**763,215**
with reporting dealers	53,65,222	4,134,363	1,915,674	2,274,216	476,149
with other financial institutions	1,988,266	1,502,218	687,051	687,804	148,926
with non-financial institutions	1,253,965	955,670	481,727	431,761	138,139
Total including gold	**8,725,589**				
Options Bought	**8,660,054**	**6,553,641**	**3,044,015**	**3,513,088**	**799,225**
with reporting dealers	5,562,573	4,286,233	1,924,685	2,371,265	505,255
with other financial institutions	1,883,611	1,365,531	681,584	717,221	162,997
with non-financial institutions	1,213,876	901,877	437,746	424,601	130,971
Total including gold	**8,890,070**				
Total options	**11,803,614**	**8,935,596**	**4,205,291**	**4,584,136**	**1,071,744**
All instruments	**48,620,200**	**40,488,016**	**18,279,772**	**10,578,767**	**7,768,973**
Total contracts including gold	**49,045,744**				

Source: BIS derivatives statistics.

Table 2.3b Foreign exchange derivatives by instruments counterparty and currency

Instrument/ counterparty	Total	US dollar	Euro	Japanese Yen	Pound sterling
	Gross market value at end June 2007, in millions of US dollars				
Outright forwards and foreign exchange swaps	**491,825**	**434,078**	**120,101**	**143,631**	**51,797**
with reporting dealers	189,900	183,562	36,892	69,594	17,017
with other financial institutions	184,913	158,019	43,320	46,110	19,761
with non-financial institutions	117,020	92,499	39,888	27,970	15,019
Currency Swaps	**616,754**	**494,819**	**278,743**	**116,631**	**110,240**
with reporting dealers	153,436	137,282	54,028	37,343	25,207
with other financial institutions	290,927	226,405	138,009	50,192	51,089
with non-financial institutions	172,392	131,131	86,708	29,096	33,944
Options sold	**175,177**	**136,692**	**40,580**	**100,112**	**8,206**
with reporting dealers	108,516	85,482	24,066	67,565	4,648
with other financial institutions	43,149	31,238	10,384	20,404	2,436
with non-financial institutions	23,525	19,973	6,130	12,142	1,122
Options Bought	**167,963**	**129,715**	**39,722**	**94,404**	**8,041**
with reporting dealers	110,552	86,520	25,227	67,668	4,992
with other financial institutions	37,695	26,566	9,870	17,895	1,777
with non-financial institutions	19,719	16,630	4,625	8,840	1,270
Total options	**234,624**	**180,925**	**56,236**	**126,951**	**11,599**
All instruments	**1,343,192**	**1,109,850**	**455,080**	**387,211**	**173,636**
Total contracts including gold	**1,390,373**				

Source: BIS, foreign exchange derivatives statistics.

7. Monetary analysis of derivatives

As I remarked earlier, monetary policy pursues financial stability in an ever-evolving financial world. Derivatives play a role in the transmission mechanism of monetary policy, and their monetary nature can be investigated from different points of view: monetary aggregates, portfolio substitution, interest rate channel and expectations setting.

There are a number of similarities between the Eurodollar phenomenon of the 1970s and derivatives in the 1990s. Eurodollars were off balance sheet items for European banks, foreign currency denominated and grew at incredible rates over a fairly short period. They were used as vehicles to invest outside the strict international capital immobility imposed by the Bretton Woods exchange rate system, and posed a number of policy problems. The Eurodollar modified the ability of institutions (i.e. central banks) to strictly control money circulation and lending, and because of that their own autonomy from the Treasury has been criticized. Fratianni and Savona (1973) argued that the Eurodollar created a new system of international flows and accounting, referred to as the International Money Base and Liquidity, breaking the boundaries of domestic money creation. The European Monetary Union created a common currency 30 years later, but financial and monetary markets were European long before that date. Derivatives, like the Eurodollar, change the effectiveness of control and monitoring by national and international authorities by circumventing rules and accounting principles.

With respect to monetary measures, it is useful to clarify the difference between money and monetary base (or high-powered money, to use Friedman's expression). The latter is under the control of central banks in industrialized countries with developed financial markets, while money is the product of money base circulation. Various domestic and external events can affect its creation process. Various economists have defined the monetary base. Friedman and Schwartz (1963) and monetarists used the institutional definition. The functional definition underlines the role of compulsory reserves by the central bank, or free reserves held by banks (Fazio 1968). The analytical definition, proposed by Fratianni and Savona (1973), looks at the short-run reaction of the central bank interest rate to monetary instruments: there is a negative relationship between the supply of the money base and the interest rate, while the relationship between money and the interest rate is positive. This difference in reaction is observable in the short run, since, in the long run, if there is no money illusion or if rational expectations hold, the interest rate incorporates inflationary expectations, and the relationship cannot be but positive. It is worth noting that financial innovation is *per se* a short-run phenomenon.

None of these definitions is of help with respect to derivatives, since derivatives are not accepted as reserves by any institution. Moreover, in order to apply the analytical definition of money, we should identify the supply of the asset, which is not possible given available data[19]. Money is, instead, the result of the interaction of the monetary base with the market; money can be defined as those liquid instruments that are accepted for "the payment of the debt," and this leads to the creation of money aggregates.

In quiet periods for financial markets investors face a stable real cash balance, which can induce them to look at more efficient forms of money, yielding a (low) return, with an acceptable dose of risk. Financial innovation can play a role in this search for new opportunities, and liquid innovative instruments can substitute monetary securities in the portfolios of sophisticated investors. If an instrument needs liquidity and a certain risk, presuming no exogenous shock happens, portfolio shift and rebalancing can move toward derivatives and away from traditional instruments, which have the same liquidity, but a less efficient combination of direct and indirect costs and risks. The equivalence between futures and bonds and time deposits can be considered the other way round to evaluate the liquidity of the two alternatives. The increase in liquidity fuels the demand for innovative financial securities, and *vice versa*.

Then the issue becomes to identify which derivatives have certain monetary characteristics. This could be addressed if comprehensive data on transactions and counterparts were available, which unfortunately they are not.

Strictly linked to this is the issue of how derivatives affect the motive to hold on to money. As Keynes explained (1936), L_1 is the money for transactions and exchange-traded futures can substitute it. In fact, firms substitute cash for periodic payments with very liquid futures, rolled over relevant expirations dates; the most liquid futures in the US are written on the Federal Fund rate, and the Eurodollar.

L_2 is the Keynesian money for speculation, and can be substituted by financial securities available. Many exogenous and endogenous forces—expectations, shocks, risk attitude and market rumors—affect it.

Financial substitution and prevalence are at the basis of the creation of money aggregates over time, but I believe that this issue cannot be analysed only from a quantitative point of view (i.e. effects on aggregates). Both portfolio substitution and the choice of liquid instruments are heavily influenced by financial innovation. If the characteristics of instruments are liquidity and risk, and no exogenous shock takes place, a portfolio shift can happen, pushing up the demand for derivatives contracts that are tailored to customers' needs, are liquid and exhibit an acceptable dose of risk. An example is the time deposit, which is financially equivalent to a portfolio with a short future on bond, and a long position on the underlying bond[20]. The spread of derivatives in portfolios is the result of the evolution of the payment system and can modify the dynamic of money and monetary base, on the basis of

---

19   A research paper by Savona, Maccario and Oldani (2000) considered only one derivatives contract, although relevant, and the analytical definition of money; the results show that this contract behaves like money base.

20   The underlying bond can be defined by the cheapest to deliver strategy. See Hull (2002) for details, and Angeloni and Massa (1998) on the economic equivalence.

the degree of substitution. Moreover, the Goodhart law, which, after observing the evolution process of money, states that once you find statistical evidence or a rule the market circumvents it, offers a powerful explanation of the behavior of financial markets, when a definition of money is imposed.

The interest rate channel of monetary policy is heavily affected by derivatives (Violi 2000; Fan et al. 2007). The structure of the banking system and financial markets determine both the speed and magnitude of the response of interest rates to monetary actions. Since markets and operators are very mature, the response of bank lending rates to monetary actions is relatively small, and longer policy actions are required to achieve the desired effect (Sellon 2002). The possibility to hedge allows firms to soften the blow if interest rates unexpectedly rise, weakening the impact of the maneuver (Fan et al. 2007). The changes in financial structure have modified the working of the interest rate channel of monetary policy, and it can now work through the capital market as well as the banking system.

7.1 Derivatives and the expectations' setting

The issue of expectation setting has been addressed in the recent literature, after observing that interest rates and financial stability are heavily influenced by it. I believe derivatives play a role here, and that the statistical poverty of data can be overcome. We need to distinguish between liquid and standardized derivatives transactions, from which market expectations can be taken with a small forecast error, and opaque and non-standardized transactions, where the error can be far bigger. I refer to the first class of contracts when considering the informative role of derivatives.

Soderlind and Svensson (1997) survey most applied techniques to extract market expectations from financial securities for monetary policy purposes. In particular, they underline the importance of implied forward interest rates and options prices to extract future time paths, or even the entire probability distribution. An investigation of Japanese data (Nakamura and Shiratsuka 1999) confirms their theory. An econometric investigation on the interest rate movements of the ECB (Vahamaa 2005) further shows that market expectations are asymmetric around monetary policy actions[21], and that they change around policy maneuvers.

The ECB (2000) explicitly acknowledges the information content provided by interest rate derivatives; derivatives prices incorporate information on different characteristics associated with market expectations. The slope of the yield curve is usually viewed as a useful indicator of expectations about economic activity and inflation. Financial markets anticipate and "price in" changes in the official rates in determining the prices of assets. Derivatives contain information on different

---

21 Vahamaa (2005) shows that market participants attach higher probabilities for sharp yield increases than for decreases around policy tightening. This confirms that expectations change around policy actions, and that they return to normal only after the change has taken place.

aspects of uncertainty, e.g. swap spreads, or the implied volatility of options. The implied volatility of German Bund future options increased during 1999–2000 while the implied volatility of three-month Euribor future options (the most important European banking rate) decreased steadily over the same period. The increase in uncertainty on German bonds failed to have a negative influence on the Euribor, while short-term uncertainty diminished. The information coming from financial markets, including the derivatives market, is taken into account in the way the ECB conducts monetary policy, but "Market expectations extracted from financial asset prices cannot be a substitute of future economic conditions." (ECB 2000) This seemingly simple statement is in fact a strong statement on the role of expectations. Those coming from financial markets cannot substitute those referring to future economic conditions. Financial rumors, or temporary deviations in asset prices, cannot influence monetary policy.

Moving further from the monetary nature of single contracts, a pioneering study (Upper 2006) looks at the existence of a statistically significant relationship between derivatives activity and the perception of monetary policy—the perception is captured by the unanticipated variation of the interest rate. The hypothesis is that derivatives are able to anticipate future fluctuations in monetary policy. Up to now, the literature has investigated the inverse relationship, i.e. how monetary policy influences future prices. The exercise is run on monthly data (February 1999–June 2006) to abstract from day-to-day fluctuations on G3 countries, the US, Canada and Japan, characterized by highly liquid and developed financial systems. Derivatives considered in the analysis are exchange traded futures contracts written on Federal Funds, Eurodollar, Euribor, and Euroyen, which are the most traded and liquid contracts in these countries. Derivatives activity is represented by the turnover of futures contracts. The limit of the exercise is the use of exchange traded contracts, which have various good substitutes in OTC contracts. Data referring to OTC contracts cannot be employed for estimates, because they are not sufficiently detailed, and the breakdown is too rough. The relationship between derivatives activity and changes in the interest rates is positive and visible in the G3 countries and Europe.

The contract-by-contract monthly estimate for each of the G3 countries is the investigation of variables influencing the turnover, and can be represented as:

$$\Delta turnover = \alpha + \beta_1 turnover_{-1} + \beta_2 turnover_{-12} + \beta_3 |\Delta futrates| + \beta_4 |\Delta unantrates| +$$
$$\beta_5 |\Delta antrates| + \beta_6 \Delta impl.vol + \beta_7 DiffOpin + u \tag{4}$$

where *turnover* refers to the turnover of the future contract and its relevant lags are used as regressors, *futrates* is the changes in implied three-month rates two months ahead, *unantrates* is the unanticipated variation in the interest rates, *antrates* in the anticipated variation in the rates, *impl.vol* is the implied volatility of the at-the-money options, and *DiffOpin* is the standard deviation of the individual forecasts for three-month interest rates in any given month. This function shows how changes in the interest rates react to the turnover of relevant futures.

Empirical results confirm that all variables are statistically significant except for the anticipated changes, which have no effect on turnover for any contract. Changes in expected interest rates rather than actual changes affect trading in derivatives on short-term interest rates[22].

Before Upper, the literature always considered futures prices as influenced by monetary policy, not the other way round. Upper's study, although limited to three countries, shed light over a reverse causation among monetary policy and financial markets that merits further research.

8. Monetary aggregates and derivatives[23]

The debate around the role played by monetary aggregates in policy making and the theory is very hot. I'd like to take a little time to explain my position, and describe the American and European (distant) approaches to financial innovation.

Monetary aggregates, widely used in monetary policy, are defined by the degree of liquidity of assets and the evolution of financial markets drives changes in their definition. Monetary aggregates are those referring to narrow money (cash, coins and sight deposits at banks). No money aggregate is considered to be the best measure of money, as observed by many central banks, but second-best solutions can be achieved. Monetary aggregates, which provide useful information about the underlying economic activity, are preferred, but the choice cannot be made *a priori*. The simple definition of assets to be computed in the aggregate is that money means all assets that can be used in settlement of a debt—but there is no special theory to identify them[24].

The decision of the US Federal Reserve, announced in March 2006, to stop the measurement and disclosure of M3[25] is justified by the lack of information the aggregate provides about the underlying economic activity, but also indirectly acknowledges the role played by financial innovation. The lack of information is due to improvements in the system of payments, where there are now better tools for the payment of debt, and to financial substitution. Derivatives play a role in both of these. By looking at single non-M2 components of M3 we can observe the actual effects of derivatives, and try to find a different approach to the relationship between monetary aggregates, economic activity and financial securities.

---

22   Upper (2006) admits that using higher frequency data might change these results, and that the econometric tests on stationarity provide contrasting evidence, suggesting that the robustness check might not support the evidence univocally.

23   I thank Michele Bagella, Emilio Barone and Francesco Nucci for their helpful suggestions.

24   A different approach is that of weighted monetary assets (Barnett 1997) where each component of the aggregate is weighted by its user cost. Nevertheless, this approach does not provide any theoretical definition of assets.

25   For a detailed definition of US money aggregates, see Table 2.4.

M3 does not appear to convey any additional information about economic activity that is not already embodied in M2 and has not played a role in the monetary policy process for many years. Consequently, the Board judged that the costs of collecting the underlying data and publishing M3 outweigh the benefits (Federal Reserve 2006).

8.1 Monetary management in the US and the EU

Table 2.4 US Federal reserve system monetary aggregates

The H.6 (Money Stock) release, published weekly, provides measures of the monetary aggregates (M1, M2, and M3) and their components.
M1, M2, and M3 are progressively more inclusive measures of money: M1 is included in M2, which is included in M3.
M1, the most narrowly defined measure, consists of the most liquid forms of money, namely currency and checkable deposits.
The non-M1 components of M2 are primarily household holdings of savings deposits, small time deposits, and retail money market mutual funds.
The non-M2 components of M3 consist of institutional money funds and certain managed liabilities of depositories, namely large time deposits, repurchase agreements, and Eurodollars.

Source: http://www.federalreserve.gov/releases/h6/about.htm.

Monetary aggregates currently used for policy analysis in the US are narrow, i.e. M1 and M2, and provide useful information on (real) economic activity. The non-M2 components of M3 consist of institutional money funds (IMFs), certain managed liabilities of depositories, namely large time deposits (LTD), repurchase agreements (RA), and Eurodollars (EU$).

$$M3 = M2 + IMFs + LGT + RA + EU\$ \tag{5}$$

Looking closely at M3, the selective replacement process has affected all of these.

Table 2.5 Growth rates of US non-M2 assets of M3

	1980–2006	1990–2006	1995–2006	2000–2006
M3	4.65	1.52	1.34	0.56
M2	5.83	1.84	1.15	0.55
LTDs	5.22	1.65	2.66	0.83
Euro$	6.74	2.99	3.73	1.43
Overnights	11.27	2.46	1.89	0.71
IMFs	102.04	9.28	4.33	0.76
Time and Saving	6.39	2.17	1.93	0.77

Source: St. Louis FRED database.

The plot of non-M2 components of M3 shows that their pattern of growth has been not homogeneous. During the past 25 years or less, the driving assets are time and savings deposits, followed by LTDs (a share) and overnights. Eurodollar and IMFs show very different patterns, since their growth rates have decreased steadily. IMFs are losing their attractiveness because there are many other liquid instruments that can accrue similar return and risk. The abundance of credit at the world level[26] has reduced the return on money funds, moving preferences toward instruments that can guarantee liquidity at low risk, but at non null return, like repos, portfolio of futures, and other types of funds (exchange traded funds, or ETFs). The Eurodollar is (negatively) affected by the (devalued) exchange rate between the Euro and the dollar (the decrease in) the financial flows to the US, and the very low interest rates in Europe during the last five years.

The decision by the Federal Reserve to quit the measurement of M3 marks the difference in strategy between it and the European central bank. In the first part of its life the ECB set an explicit growth target for M3 (i.e. the second pillar) of 4.5 percent, which has never been achieved since 2002. The ECB modified the definition of assets to be included in M3 (Table 2.6), and at the present M3 includes expiring bonds and securities held only by EU residents, and not by foreigners, based on the fact that the relationship with consumption, and core inflation, should be weak. The definition of European M3 considers debt securities of up to two years' maturity. This last part of the aggregate is vague enough to let the ECB consider different securities in the computation, according to the evolution of the financial and payment system.

---

26   Federal Reserve chairman Ben Bernanke has defined this phenomenon as "saving glut."

Table 2.6 Definitions of euro area monetary aggregates

Liabilities	M1	M2	M3
Currency in circulation	X	X	X
Overnight deposits	X	X	X
Deposits with an agreed maturity up to 2 years		X	X
Deposits redeemable at a period of notice up to 3 months		X	X
Repurchase agreements			X
Money market fund (MMF) shares/units			X
Debt securities up to 2 years			X

Note: (1) Liabilities of the money-issuing sector and central government liabilities with a monetary character held by the money-holding sector.

The ECB's definition of euro area monetary aggregates is based on the following:

- A harmonized definition of the money-issuing sector. It consists of those entities which issue liabilities with a high degree of moneyness to non-MFIs located in the euro area (excluding central government). This sector comprises MFIs resident in the euro area.

- A harmonized definition of the money-holding sector, which comprises all non-MFIs resident in the euro area (except central government). In addition to households, non-financial corporations and financial institutions which are not MFIs are included, as well as state and local governments and social security funds. Central governments are considered to constitute a "money-neutral" sector, with one exception: central government liabilities with a monetary character (Post Office accounts, national savings accounts and Treasury accounts) are included as a special item in the definition of monetary aggregates.

- The harmonized definitions of MFI liabilities categories. These make it possible to distinguish between MFI liabilities according to their degree of moneyness, while also taking into account the features of different financial systems.

Source: ECB Statistical Warehouse: Monetary Statistics.

In its July 2007 monthly bulletin the ECB states that financial innovation, namely derivatives, has modified the way monetary analysis is conducted. It affirms that:

> ... holdings of retail derivatives and/or easier credit supply conditions resulting from increased securitization of bank loans represent financial innovations that change the structure of the monetary sector and thus their impact should be discounted in assessing monetary developments. However, such an approach would ignore how these innovations have increased the aggregate liquidity of the domestic private sector and eased overall financing conditions, both of which may lead to stronger aggregate spending and thus ultimately inflationary pressures. (69)

The boundaries of liquidity change according to the needs of the private sector, which looks for moneyed debt securities. This consciousness seems to widen the gap between the monetary analysis developed at the central bank, and its active monetary management, which considers only the relationship between the growth rate of money and inflationary pressures over the medium term (Trichet 2006), and not other relevant financial driving forces.

8.2 Replication of monetary assets and selective replacement

Financial replication and selective replacement explain reduced interest in traditional payment instruments, and justify the lower informative ability of monetary aggregates with respect to the underlying economic activity observed by the Federal Reserve.

Institutional money funds (IMFs) are operations through which large institutions provide cash to a money market fund, and earn the overnight rate. IMFs can be replicated by means of rolled over forwards, futures and options contracts, written on US short-term bonds (treasury bills). Futures have short maturities (days, weeks or months), the underlying rate is "risk-less," and the contract is very liquid. A large (in excess of US$100,000) time deposit (LTD) is a repurchase of (usually) government securities over a certain term or period of *time* and earns the repo rate. The cash receiver (repo seller) sells *securities* in return for *cash* to the cash provider (repo buyer), and agrees to repurchase those securities from the cash provider for a greater sum of cash at a later date, that greater sum being all the cash lent and some extra (constituting the implicit interest rate or repo rate). There is little that prevents any security from being employed in a repo, so, corporate, treasury or government bills, corporate and treasury bonds, and corporate bonds or shares may all be used as securities involved in a repo.

The IMF-LTD final price is the compound price (S_0) of the security plus, considering the risk free interest rate.

$$F_t = S_0 e^{rt} \tag{6}$$

By imposing the "no arbitrage" condition, the present discounted value of the payoff is such that $S_0 = F_0 = F_t e^{-rt}$. This is also the simplest pricing rule of the forward contract in the presence of the risk-less rate (r) and in the absence of friction and costs. In real financial markets, the risk-less rate would be substituted with the repo rate, and the length of the operation can vary from intra-day to months. The formula should incorporate various costs that sum negatively to the interest accrued. It is clear that a simple future-forward strategy can efficiently replicate IMF-LTD[27].

---

27 For more complex strategies, including different currencies, see Avellaneda and Laurence (2000), and Hull (2002).

Eurodollars are deposits in dollars at banks headquartered outside the *United States*, or in foreign branches of banks headquartered within the United States. The rate of return of these deposits is the Eurodollar rate, which is driven by the US Federal Reserve. Deposits usually exceed $1million and involve financial institutions, not private investors. Eurodollars can be efficiently replicated by means of their own futures and options contracts, OTC or exchange traded[28]. This explains the diminishing demand for the underlying deposit.

The end of M3 measurement means that non-M2 assets do not bring additional information to the central bank. I believe it is basically a demand-driven phenomenon, where the evolution of financial and money markets changes the asset, and players use other tools for "the payment of debt," modifying the relationship with the underlying economic activity. Wide money aggregates in a stylized money demand function can be informative because of the modified environment in which they are put, and lose their overall relevance.

One economic consequence of financial replication is the selective replacement of inefficient assets. In consumer-portfolio theory[29], individual preferences are set toward special characteristics, like liquidity, profit (or costs) and risk. Introducing more attractive financial assets in the market crowds out less efficient and less attractive securities, improving the liquidity and pricing process of the innovative assets. This process is demand driven, in the sense that the finance industry introduces innovative instruments on a daily basis to satisfy customer needs; the market decides which innovation is going to survive, and "kills" other securities, by eliminating the demand. The demand for innovative and attractive securities increases, indicating investor preference, so the market amplifies the initial advantages of the innovative instruments. The possibility of using different assets as collateral (for the payment of debts) is the key to opening the door to innovation. At present, OTC contracts (swaps, forward) are not accepted as collateral because of the counterparty risk they exhibit. But some financial institutions can accept exchange-traded contracts, like futures on special underlying[30].

8.3 Money and the relation with the underlying economic activity

Monetary aggregates are useful for policy making because of their ability to provide information on underlying economic activity, and the relationship between variables and their stability. Money aggregates evolve according to the changing habits of payments and investments, and wide aggregates include relevant financial securities. The recent debate about the importance of money aggregates is well

---

28   Replication is likely to work better with ET contracts, which are more liquid and transparent than OTC.

29   Lancaster utility model (1971).

30   The choice of derivatives contract can be based on the "cheapest to deliver" strategy, where the value of the contract depends on the quality of the underlying on which is written (e.g. on sovereign states' bonds with a high credit standing).

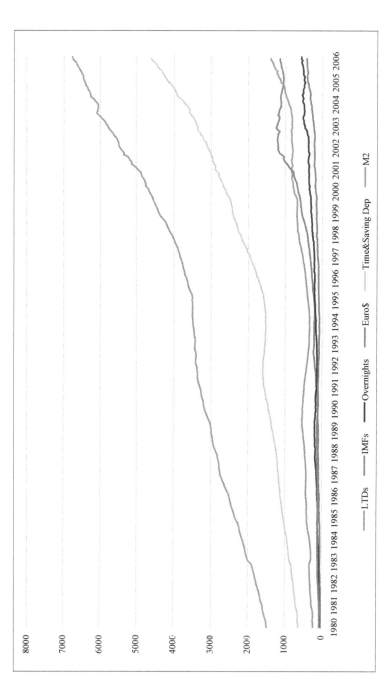

Graph. 2.3 Components of US monetary aggregates (monthly, $US billions)
Source: St. Louis FRED data.

founded, because a number of central institutions recognize an ever-increasing distance between liquidity measures and monetary aggregates. There is an active and disruptive circularity, but generally speaking real money demand (i.e. deflated money aggregates) and other money demand-related measures are useful informative variables for monetary analysis, in the pursuit of stability.

Money has played a special role in monetary theory, but the neoclassical interpretation (i.e. "the veil of money") denies it has played any role in the economic system. Michael Woodford (2006), a prominent exponent of NK economics, in his contribution to the fourth ECB conference on the (ir)relevance of money, stressed how NK models[31] can be easily represented as neoclassical: the quantity theory of money in the Cambridge version can be added to other equations (IS, Phillips and so on) without affecting the solution. This argument is coherent with the irrelevance of money, which is the conclusion of most general equilibrium models. The quantity theory is interpreted as the money demand function, linking money and inflation via interest rates, and does not affect any other piece of the model, since monetary policy is governed only by the Taylor rule. I strongly agree with Woodford's theoretical synthesis[32], but want to underline the fact that in the short run (i.e. away from equilibrium) money can play a signaling role for the central bank. In the long run, equilibrium money and money demand do not influence growth and income—but in the long run we are all dead!

The fact that liquidity drives innovation can be viewed from the opposite approach: innovation sustains the demand for liquidity, and the causal relationship is broken. This endogeneity, very common in macroeconomic models, can be addressed with special econometric techniques, which however an only be used to interpret data.

Stock and Watson (2003) review the literature on the ability of financial variables to forecast output and inflation, and argue that some asset prices have been helpful in predicting inflation and output growth in some countries during some periods, but generally speaking instability among bi-variate and tri-variate predictors is detected when asset prices are considered. Asset prices are basically the prices of stock exchange securities, like shares and bonds. Their predictive ability justifies their use in the forecast. Asset prices taken together have predictive power but lose it at individual level, rendering the robustness check very difficult. Moreover, various econometric problems arise when asset prices are considered, since they exhibit non-stationarity and suffer excess volatility[33]. I suggest the use of a class of financial securities, which embed market expectations (Soderlind and Svensson 1997, Upper 2006 and the ECB, 2000). Derivatives, among them exchange traded futures, have price discovery properties and can extract market expectations over

---

31 These are dynamic stochastic general equilibrium (DSGE) types of model.
32 Further details are given in part 9 of this chapter.
33 This weakens the stability of parameters and the reliability of results.

relevant prices[34]. Since derivatives contracts price market expectations, they can be used as substitutes for underlying securities and securities that can be replicated efficiently.

The next step, after having observed the death of M3 and traditional moneyed instruments, should be to think critically about useful alternative measures of money demand that can satisfy the policy purpose, i.e. looking at information on economic activity and stability. The US Federal Reserve is confronting its actions with a number of inflationary and financial risks, and its new approaches are coherent with the emergence of unknown risks. According to various speeches from the Federal Reserve's chairman, the increase in real estate prices does not correspond to a bubble, and the main risks come from the financial sector (e.g. hedge funds and subprime—Bernanke 2006 and 2007).

Financial variables have a strong link with economic activity, as surveyed by Stock and Watson (2003), and should be considered in policy-making. Informative power comes from derivatives, and not from their underlying. In consequence, they should not be added to other monetary assets, but allowed to play an informative role in the pursuit of stability.

8.4 Futures and money demand

The ability of certain types of derivatives to incorporate current market expectations, and signal the future[35] can be employed as an informative tool for monetary authorities. Financial innovation, which provides information to policy authorities, should be incorporated into policy making. Usually, policy making considers a model to explain forces, which represents long-run structure and temporary deviations from the equilibrium path, and innovation is, by definition, a temporary deviation from traditional equilibrium, or the demands of securities. Once the innovation is well established, it is no longer innovative. In other words, financial innovation cannot be considered a determinant of monetary aggregates, since its effects vanish in the long run. Nevertheless, derivatives can explain short-run deviations in money demand.

Liquid and efficient derivatives contracts, written on relevant underlying assets, in terms of relative size, and monitored by the central bank, can be employed in the pursuit of financial stability.

Very liquid and representative derivatives are ET futures—the "measurement" of the contribution of futures is the next step. Statistics on futures, other than prices[36], refer to notional value and open interest (OI): the notional value is never

---

34   Econometric problems can be still present, since derivatives' prices are non-stationary.

35   Among others see Cohen (1999), Kearney and Lombra (2004), Hung-Gay and Leung (1993), Herbst and Maberly (1992), and Yiuman (1999).

36   Variables are usually taken in logs, but the log of derivatives' prices is null by definition. The log of the price of an asset approximates its return, and, in perfect financial

exchanged between the parties for these contracts, which are cash settled on the difference or rolled over. Conversely, open interest is a measure of demand and transaction, and can satisfy our need for a signal.

Another problem frequently raised in the monetary literature is endogeneity; models should be represented with at least one identifiable exogenous variable but many macroeconomic variables are not. Money, regardless of how it is measured, is the result of circulation and demand, and is endogenous. CPI and GDP are endogenous too. At the present we cannot identify a model that incorporates different endogenous variables, and adding innovation does not make the exercise any easier.

Instead I will look at relationships between variables, understand whether the innovation is linked to the policy variables, and can be considered a signal for the authority (i.e. reflects market expectations).

Since the Federal Reserve looks at information on economic activity, and relies on the relationships between narrow aggregates (M1 or M2) and the underlying economic activity (GDP and CPI), we can introduce financial variables, which are "expectation catchers," to overcome the low informative power of wide aggregates and consider the evolution of habits of payment and investment.

The approach to modern monetary policy, testified at the fourth ECB conference in November 2006[37], is not based on quantity of money but on capital ratios and risks. Ratings and risk-weighted coefficients, not multipliers, are the tools of central banks[38]. The fact that we analyse the informative contribution rather than the quantitative effect is consistent with the evolution of monetary policy.

The informative relationship between money demand and economic activity can be described implicitly as:

$$M=f(GDP,\ CPI,\ signal) \tag{7}$$

where M is narrow money M2 (or M1), CPI is the inflation rate, GDP is the growth rate of output, and *signal* is the variable that reflects market expectations. In the long run the *signal* vanishes, since it is incorporated into the previous two.

According to Stock and Watson (2003) the use of (single) financial securities for forecasting economic activity provides econometrically weak results, but if the financial variable is less volatile, results should improve. Moreover, the chosen asset has to be relevant in terms of liquidity, demand and efficient pricing.

---

markets, the return on derivatives is null (the return is due to the underlying asset price and not to the derivative contract). Considering non-null returns implies the presence of arbitraging opportunities, which is coherent with the hypothesis of inefficient market, where monetary policy cannot pursue price stability.

37   The conference title was "The role of money: money and monetary policy in the twenty-first century," Frankfurt am Main, November 9–10, 2006.

38   This is exactly the difference between Basel I Capital Accord, based on fixed risk and capital ratios approach, and Basel II, which considers a risk-weighted approach.

Futures are relevant in US financial markets, and chosen contracts are written on the Eurodollar and the Federal Fund rate; the former reached US$4 trillion notional amount in 2006 at the CME, and the second US$5 trillion at the CBOT. As Yiuman (1999) and Hung-Gay and Leung (1993) showed, futures have good price discovery ability on the underlying asset price, and this can be used to extract market expectations for relevant prices. Herbst and Maberly (1992) show that this ability can be employed on US stock indices futures to extract market expectations. Futures have an efficient pricing system, but we want to address and get rid of the econometric weakness due to the use of prices and rely on demand measures and open interest instead of price measure to extract information. In this way we satisfy the need for an efficient financial security to proxy market expectations, but avoid the excessive volatility of prices.

8.5 Empirical investigation

The informational contribution of financial securities to underlying economic activity can be detected through a cointegration money demand relationship. The non-stationary nature of the variables involved has been deeply discussed in the literature, and the econometric problems, mainly related to weakness of coefficients, are addressed in order to advance a different approach to the problem. Cointegration is a way to analyse the relationship between un-stationary (i.e. integrated) variables[39], in order to find a stable representation among them. This procedure is useful when problems of endogeneity arise, breaking causal relationships among the variables.

I investigate the informative role played by financial securities with respect to US economic activity in the period 1982–2006, considering quarterly data. The estimate is limited by data availability; because financial derivatives have only recently been traded, and OTC transactions cannot be considered in the empirical exercise. The choice of contracts reflects their overall relevance in the American financial system, and in relation to the international financial system.

The Federal Reserve's statement about the lack of information of M3 (i.e. non-M2 securities) is taken for granted, and not investigated further. I first check whether M2 has the required informative power, then focus attention on the informative ability of other securities, which provide reliable and long data, are free of excess volatility, and representative of the US financial system. In this way I explicitly address Stock and Watson's (2003) problem of econometric weakness of financial time series estimates for the monetary analysis, but consider securities that are relevant in investors' portfolios.

The first step is verification of M2 informative power. Data are quarterly, taken in logs, refers to the US, and go from 1970Q1 to 2006Q2[40]. The GDP is the quarterly time series supplied by the US Bureau of Economic Analysis, measured

---

39   See Hamilton (1994) for time series analysis of non stationary series.
40   Complete econometric results are available from the author on request.

in US$ billion at current prices. The CPI is the time series of the consumer price core index, excluding food and energy, supplied by the US Bureau of Labor Statistics, 1982 = 100. M2 is the times series of the monthly supply of M2 supplied by the Federal Reserve, measured in US$ billion, at current prices. The first check confirms that M2 has a strong relationship with the underlying economic activity, proxied by the GDP and the CPI[41]. This superiority has also been shown for the US economy by Elger et al. (2006). Following the literature, I expect that nominal income will have a positive relationship with nominal money, and that inflation will have a negative relationship. These signs hold in the absence of money illusion, or structural breaks in productivity[42].

The cointegration relationship (Johansen) among money, income[43] and inflation can be written as follows:

$$\text{Log}(M2_{-1}) - 38.58\text{Log}(CPI_{-1}) + 18.81\text{Log}(GDP_{-1}) + 41.41$$
$$\text{S.E.} \qquad (11.96) \qquad\quad (8.19) \qquad\qquad\qquad\qquad\qquad (8)$$

Results show that in terms of magnitude inflation affects money more than income, but the signs are not the anticipated ones[44].

The second step is the investigation of the informative power of the chosen financial variables. The most traded and liquid exchange traded futures in the US market are written on the Eurodollar, the Federal Fund rate, the Dow Jones industrial average index, and the Euribor rate. Financial replication is clear for the Eurodollar future, and for the Federal Fund future. The Euribor rate is the European interest rate and its demand (spot and future) is fuelled by perfect international capital mobility, and the difference between US and EU interest rates. The DJIA is written on one of the most important worldwide stock indexes; its underlying is not a component of money aggregates, but the wealth invested in it (spot and futures) testifies its importance.

The future on Eurodollar is traded at the Chicago Mercantile Exchange (CME). Its notional amount reached US$4 trillion in 2006, it has a notional value of US$1 million, it is cash settled on the basis of the LIBOR rate, and has three-monthly expirations (March, June, September, and December). The underlying is the deposit of US$ in Europe, i.e. the return corrected by the exchange rate between the Euro and the US$. The future on the Federal Fund rate is traded at

---

41 The Phillips and Perron test confirms that variables are I(1). The length of VAR has been chosen on the basis of Akaike information criteria.

42 According to various speeches by the chairman of the Federal Reserve, there was a structural change in productivity in the US during the 1990s (Greenspan 2000).

43 The entire exercise has been run considering also filtered measures of the GDP, but results are very similar.

44 A number of empirical investigations detect instability of parameters in the 1980s, because of deregulation, financial innovation and changes in productivity (Cesarano 1990; Glennon and Lane 1996; Ireland 1995).

the Chicago Board of Trade (CBOT) and has a notional value of US$5 million. It is cash settled according to the last working day Federal Reserve fund overnight rate, settled by the New York Federal Reserve Bank, and has 30-day expirations. It is priced at 100 minus the Federal Fund rate. The Dow Jones Industrial Average future is traded at the Chicago Board of Trade (CBOT) and its value changes of US$10 each tick movement of the index. The Euribor future is traded at the London International Financial Future Exchange (LIFFE), with €1 million notional value, three-monthly expirations, priced as 100 minus the Euribor rate, and is cash settled. Its underlying is the European Inter Bank Offer Rate (Euribor), and its derivatives accounts for more than 99 percent of the whole European derivatives market activity. The future reached US$29 trillion turnover at LIFFE in November 2005, after the pick of US$32 trillion in June[45]. The Johansen cointegration procedure is a way to investigate the relationship between non-stationary variables. Its use in the presence of financial variables usually yields weak results, because their volatility is hardly captured. Using data on open interest of derivatives, which proxy the size and activity of the market, but are free of (undesirable) high volatility, solves this difficulty. The plot of the variable, for different (relevant) US contracts, supports this choice.

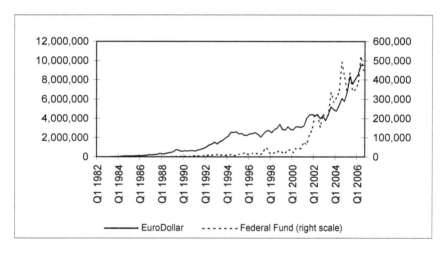

**Graph 2.4 Open interest of EuroDollar and Federal Fund futures
(quarterly, number of contracts)**
Source: Thomson Financial Datastream.

Moving to the estimation, a restriction that cannot be overcome is the length of data, and this allows us to choose those contracts that are representative in relation

---

45   Source: BIS Quarterly Review, March 2006.

to the US economy, and old enough to enable us to run the estimate. The chosen contracts are the Eurodollar future, which has been traded since 1982, and the Federal Fund future, introduced in 1989.

The econometric procedure starts with the simple (unrestricted) VAR, and the Johansen cointegration test. The Akaike information criterion shows that the length should be equal to 4. Results with the Eurodollar confirm the existence of two cointegration vectors; the first vector of the VAR(4) can be written as follows:

$$\text{Log(M2)-2.993Log(GDP)+3.12Log(CPI)+0.153Log(Eurodollar OI)}$$
$$\text{S.E.} \quad (0.23) \qquad\qquad (0.439) \qquad (0.033) \qquad\qquad\qquad (9)$$

These results confirm that the Eurodollar is relevant in the adjustment process, and is informative about money, income and inflation; the positive coefficient suggests that the derivative has a monetary nature[46].

The second econometric estimate considers the Federal Fund future. The VAR(4) procedure suggests the existence of one cointegration vector. The vector can be represented as:

$$\text{Log(M2)-3.78Log(GDP)+7.39Log(CPI)-0.070Log(FedFund OI)}$$
$$\text{S.E.} \quad (0.447) \qquad\qquad (0.935) \qquad (0.017) \qquad\qquad\qquad (10)$$

The coefficient of the Federal Fund deserves special attention. The underlying asset is the instrument of the Federal Reserve bank and its relationship with the supply of money should be negative. This result is also verified for its derivatives; this confirms the efficient pricing mechanism on the one hand, and the informative power of the future on the other.

The results do not reject the existence of a relationship between the variables. In particular, the future coefficient is always significantly different from zero, both in the Eurodollar and the Federal Fund; it is small and has a significant elasticity with respect to money. The GDP and CPI have the expected (opposite) signs and coefficients are always statistically different from zero. The residuals lie by and large in the area ±2 standard deviations with variability around zero, which is acceptable in order to avoid spurious regression.

Now we move further and look at market expectations all together rather than singly. In this way we solve the Stock and Watson financial instability (2003), and consider market expectations free from undesired excess volatility. The empirical exercise was run considering both future contracts in the function. The cointegration test confirms the existence of one vector, which can be represented as:

---

46 By considering the OI as an explanatory variable in the function, income and inflation show up with the expected sign. This feature supports the importance of financial innovation.

Log(M2)+7.39Log(CPI)-3.91Log(GDP)-0.06Log(FedFun_I)+0.014Log(Eurod_OI)
S.E.   (0.69)   (0.29)   (0.016)   (0.044)   (11)

Residuals lie in the area ±2 standard deviations, with variability around zero, confirming that the regression is not spurious. Coefficients of the macroeconomic variables, money income and inflation, have the expected sign. The Federal Fund future has negative and the Eurodollar positive elasticity. This very important result shows that taking market expectations either singly or together does not affect their informative power. In fact, the coefficients are very similar in the single contract result and in the two contracts, confirming that the relationship is robust.

These results confirm that future contracts are relevant "expectation catchers," both singly and together. The Federal Fund underlying rate is the instrument of policy action, and has a negative relationship with money demand, because a restrictive monetary policy is reflected in an increase in the Federal Fund rate. The Eurodollar has a positive relationship, and is not a monetary policy instrument; an increase in its demand pushes up money. Moreover, the difference in the sign can be due to different expectations influencing the open interests of the contracts (i.e. demand), which play different roles in portfolios.

9. Monetary policy: An expectations' management exercise

Modern macroeconomics considers monetary policy as a way to guarantee price stability (of goods, services, and markets) and safeguard the monetary and financial system through regulation and monitoring. The interactions among macroeconomic variables in the transmission mechanism can be affected by operators' expectations, which can influence the allocation of resources and the authority's performance. Three theories can explain the expectation setting.

The simplest is extrapolative, where a variable's future value is corrected of an small alpha from its historic value. There are systematic errors and turning points are not forecasted.

$$X^e_{t,t+1} - X_t = \alpha(X_t - X_{t-1}) \tag{12}$$

Autoregressive expectations are formulated to correct the prediction error, rather than the past value of the variable. Still turning points are not forecasted.

$$X^e_{t,t+1} - X^e_{t-1,t} = \beta(X_t - X^e_{t-1,t}) \tag{13}$$

Expectations are rational if based on the set of complete information (I) available at null cost to all operators. Rational expectations represent complete rationality and are widely employed in general equilibrium models.

$$X^e_{t,t+1} = E[X_t/I_t] \tag{14}$$

Rational expectation theory (Lucas 1980) has changed dramatically the way economics is studied, introducing redundancy for economic policy. In the presence of perfect and complete markets, rational expectations and no transaction or information costs, monetary and fiscal policies are only sources of distortion, and generate net wealth losses.

Reality is not so perfect and does not follow literally the Lucas paradigm; monetary policy can contribute to enhance efficiency and increase wealth. Fiscal policy allocates wealth by means of taxes and debt, resulting from excessive deficits.

A recent approach to macroeconomics, i.e. New Keynesian (NK) economics, synthesized by Michael Woodford in his *Interest and Prices: Foundation of a Theory of Monetary Policy* (2003) is a stylized dynamic stochastic general equilibrium (DSGE), where rational agents face different frictions and rigidities (in wages, prices, preferences). The main advantage of these models is that they can approximate the reality of economics to a good extent; the disadvantage is probably their mathematical complexity, which makes solutions difficult to be interpreted[47].

The presence of rigidities, or of certain *a priori* preference schedules other than opening the economy, represents the evolution of the model with rational expectations (see Woodford 2003).

A standard reduced-form NK model is made by three equations: the IS curve, which describes the real sector of the economy, as the relationship between the deviations from potential output, i.e. the output gap ($x_t = y_t - y_e$); the natural interest rate in the previous period (r_{t-1}); and the exogenous demand of the economic system (A_t), with $i=0,1$.

$$x_t = (A_t - y_t) - ar_{t-1} \tag{15}$$

The NK Phillips curve describes the equilibrium inflation mechanism on the basis of an imperfect competition hypothesis, which can be further specified as oligopoly or monopolistic competition[48].

$$\pi_t = \pi_{t-1} + \alpha x_{t-j} \tag{16}$$

A monetary rule, needed to close and solve the model and of particular interest for our purposes, can be specified in different ways. In particular, the loss function (*L*) of the monetary authority shows preferences toward target variables (inflation, output gap). The literature has identified some basic rules, such as[49]:

---

47   For an example see Benigno and Woodford (2003).

48   The competition depends on the structure of the industry, or consumer preferences.

49   This synthesis is taken from Carlin and Soskice (2004).

$$L = x_t^2 + \beta\pi_t^2$$
$$L = x_t^2 + \delta\beta\pi_{t+1}^2$$
$$L = x_{t+1}^2 + \beta\pi_{t+1}^2$$
$$L = x_{t+1}^2 + \delta\beta\pi_{t+2}^2 \tag{17}$$

The functions shown here are, respectively, those of Walsh, Romer and Taylor, Carlin and Soskice, Svensson and Ball. The NK model can be solved by minimizing the loss function with respect to output (x_{t+1}), under the conditions set by the Phillips curve on inflation (π_t), providing the following results:

$$x_t = -\alpha\beta x_t$$
$$x_t = -\delta\alpha\beta\pi_{t+1}$$
$$x_{t+1} = -\alpha\beta\pi_{t+1}$$
$$x_{t+1} = -\delta\alpha\beta\pi_{t+2} \tag{18}$$

Results show how monetary policy should act optimally. Relevant parameters are the *ex ante* preference toward inflation (β), i.e."hardnosed" or "wet"[50], and the inflation rate target (π^e), the slope of the Phillips curve (α), the elasticity of aggregate demand to interest rate (a), the equilibrium output (y_e) and the natural interest rate (r_{t-i}).

John B. Taylor's rule, introduced in the literature in 1993, describes the reaction function of the monetary authority in the presence of forward-looking agents. The central bank acts on the interest rate following deviations between effective and potential output and between effective and expected inflation. This rule is sub-optimal, since it contains forward variables, the expected inflation, and lagged variables, the lagged interest rate, which describes the *inertia* of the policy. I will discuss Taylor's rule later in this chapter.

NK models can be complicated in many ways, inserting market rigidities (of labor, costs or of goods), introducing preferences by group of households, proportional income taxes, and the issuance of public debt by the government, which influences wealth allocation. The complexity of these models is frequently criticized .

Michael Woodford (2006) states that these models can be completed with a money demand equation of the form:

$$\log(M_t / P_t) = \eta_y \log Y_t - \eta_i i_t + \varepsilon_t^m \tag{19}$$

where M_t is the nominal money supply, the coefficients η_y, η_i are income and interest rate semi-elasticity of money demand, and ε_t is the exogenous disturbance to the money demand. The solution of NK models is compatible with this equation,

---

50   The parameter is $0<\beta<1$. If the preference is higher toward inflation the government is hardnosed, otherwise is wet.

in the sense that it can be added or not, and the equilibrium of inflation, output and interest rate is not affected either way. Empirically, the correlation between inflation and money is verified and can be modeled coherently. Woodford's equation of money demand is the Cambridge version of the quantity theory of money, and is usually considered to be neoclassical. The money side of the NK model is perfectly compatible with a neoclassical interpretation, which is of great help in policymaking and interpretation, in case inflation targeting is mixed with another strategy (like in the ECB case).

The NK school has solid European roots and academia has started to introduce it in undergraduate textbooks and courses, but in the US it is not yet widely accepted. The NK model is apparently antithetical to the American approach, with headquarter in the Chicago school, according to which markets are the endogenous engines to fuel growth and guarantee efficiency. Rational expectations come with perfect competition, absence of friction and rigidity, and the uniqueness of equilibrium. The free-market approach has been an inspiration for many authorities, such as the US Federal Reserve Bank and the European Central Bank.

In both the NK or Chicago school economic frameworks market expectations influence the achievement of equilibrium, and in the NK also its uniqueness. Expectations are target variables of monetary policy. George Soros, a well known currency speculator in the 1980s and 1990s, famous for having bet heavily on the Italian and British currencies leaving the European Monetary System in 1992, states that expectations influence the fundamentals, rather than the other way round. Fundamentals are the most representative macroeconomic variables, like growth, interest or inflation rate, trade deficit and wages; expectations can be influenced by many factors, but according to Soros, are a driving force in the economy, and influence these macroeconomic variables. An example is a currency attack where the market, based on its expectations and valuations, considers that the relative price of two currencies is misaligned and suddenly takes positions to correct it. International confidence in the currency (and country) and external events (like contagion or domino effects) can influence the valuation process. With a currency attack, fundamentals change irreversibly as a result.

9.1 Effects on channels and policy

Financial innovation enters this process of evolution in different ways. From an institutional point of view, it renders regulation far less rigid and gradually more obsolete, contributing endogenously to its modification. Different customer needs are satisfied with new instruments, not directly included in traditional definitions. Markets decide which innovation will survive, based on profitability; markets are moreover positively influenced by innovation, which increases the liquidity and size of the market. Financial derivatives have various effects on financial markets, in terms of liquidity, better pricing and contribute to endogenously modify the regulation. On a macro-level, they modify the transmission mechanism of monetary policy.

As shown by the Banca d'Italia (1995), one of the first central banks to address the issue, derivatives improve substitution among banking credit, money and bonds[51].

In a global world, markets have no boundaries and capital moves where profits and efficiency are provided. There is a limit to the extent to which the central bank can influence the holding of credit, bonds or money, since it is mainly market determined. Improved substitution diminishes the ability of the central bank to influence the allocation of wealth by market agents. The demand for money, a liquid asset with a very low return, is influenced by the development of payments system and innovations. The substitution between credit and bonds depends on the structure of the financial system, on the openness of market and on economic convenience: all structural variables that influence substitution. For more efficient markets (banking) credit is a less attractive means of financing (for firms) with respect to market capital.

The demand for credit diminishes and demand for bonds increases. The ability of the central bank to influence or drive the demand for bonds is far smaller, since, outside ordered market conditions, it cannot directly control any relevant variable influencing bond demand. The toolbox of monetary policy changes, following the evolution of financial and monetary systems. Vrolijk (1997) observes that another instrument of the central bank, the surprise effect, is much more difficult to use in the presence of derivatives. Markets are becoming increasingly more sophisticated and it is very difficult to surprise them. Monetary maneuvers are anticipated and priced on forward values of assets and rates; only undeveloped systems can be "surprised" by monetary policy moves. Market expectations are embedded in prices and it is not possible for the central bank to drive them exogenously, without a strong credibility or reputation, which only a few banks have. Monetary policy becomes an exercise in expectations management, and is less and less a matter of interest rate changes.

According to Estrella (2001) derivatives have a number of effects.

Table 2.7 Monetary policy channels and effects

Interest Rate	Market Liquidity
	Cost of Capital
Valuation	Wealth (Consumption)
	Cost of Capital (Investment)
	Exchange Rate (Net Exports)
Credit	Bank Lending
	Balance Sheet

Source: Estrella, 2001.

---

51   See also Angeloni and Massa (1998), Driffil et al. (2005), Estrella 2002, ECB (2000), von Hagen and Fender (1998), Upper (2006), Violi (2000) and Vrolijk (1997).

The interest rate channel is influenced by derivatives. The cost of money and capital diminishes because derivatives contribute to lower volatility and improve the pricing mechanism of securities. Other than improved pricing, market liquidity is positively influenced by the introduction of other markets where assets are traded (Bartram and Fehle 2006).

A relevant issue is to what extent derivatives affect the short- and long-term interest rate. The short-term rate is influenced by monetary maneuvers and market expectations; the long-term rate is market determined. From a microeconomic point of view, derivatives improve pricing mechanism, reduce noise and increase liquidity; these should lower the volatility of interest rates, and should result in lower bid-ask premium. However, the recent experience of European and US rates is not entirely explained by these simple forces[52].

The valuation channel can be considered through three main effects. The allocation of wealth can be improved, thanks to the availability of instruments, which satisfy the needs of customers, inducing an increase in consumption (of financial instruments). Investments increase because innovation can finance them better (Gorton and Rosen 1996). The exchange rate pricing improves if markets are more efficient and liquid, and exports are facilitated.

The credit channel should work in a more efficient way. Bank lending, thanks to improved substitution between money, bonds and credit, allocates resources more efficiently, ameliorating the performance of the banking system (Banca d'Italia, 1995B). These have positive effects on the entire economic system. From a macroeconomic point of view, the presence of derivatives improves the speed of adjustments in response to shocks and endogenously contributes to stabilizing rates and expectations. This virtuosity is possible if and only if regulation is perfect, i.e. derivatives are not misallocated, otherwise the leverage effect and risks embedded expose market participants to a worsening of their wealth, consumption and exposure. Mismanaged derivatives exacerbate negative effects due to shocks, rumors or hazard. The limited rationality of investors, regulators and markets can eliminate most of the advantages of derivatives, as famous crashes testify.

10. Derivatives in New Keynesian models

Monetary policy should concern itself with financial innovation because it modifies the effectiveness of policy implementation and its ability to achieve predefined goals (e.g. price and financial stability) (Vrolijk 1997). The NK model (Woodford

---

52   I refer to the *conundrum*, i.e. the very low return on long-term bonds detected in the yield curve between 2003 and 2007, and to the credit crunch of 2007 (known as the subprime crisis).

2003) represents optimizing conditions in the presence of real frictions. Modern financial systems rely on qualitative (i.e. risk-adjusted measures or capital ratios) rather than quantitative rules; transparency is necessary for the regulation to succeed in guaranteeing stability. The aim of the central bank is to ensure financial stability, and growth; this can be subordinated to price stability, or to foreign exchange rate management. Final objectives can be achieved by means of those instruments, which work better in influencing the pre-defined target. Quantitative instruments are bank lending, money supply, deposits, and compulsory reserves.

Significant financial innovation should be considered in both fiscal[53] and monetary policy making, and with respect to coordination for the purpose of controlling inflation and achieving market stability. Carare and Tchaidze (2005) point out that a simple monetary policy rule like Taylor's has been abused as a tool for policy setting. After observing the poor data fit yielded by the simple Taylor rule, numerous authors have tried to add lagged or forward-dependent variables. I do not agree with the Carare's skeptical view, since the evolution of markets and agents cannot be captured by variations in inflation and output gaps alone. Financial innovation is the manifestation of the evolution of markets.

The very first pioneer paper considering derivatives as modifying the monetary rule, is that by Driffil et al. (2005), which considers a monetary policy rule of the form:

$$r_t = \rho r_{t-1} + \phi_\pi E_t \pi_{t+1} + \phi_y y_t + \phi_{br} \left[(\log P_t^A - \log F_t) - (\log P^{A*} - \log F^*) \right] \qquad (20)$$

where r is the interest rate (of the US Federal Reserve), y is the output gap, π is the inflation rate, F is the future price and P^A is the price of its underlying; * denotes desired or target values. The weight put on price stability, expected output and financial stability is represented respectively by ϕ_π, ϕ_y, and ϕ_{BR}. To simplify the policy rule, the authors add the hypothesis that the difference in returns between the derivative and the underlying is given by:

$$(\log P_t^A - \log F_t) = -\log R_t$$
$$(\log P^{A*} - \log F^*) = -\log R^* \qquad (21)$$

Substituting (21) into (20) the interest rate rule looks like the usual Taylor version, the NK reduced model can be easily solved and its results straightforward interpreted. However, the implicit assumption in (21) is that the log of the price of futures (*logF*) is a proxy of its return. But most literature has strongly rejected this assumption, because the future price is considered to be a very bad predictor

---

53   See Piga (2001), Oldani and Savona (2005) on the use of derivatives by European governments, and Oldani (2004) for a survey on the use of derivatives in economic policy.

of futures market trends and cycles[54]. Most studies use turnover or open interests instead, which are better measures of demand and can be used for this purpose.

Equation (21) is based on a strong assumption, since the equivalence is true if and only if there are no arbitraging opportunities (i.e. efficient market hypothesis and perfect capital market), and interest rates are constant at all times. But since we are dealing with an interest rate rule, the second part of the hypothesis cannot be satisfied *a priori*.

I now move to a small and tractable model to consider derivatives explicitly into the monetary rule; the key variable is the implied volatility of options contracts[55]. Implied volatility is the volatility implied in the price of derivatives, and is used to price other contracts. Interestingly, the historical values of volatility of derivatives' prices never match the implied volatility exactly, since it includes the expectations on future prices, which are not incorporated into the historical volatility[56].

The New Keynesian monetary policy rule specified by Taylor (1993)[57] can be described by an augmented interest rate rule taking the form:

$$r_t = \mu + (1+\alpha)\pi_{t-1} + \varphi x_t + \delta\sigma_t$$
$$\mu = r^* - \alpha\pi^* \tag{22}$$

where x is output gap, r is the nominal interest rate, π is the inflation rate, π^* is the target of inflation, r^* is the natural interest rate, and σ_t is the implied volatility of options. The lagged interest rate can be plugged into the function to consider the *inertia* of monetary policy, and its coefficient (ρ) should be less than one, but greater than zero.

The implied volatility is supposed to behave like an AR(1) shock, i.e.:

$$\sigma_t = \omega\sigma_{t-1} + \varepsilon_t$$
$$\varepsilon_t \approx (\mu, SD) \approx \chi^2 \tag{23}$$

The error term of the monetary rule (ε_t) is a random shock, with a given mean (μ) and variance (*VAR*), and it is distributed like a χ^2, which is a positively skewed distribution and allows for asymmetric effects of increasing versus decreasing volatility. In fact, the authority should react to higher (increasing) volatility by acting on the (nominal) interest rate, while in the case of decreasing volatility, a soft monetary reaction is probably necessary to support the ordered market conditions.

---

54   Moreover, the return of futures is zero by definition, if arbitrage between spot and future markets is absent.

55   It is worth noting that the law of iterated expectations holds, and we can make an assumption about the implied volatility.

56   This is another argument against the use of market prices, from which historical volatility is computed.

57   A previous version of this study can be found in Oldani (2007).

Expectations about the interest rate influence the behavior of investment demand and supply, affecting aggregate demand, growth and prices. In the standard New Keynesian model the last term of equations 22–23 ($\delta\sigma_t$) is not present because the monetary policy rule is not supposed to react to expectations in the financial market. My intention in introducing expectations about the interest rate into the monetary rule is to stress the informational content of options, which are used by policy makers to extract future expected price patterns. This is a rational behavior because it acknowledges their economic and informational content, together with their high liquidity, efficiency and diffusion across worldwide markets.

Modern monetary policy considers targets of inflation (π) and growth into the policy rule. The Austrian School recognized that human manipulation influences the level of the natural interest rate, because it is determined by the interaction between demand and supply and is heavily affected by expectations. The behavior of monetary policy is subject to expectations-setting mechanisms and their volatility. The Taylor rule is itself sub-optimal, regardless of its specification, and the relevance is put over stabilization and expectations management. Changing expectations about growth affect the natural rate of interest desired by the authorities, and, in this specification, it affects the interest rate rule via the equilibrium setting.

If the implied volatility of options is subject to instability (e.g. it increases or decreases because of unanticipated shocks), the behavior of monetary policy should not be specified in such a way that the interest rate will jump the same amount. The Taylor rule is not an automatic policy rule; rather, it is a behavioral function of policy authority in an environment that changes in response to shocks and innovation.

10.1 The long-run solution

The macro model can be solved in the long run, starting from the reduced form:

$$E_t Z_{t+1} = AZ + ar_t^n + b\varepsilon_t \tag{24}$$

where A is a 4X4 matrix and a, b are 1X4 vectors. As shown by Woodford (2003, 721) a stable equilibrium exists if and only if two eigenvalues of matrix A are inside the unit circle.

Matrix A is:

$$
\begin{matrix}
1/\alpha & 0 & 0 & 0 \\[2mm]
\dfrac{-\theta+\varphi\gamma}{\alpha\beta}-\dfrac{\lambda}{\alpha} & \dfrac{1}{\beta} & \dfrac{\varphi}{\beta} & 0 \\[2mm]
-\dfrac{\psi}{\alpha}+\dfrac{\rho\gamma}{\alpha} & 0 & \rho & 0 \\[2mm]
\dfrac{\omega\delta\gamma}{\alpha} & 0 & \omega\delta & \omega
\end{matrix}
\tag{25}
$$

Eigenvalues of matrix A can be represented as:

$$\left(\rho \quad \omega \quad \frac{1}{\alpha} \quad \frac{1}{\beta} \right) \tag{26}$$

and, since $\rho<1$, and $\omega<1$ the equilibrium condition is satisfied. ρ is the *inertia* of the interest rate and ω is the *inertia* of the implied volatility. Both *inertias* are less than 1, otherwise there would be overshooting phenomena. Provided that a stable long-run solution exists to the modified model, the stylized NK model can be employed to draw further policy implications.

10.2 Empirical evidence

As an empirical exercise I estimate the Taylor rule on US quarterly data 1990–2005: the Greenspan era. The theory tells us that monetary policy in the presence of rational optimizing agents can set a linear rule of contemporaneous or lagged variables, because the forward-looking component is incorporated into the agents' behavior (the Taylor rule). In my framework, the implied volatility of options serves the purpose of incorporating the expectations of financial markets and then signals the expected future behavior of markets.

I run different estimates to check for robustness of results. As a first step I estimate the Taylor rule over the longer time period (1990–2005) without the volatility term. This is a first check of the coherence of the rule on US data and policy. As a second step, I introduce the implied volatilities in the rule, chosen for their relevance in the US financial market.

With two exercises, over different time spans, and considering different implied volatilities, I check for the informative ability of different contracts. I consider the implied volatility computed from the Dow Jones Industrial Average Index (DJX), and that of the Chicago Board Option Exchange Implied Volatility Index (VIX). The DJX refers to the call and put contracts, plotted in Graph 2.5; the DJIA index is considered to be very volatile, and its main constituents stocks change very frequently. The VIX has been created by the Chicago Board Options Exchange as a measure of equity market volatility; the computation of the value of VIX is based on the implied volatility of eight option series on the S&P 500 index, and is quoted in percentage points per annum.

The increase of the implied volatility above certain values signals financial market turbulence and not simply an increase in securities prices[58]. Monetary policy should react by strengthening the money stance (increase the interest rate) to counterbalance turbulence. If volatility is below certain value, the reaction may be asymmetrical in that it does not reduce the interest rate. This stylized fact is incorporated into the asymmetrical shape of the epsilon shock.

---

[58] As in the last five months of 2007, market turbulence reflects a stable increase in volatility and price variance.

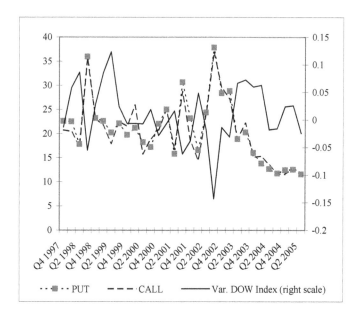

**Graph 2.5 DJX, put and call, and the variation of the underlying stock
index (quarterly, 1997–2005)**
Source: Own elaboration on Bloomberg and Thomson Financial Datastream data.

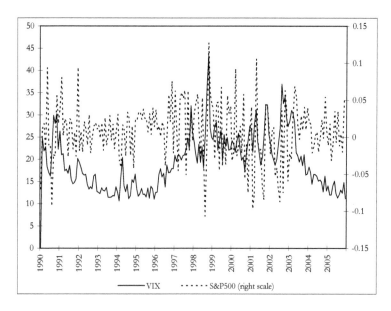

Graph 2.6 The variation of the S&P500 and the VIX (monthly, 01/1990–12/2005)
Source: Thomson Financial Datastream.

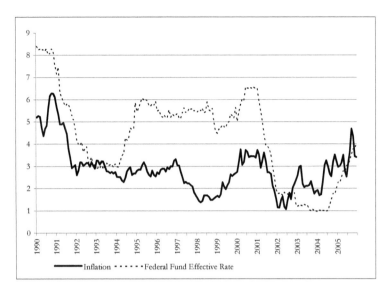

Graph 2.7 US inflation rate and Federal Fund effective rate
Source: Thomson Financial Datastream.

The Federal Fund's effective rate (r) is expressed in percentages, and its values vary between 8.38 and 0.99 over the period of observation. The inflation rate (π) is computed from the consumer price index on all areas of the US; it is expressed as a percentage, and its value is very low over the period (between 6.3 and 1). Both are represented in Graph 2.7. The output gap (x) is measured by the OECD, and is the deviation of the actual GDP from its potential value, both expressed as a percentage. The output gap is positive for a part of the period, in particular between 1998 and 2001, confirming that the US economy enjoyed very good performances.

The Greenspan era was characterized by extremely low inflation, and output featured largely in a number of Chairman speeches. The coefficient over inflation might be expected to be small, or even not statistically significant.

Following the possible effects of un-stationarity of variables in the Taylor rule (Siklos and Wohar 2004) I first checked for unit roots, finding that all but the output gap are I(1) series; however, the Johansen cointegration test rejects the presence of cointegration among the variables. I then choose econometric estimators, which consider non-stationarity to represent the relationship among the variables. The presence of heteroskedasticity cannot be rejected, and I use the ML-ARCH and

Table 2.8 Phillips Perron unit root test

Null hypothesis: Stationarity	
MacKinnon (1996) one-sided p-values	
Variable	Prob.
π	0.183
diff(π)	0.000
x	0.047
diff(x)	–
r	0.105
diff(r)	0.000
VIX	0.215
diff(VIX)	0.000
DJX_call	0.263
diff(DJX_call)	0.000
DJX_put	0.255
diff(DJX_put)	0.000

GMM estimators[59]. According to the literature[60] and the model, the function should be specified in terms of contemporaneous variables, but the lagged interest rate is meaningful and represents the *inertia* of the policy. I estimate the function first without the implied volatilities, then include the implied volatility of call and put of DJIA[61] and that of VIX.

Empirical results are presented in Table 2.9, panels A, B, and C.

DJX data are available over a shorter period (October 1997–June 2005). The Bloomberg algorithm computes the implied volatility on the DJIA (σ_t)[62]. Macrodata are the same as above, and it is important to underline that over this shorter period the inflation rate was extremely low (between two and four percent) in the presence of sustained growth[63].

---

59 As observed by Siklos and Wohar (2004) and Carare and Tchaidze (2005), having non-stationary variables in the Taylor rule raises a number of econometric problems. The order of the ML-ARCH was selected according to the Akaike information criteria.

60 See Carare and Tchaidze (2005) for a survey of econometric results.

61 The DJX was estimated separately in the function, since considering put and call options together yields statistically insignificant results, because of the put-call parity used to compute the implied volatilities (Hull 2002).

62 For a definition of implied volatility see Hull (2002).

63 According to the Federal Reserve board members and chairman, closest attention was paid to economic growth, asset prices, and financial market stability. From 2006 on, the Federal Reserve chairman, Ben Bernanke, has been more concerned with inflationary pressures due to accelerating energy prices.

Table 2.9   Taylor rule econometric estimates

A 1990–2005	Coeff.	z-stat	Prob.
Method:	ARCH-ML		
$r_t = \mu + (1+\alpha)\pi_{t-1} + \varphi x_t + u_t$			
μ	2.628	19.665	0.000
$(1+\alpha)$	0.891	24.389	0.000
φ	0.481	16.577	0.000
B 1997–2005	**Coeff.**	**z-stat**	**Prob.**
Method:	ARCH		
$r_t = \mu + (1+\alpha)\pi_t + \varphi x_t + \delta\sigma_t + u_t$			
μ	-3.955	-4.785	0.000
$(1+\alpha)$	0.254	2.123	0.034
φ	1.312	18.841	0.000
δ (DJX PUT)	2.352	9.312	0.000
C 1990–2005	**Coeff.**	**z-stat**	**Prob.**
Method:	GARCH		
$r_t = \mu + (1+\alpha)\pi_t + \varphi x_t + \delta\sigma t + ut$			
μ	1.473	4.560	0.000
$(1+\alpha)$	0.945	49.202	0.000
φ	0.515	22.745	0.000
δ (VIX)	0.292	2.56	0.015

Taylor rule coefficients (panel A of Table 2.9) are consistent in terms of sign and magnitude with those already present in the literature. The Taylor rule with the implied volatility over the shorter period (panel B) provides encouraging results, in terms of sign, magnitude and significance. Results with the VIX (panel C) over the entire period support my idea. In particular, estimates with the VIX show that the effect of the implied volatility is not negligible; its coefficient is small, a finding that can be explained by the fact that the informative content deriving from these options is a portion of the entire information set available to the US economy[64].

If the goal of monetary policy is to achieve financial stability, the information provided by options seems to be important, because the wealth invested in the stock exchange is a large share of the total.

The econometric results are consistent, interesting in terms of magnitude, and confirm that inflation was not a cause of concern for the Federal Reserve. Over the period of my analysis, public statements by the Federal Reserve focused mainly on growth and the maintenance of financial stability rather than inflationary pressures[65]. Stock exchange exuberance, the consequent financial turbulence and a

---

64   This result is fairly common in the literature.
65   This is confirmed by the magnitude of the coefficient of the output gap.

number of corporate crises experienced by the US during the period were the main sources of concern for the Federal Reserve.

The econometric findings can be briefly synthesized as follows:

- inflation was not a concern for the US monetary policy authority during the period 1998–2005;
- the output gap was the main goal of Federal Reserve policy;
- the implied volatility of options written on stock indices can be a useful source of information and could be used to implement the policy rule.

The first two results confirm the established literature; the third, although limited, is the only possible inference to be drawn from the Taylor rule, given the lack of complete data on derivatives, especially OTC, regarding counterparty, amounts outstanding, and balance sheet effects.

11. Conclusion

Monetary theory has evolved from the changing conditions in which it operates, with respect to instruments, operators, and regulation. The ability to catch up with innovation, together with credibility, is the main reason to devote the monetary power to a separate and independent authority, other than the elected treasury.

At the micro-economic level, monetary policy faces more perfect financial markets, which are more difficult to influence unilaterally; substitution in portfolio works better, and wealth moves without barriers at a global level. Derivatives play a role in the transmission mechanism of monetary policy, and their monetary nature is investigated from different viewpoints: monetary aggregates, portfolio substitution, interest rate channel and expectations setting. Derivatives help in exchange rate management, but cannot be used to fight a speculative attack in the market. Credit derivatives are very powerful tools to separate risk from credit, but their opaqueness and deregulation can dramatically reduce global stability, as testified by the 2007 subprime crisis, and ultimately represent a danger to economic development. As far as their monetary role is concerned, derivatives can provide relevant information on market expectations; in particular, there is a statistically significant relationship between derivatives activity and the perception of monetary policy captured by unanticipated variations of the policy interest rate. The informative relationship between money demand, measured through monetary aggregates, and economic activity can be enriched with the financial signal. Empirical results on US data confirm the role derivatives (exchange traded futures) play in the American system. Monetary policy is concerned with financial innovation because it modifies the effectiveness of policy implementation and its ability to achieve targets. The Taylor rule can be augmented to consider financial stability, which is a relevant target of monetary authorities. To sum up derivatives effects are that they modify monetary control by rendering evanescent (wide) monetary aggregates; thanks to their virtues, they accelerate the portfolio substitution process and endogenously modify the equilibrium of the financial system. As a result of these endogenous forces, the interest rate channel is much more difficult to be used by the central bank; expectations influence the monetary policy and vice versa, but the authority has far smaller resources than those at the disposal of the market. Monetary policy in the presence of derivatives is basically an expectations management exercise.

Chapter 3

Derivatives and Fiscal Policy:
Risks and Hazard

1. Introduction

Fiscal policy sets out the principles of a government in fixing the level of public expenditure, and the ways to fund it; it manages public spending, revenues (taxes) and any borrowings (debt) resulting from excessive spending or smaller revenues, and ultimately influences the growth of the economy.

Public finance is the oldest branch of economics; its roots go back to the sixteenth century, and its principles should be coordinated with those governing the market[1]. The fiscal system can modify capital formation in the economy by means of public investments, by affecting the growth path and influencing the incentives to save. In order to finance expenses, the government can raise taxes, issue money or debt. With public debt, the government has a legal obligation to make interest or amortization payments to holders of claims, in accordance with a defined time schedule. In simple balance-sheet terms, public debt is a liability for the government and an asset on the account of holders of debt instruments (firms, households, domestic and foreign financial investors).

Modern governments interact with financial markets in order to raise funds and manage expenses, taxes and outstanding public debt. Various constraints limit the actions of the government, while financial innovation can be interpreted as another resource at their disposal. The use of financial innovation by taxpayers is an example of the development of the financial system, although it is not particularly new to the literature or to the historical experience of most countries. On the other hand, the active use of innovative financial securities to manage outstanding public debt and risks is fairly recent in the experience of most countries. What deserves our attention is how the public sector uses these securities, and how it deals with associated risks, in the presence of peculiar accounting and monitoring rules. The public sector is probably the most interesting player in the derivatives market, and not only for the amazing fees it guarantees to financial intermediaries.

Derivatives have different effects on the stock or flow of debt. They can be used to hedge interest payments (i.e. flows), although the advantages this brings can be analysed only at expiration. Derivatives can also be used to restructure outstanding debt (e.g. lengthening the maturity) and then their effect can be immediate.

---

1   The definitions of various concepts are taken from the *New Palgrave Dictionary of Economics*.

Accounting and monitoring rules and principles should be updated in order to cope with the effects of innovation, whether used by taxpayers (i.e. tax timing), or by the public sector as a tool to manage (scarce) resources. The financial stability of the public sector is a necessary condition to safeguard growth and avoid excessive and unconscious risk taking, whose effects remain a burden for present and future taxpayers, violating the democratic equilibrium principle of no taxation without representation.

2. Tax timing options with derivatives

Financial and non-financial firms can benefit from hedging strategies if taxes are progressive (Fan et al. 2007). In these circumstances, firms that "have larger tax loss carry-forwards would be more likely to hedge in order to maximize the tax savings". This evidence is probably the basis for the FSAS and IAS regulations, which aim at decreasing asymmetries among financial and non-financial firms.

The possibility of postponing revenues and anticipating losses for fiscal purposes is a very controversial issue in the literature. The SEC sustains the existence of tax circumvention practices in the US, but no data is available to help describe the phenomenon. In the first chapter I presented the main issue related to the accounting of derivatives at fair value which can create a gap between market and corporate valuation of the same security. Fiscal policy can add another gap, since tax rules can affect the way firms (banks, financial or nonfinancial-institutions) treat their financial trading. In some countries, such as Italy, the taxes on financial investments (paid by households) are simplified by applying a single proportional capital gain tax rate (12.5 percent), which aims to increase financial investments and the transparency of transactions. Firms (financial or not) should account their investments at fair value. They can sometimes apply the hedging accounting rule, which is more favorable in terms of tax burden, but which can be used only in a very limited number of cases. After the valuation of the security, the tax rate is relevant to corporate choices, since tax arbitrage[2] cannot be avoided especially with global corporations. Derivatives are no exception, and their amazing growth can affect the final revenues of the fiscal authority[3]. Domestic regulation and tax laws aim at increasing competition and decreasing opacity, together with international rules.

Taxpayers usually have a negative attitude toward taxes (i.e. disutility of taxes); the search for different ways to pay fewer taxes fuels the industry of accounting consultancy. To pay taxes you need a taxpayer (firm, household, bank

---

2   Tax arbitraging is the exploitation of asymmetries in tax rules among different states, e.g. in the EU or the US. The exploitation never causes a violation or a fraud.

3   The SEC (2000) testified at the US Congress that derivatives can be used for tax avoidance, but did not provide data.

or financial institution), a government to collect money[4], and a certain flow of funds to be taxed. Taxes are paid on flows of income and on certain types of stocks (e.g. real estate). The way to calculate the tax is not homogeneous worldwide nor often within a country depending upon the industry and other factors; what is relevant is whether there is a hole in the tax system (i.e. a flow of funds which is not explicitly subject to taxation). Derivatives represent an example of this in different ways: first if OTC derivatives are not reported in the balance sheet of firms, the tax burden is modified and not homogeneous among financial securities. The Financial Accounting Standard Board (FASB) introduced the Financial Report Standard (FRS) No. 13 in 1998 to meet the demand for information on derivatives usage (Dunne, Helliar and Power 2003). The aim of the FRS no. 13 is to ensure that firms "provide in their financial statements disclosure that enable users to assess the entity's objectives, strategies and policies for holding-issuing financial instruments". Entities should provide narrative information on their use of derivatives, to let stakeholders evaluate the role that these instruments have played in the overall risk management strategy of a company. The Financial Accounting Standard (FAS) No. 133, effective after 2001, "requires specified numerical disclosures to be provided about:

- interest rate risk;
- currency risk;
- liquidity risk;
- the fair values of financial instruments;
- the use of financial instruments for trading;
- the use of financial instruments for hedging;
- details of specified commodity contracts."

There was a large gap between the requirements of FSR no. 13 and the practice prior to its introduction. The Financial Accounting Standard (FAS) No. 133, issued in June 1998, requires that: (1) an entity recognize all derivatives as either assets or liabilities in the financial statements; (2) derivative financial instruments are measured at fair value; (3) accounting for changes in the fair value of a derivative (that is, gains and losses) be dealt with through the earnings statement; and (4) special rules exist for hedge accounting. These hedge accounting rules state that there must be formal documentation commencing at the inception of the hedge that explains how the hedge will work and how effectiveness will be measured" (Dunne, Helliar and Power 2003, 2).

The International Accounting Standard (IAS) 39 became effective after 2001 but some countries delayed its introduction. In fact, the European Union delayed it up to 2005, and states that all EU listed companies "must recognize all financial assets and liabilities on the balance sheet, including derivatives. They are initially

---

4 This point is not secondary, since in the world there are a few countries with no taxes, which are extensively used by smart taxpayers (i.e. tax heavens).

measured at cost, which is the fair value of whatever was paid, or received, to acquire the financial asset or liability, and are then regularly re-valued to reflect their fair value" (Dunne, Helliar and Power 2003).

The FRS No. 13 is a disclosure-only standard, while the FAS-IAS deals with the evaluation and the definition of derivatives accounting. There are essentially two treatments of financial instruments: fair value and hedge accounting. Fair value accounting states that the value of the derivative is recorded on the balance sheet (as asset or liability) and any unrealized loss–gain is reported in the profit and loss, irrespective of the accounting of the item being hedged. Hedge accounting, which is preferred by firms but very restrictive in its application, accounts derivatives as assets–liabilities, while gains and losses are reported in the profit and loss if the corresponding loss or gains on the item being hedged are clearly recognized. Critics of the FAS No. 133 stress the increase in the volatility (of earnings) that the company exhibits under these rules, which makes firms appear riskier that they are. Hedge accounting can modify relevant debt and equity ratios, making comparisons (across companies, industries and years) very difficult.

Fitch Ratings (2005) studied the effects of derivatives accounting on non-financial institutions; the survey was carried out on 57 global firms worth $US1 trillion debt. Companies had $US508 billion notional amount of derivatives positions, which correspond to $US39 billion at fair value, and $US6 billion of deferred derivatives gains (hedge accounting). The most popular contracts were the interest rate swap (on the basis of the notional amount) and currency contracts (measured with the fair value). Commodity derivatives were concentrated in the energy and oil sectors. Fitch Ratings found that firms were not engaging in widespread speculation with derivatives; the use of credit derivatives was limited, and some firms had derivatives on their own shares[5]. A source of concern is the disparities in the disclosure across companies and industries, even for most generic instruments (e.g. interest rate swaps). The difficulty in reporting, and restatement risk across corporate sectors are other concerns[6].

A different tax rule is applied to single tax payers (i.e. households); the regulation on capital gains–losses varies worldwide and it is very difficult to generalize, even in Europe, where the harmonization of taxes should have been one of the aims of the EU. Zeng (2003 and 2004) analysed the US tax system and observed that smart taxpayers, usually high income households, buy and sell out of the money options to lower the burden of taxes to be paid. This is done especially at the end of the fiscal year (March in the US and the UK, and December in continental Europe).

---

5   In some countries it is explicitly prohibited for a firm to own more than a certain (small) amount of its own shares; often derivatives are not included in the quota, and this can be considered as another type of rule avoidance.

6   Nicolò and Pelizzon (2006) show that in the presence of opaque OTC credit derivatives, moral hazard behavior cannot be ruled out *a priori*. This changes dramatically the optimal contract's rules and conditions to be imposed for the system to be safe.

3. Public finance and moral hazard

The management of public resources is modified by the evolving environment. When the government issues debt on the financial market, it accepts the markets' rules, and competes with other fund raisers (e.g. corporations). However, because of its special role in the economy and its ability to change the rules of the game, the financial structure should be designed in order to lower the potential sources of moral hazard by the state. Fiscal policy of industrialized countries, after the experience of the Keynesian approach and excessive debt accumulation, is mostly inspired by liberal principles following the Anglo-Saxon countries' liberal experience. After the 1980s, the welfare state was radically revised and it was reduced in size. In continental Europe, the state's role continues to be more proactive, through public firms and public debt issuance. In Japan, the role of the public sector needed to be increased after the severe economic downturn which started in the 1990s. These approaches are the result of historical experience, economic contingency and the international environment, but the background is fairly similar. The emergence of derivatives represents a unique opportunity for sovereign states to actively manage their debt and costs, in a similar way to other bond issuers. What is completely different is the risk attitude a government should exhibit. Financial markets and derivatives "do not add new risks" (Group of Thirty 1993) but can hide the existing risks, while the examples of crisis and hangover with derivatives should act as a warning to adopt proper risk-monitoring procedures.

I shall briefly describe the financial management of the public sector, starting with specifying its yearly budget, which gives rise to a deficit (or surplus). This is expressed as the difference between revenues (T) and costs (G):

$$DEF_t = G_t - T_t \tag{1}$$

The debt (B) evolves according to the following law of motion:

$$B_t = B_{t-1} + I_t + DEF_t \tag{2}$$

The Ricardian theorem states that the effects of taxation and government borrowing are equivalent; this is a static analysis, which has recently been taken further by Robert Barro, and developed into the New Classical Macroeconomics. Following an increase in spending financed by debt, households react by increasing savings to fund future tax increases, thus eliminating any expansionary effect due to the fiscal maneuver.

The simple rule of thumb when looking at static sustainability of debt is that the interest rate (r) to be paid on debt should be lower than the growth rate of the economy (g) (i.e. Ponzi game)[7];

---

7   This rule was also discussed Chapter 2, paragraph 3.

r<g   (3)

If, as in some European countries that enjoy very poor growth and pay interest on large outstanding debts, that is not the case, an inter-temporal sustainability evolution is necessary.

To look at the inter-temporal sustainability of debt, let's express all variables with respect to GDP, considering its growth rate as between *t-1* and *t* as g_t so that:

$$\frac{B_t}{Y_t} = \frac{(1+r_t)B_{t-1}}{(1+g_t)Y_{t-1}} + \frac{DEF_t}{Y_t}$$ (4)

If we simplify the notation, and use $b_t = B_t/Y_t$ and $def_t = DEF_t/Y_t$ we can rewrite the above equation as:

$$b_t = \frac{1+r_t}{1+g_t}b_{t-1} + def_t$$ (5)

$$\Delta b_t = b_t - b_{t-1} = \frac{r_t - g_t}{1+g_t}b_{t-1} + def_t$$ (6)

Moving to the infinite time horizon, we should satisfy some constraints in order for the economy to be dynamically efficient. The No Ponzi game condition can be written, assuming a constant interest rate r^8, as:

$$\lim_{N \to \infty} \frac{B^{N+1}}{(1+r)^{N+1}} = 0$$ (7)

By imposing the No Ponzi game condition, it comes out that at any point in time the value of the debt must equal the present value of its expected primary surpluses (*SURP*):

$$B_{t-1} = \sum_{j=0}^{\infty} \frac{SURP_{t+j}}{(1+r)^{j+1}}$$ (8)

If these dynamic conditions are not satisfied, the sustainability of debt is not achieved and the economy is dynamically inefficient and unstable. The credit rating of the government is influenced by these conditions and its ability to raise funds internationally can be accordingly modified.

Derivatives in public finance can be used by taxpayers, to lower the burden of taxes to be paid under temporary circumstances, and by the public sector, centrally and locally, to manage scarce resources, and outstanding debt. The use of these

---

8   The interest rate should be positive at all times for the whole model to provide finite solutions.

securities at the central or local level depends on the structure of the state and the administration. The hedging of outstanding debt implies a certain amount of hedging costs, which are usually a fraction of interest payments, plus fees for the financial intermediaries selling the hedge or acting as counterpart. The fee is a very relevant information in the contract, is an amount set *ex ante*, and varies across different products and sellers. In order to avoid excessive costs the Italian treasury has limited its size to a maximum of 4 percent of the nominal value of the swap to which it refers. Costs reduction, deriving from the hedging strategy, less hedging costs (fees and other administrative expenses), should produce an effective reduction of overall costs. However, this figure varies over the life of contracts, and a comprehensive evaluation can be given only at expiration.

A pervasive problem in economics and public finance is moral hazard. This can be defined as actions of economic agents in maximizing their own utility to the detriment of others, in situations where they do not bear the full consequences or do not enjoy the full benefits of their actions, due to uncertainty and incomplete or restricted contracts, which prevent the assignment of full damages (benefits) to the agent responsible. Incomplete contracts are a special case, since they create conflicts between the agent's utility and that of others; if they involve complex transactions and long time periods, the resulting inefficiency and costs can be heavy. If contracts enforcement is very costly, it can be better to live with the inefficiencies generated by the moral hazard.

Moral hazard involves contracts with hidden or asymmetric information; problems to be addressed in (public) moral hazard are:

a. the nature of optimal contracts in the presence of moral hazard;
b. market and institutional-legal response to mitigate these problems;
c. welfare consequences.

Sub a) Optimal contracts require risk sharing between principal and agent, which creates a moral hazard problem in the form of insufficient incentives. Sub b) Efficient contracts should utilize all the information available, i.e. they should be constructed on the basis of statistical inference from the information available on the hidden action of the agent. Monitoring, which reduces inference errors, is efficient and productive. Sub c) The nature of the reward schedule is sensitive to the information available, the residual uncertainty, and the degree of risk aversion of the principal and agent. Standardized contracts are usually simple and uniform, and applied to a wide variety of agents. Long-term contracts tend to mitigate the moral hazard by introducing a reward for not exploiting short-run information advantages, and because cumulative information reduces uncertainty.

In the rest of this chapter I will focus on the problems raised by the use of derivatives by sovereign states (or local public administrations) with respect to moral hazard, which can emerge due to the peculiarities of agents involved and inefficient rules. The public sector, given its relative size, can be affected by the illusion of control. This is the illusion of being able to control or at least influence outcomes by shifting costs and revenues back and forth. It is a form of overconfidence, sustained by the ability of the public sector to change the rules of the game.

The consequences of moral hazard in political processes have been neglected in the literature, except in some remarkable studies (Stigler 1971 and others). A recent stream of the literature, inspired by psychology and game theory, has tried to analyse the effects of the limited rationality of agents (i.e. behavioral economics and finance).

Psychology refers to the application of the study of mind and behavior to various spheres of human activity, including the problems of individuals' daily lives and the treatment of mental illness. *Oeconomia*, a Greek word meaning "the govern of the house" is a social science, and can gain from psychological findings. Behavioral finance (Schleifer 2000) is the study of the influence of psychology on the behavior of financial practitioners and operators, and the subsequent effect on markets. Individual investors, fund managers and corporate managers are affected by a number of psychological behaviors, which reflect in inefficient investment decisions, whose effects do not always compensate once all enter the market. The neo-classical finance theory, which supposes the existence of perfect financial markets, information and operators, maintains that individual violations of the perfect market hypothesis do not affect market prices, since the (positive) misunderstandings of some players are added to the (negative) misunderstandings of other market players to equal zero. Behavioral finance uses some human irrationality to explain well-known financial puzzles (equity premium, risk-free rate, long-run prediction, home bias and so on). The critics' response to the psychological approach to finance is that it starts from the consequence to explain the reality (i.e. hypothesis is related to results) while financial economics, although artificial and far from reality, is a more complex mental exercise where hypotheses are far from results.

It is interesting to focus on the choice of whether or not to hedge with derivatives. Table 3.1 synthesizes the main stylized effects. The decision to underwrite such contracts modifies equation (8) into

$$B_{t-1} = \sum_{j=0}^{\infty} \frac{SURP_{t+j} + HEDGE_{t+j}}{(1+r)^{t+j}} \qquad (9)$$

The hedge term represents the effect of derivatives and can have a positive or negative impact on outstanding debt. If the country engages in derivatives, and the result of its hedge is positive (i.e. it successfully diminishes the cost of debt), it contributes to stabilizing its credit rating and then the dynamic of debt improves. On the other hand, if the hedge is unsuccessful (i.e. it aggravates the cost of debt), then the debt and its costs increase, and the credit rating worsens. If a country does not engage in derivatives, but could gain from their use, the result can be a worsening credit standing.

Table 3.1 Effects of derivatives' hedging

	Country hedging with derivatives		Country not hedging with derivatives	Country not hedging but could do it
Variable/Effects	Hedge>0	Hedge<0		
Debt (B)	decreases	increases	null	increases
Interests (I)	decreases	increases	null	increases

4. Fiscal policy: An incentives management

Fiscal policy is the management of public resources; in the nineteenth and twentieth centuries it was conceived as an active resource management, supported by the spread of Keynesian economics. The resulting deficit spending has been criticized because of inefficiencies and misallocation of resources, and after the defeat of centralized economies, fiscal policies have been used for incentive management.

The public sector in European countries is diminishing its active presence in the economy, leaving room for private entrepreneurs, and stimulating the conditions for competition. Organization, monitoring and supervision are the remaining duties to be implemented, and these can be done at central or local levels. Incentives, rules and supervision are can determine success, in terms of growth of a country in the globalized world.

Governments can be grouped according to their burden of outstanding debt, limiting their present and future fiscal spending[9]. The debt condition is even more binding if the state takes part in super-national agreements, such as the European Union[10]. For highly indebted countries, with a debt over GDP ratio exceeding 60 percent, the Ponzi game condition is binding, and influences their international credit rating; for less indebted countries, the Ponzi game condition can be violated in the short term. The US is an example of (sustained) violation of the rules. It has run into twin deficits (external and domestic) and exhibits a growth rate which is lower than the rate paid on Treasury Bills. The external deficit is due to excessive imports, while public spending increased because of homeland security and war expenses. However, its public outstanding debt is less than 50 percent of GDP, so interest payments seem fully sustainable.

---

9   Equation 8 states that if there is excessive outstanding debt (B_{t-1}), the government is compelled to obtain surplus for some $t+j$.

10   The Maastricht and Amsterdam treaties impose fixed values on these constraints.

Table 3.2   US debts and no Ponzi game

Year	Current account balance as percent GDP	Gross public debt as percent GDP	Foreign debt as percent total debt	GDP real growth rate	Treasury Bill rate
1998	-2,40	53,78	33,60	4,2	5,06
1999	-3,20	50,63	34,18	4,4	4,5
2000	-4,20	45,45	30,30	3,7	5,83
2001	-3,80	42,75	30,97	0,8	4,08
2002	-4,50	44,10	34,18	1,6	1,78
2003	-4,70	46,85	38,03	2,7	1,09
2004	-5,70	48,43	44,36	4,2	0,93
2005	-6,60	49,00	43,39	3,5	2,73

Source: Thomson Financial Datastream.

The necessary conditions to be pursued by governments are efficiency, competition, fair trade and market conditions, cooperation and security. Efficiency, competition and fair market conditions are influenced by the domestic structure of production, and by external competitors. Countries offering low wages induce a form of unfair competition, since social security and the welfare state cannot be cancelled after centuries of economic evolution have introduced them into our lives. Cooperation and fair trade influence the stability of international relations, and agreements and treaties are usually the ways to implement them effectively. For example, the Doha Round[11], that is, the negotiation on trade at the World Trade Organization, which aims at mitigating the effects of regional trade agreements, such as NAFTA, MERCOSUR or the EU, which influence preferences and are barriers to free trade at a world level.

Moreover, recent international events have changed the scale of priorities for many states, and security and homeland defense play an increasing role in public spending and cooperation agreements[12]. These various forces, working in a very

---

11   The Doha Round is stuck on a few important policy problems: the reduction of European barriers in the domestic market, on the internal subsidies to agriculture in the USA, and the reduction of tariffs on non-agricultural goods in developing countries (India, Brazil and China above all). Rich countries perceive competition from emerging countries and try to control its negative domestic effects, such as increasing unemployment in certain sectors (manufacture and agriculture), while emerging countries want to exploit their comparative advantages to fuel growth.

12   In March 2006, India and the US signed a treaty for nuclear energy. This agreement is extraordinary remembering the diplomatic relationship between the two only a few years ago.

complicated way with respect to one another, lead fiscal policy to be a complex exercise of sovereignty. Fiscal policy is an incentive management exercise in a global environment; financial innovation can be a useful tool for reaching financial targets on deficit and debt, as discussed in the rest of the chapter.

5. Constraints on fiscal policy

Modern fiscal policy faces various forces linked to the main economic variables. For instance, an ageing population modifies the inter-temporal financial stability of the social security system while immigration modifies the labor market dynamic and influences social relationships and organization. In addition, the increasing importance of the services sector modifies the structure of education and social organization, while the welfare state leaves little room for quick cuts in expenses.

The main risks faced by governments of industrialized countries are linked to the demographic evolution of the population, to the macroeconomic situation and to the presence of various rigidities and inefficiencies.

The main fiscal variables are expenses (G), revenues (T) and interests to be paid on outstanding debt (I). The ageing population increases social security expenses (G) and can lower tax revenues (T) at the same time. Immigration has opposite effects, increasing tax revenues (T) and positively influencing expenses (G); since immigrants are usually younger, immigration can be considered as an economic solution to the ageing population trend. Rigid laws or bad immigration policies can exacerbate the situation, and negatively influence the credit rating of the state, increasing the interest payments (I).

The composition of the population and the stability of the proportion of those working and not working is fundamental for forecasting future tax revenues and expenses. Public sector finance can be heavily influenced by ageing population and low productivity, but it can benefit from education and technological improvements.

The labor market in globalized economies should be oriented to promote efficiency and productivity, and find new ways to remunerate workers. Benefit plans and productivity premiums are normal incentives in the private sector, but not in the public sector. Given the high number of public employees in Europe, and Italy is no exception, this issue is not of secondary importance, since the lack of incentives constitutes inefficiency and contributes to further decrease the productivity of the labor force. This, in turn, negatively influences public spending (G) and indirectly pushes toward other ways to manage the deficit, such as financial innovation, which is far more flexible and less regulated.

The Italian situation is interesting in that respect since the population is ageing fast; the birth rate is one of the smallest among industrialized countries; two pension reforms have taken place over the last decade to make the system sustainable after 2010, and the public debt exceeds the GDP. All these phenomena influence the working population (N), its ratio with the total population, and public expenditure.

The flexibility of the labor market should have pushed up productivity, but this positive effect is not yet present in the statistical data. The compensating difference between new workers with high productivity and previous workers (who are very difficult to fire or adapt to different duties due to rigid regulation, especially in the public sector), sometimes characterized by lower productivity, is not enough to raise the national productivity average and measure[13]. Over the last five years the governments have managed (increasing) expenses (G) by increasing taxes (T), but the dynamic of debt has not reversed, no matter what hedging and cost-reducing financial strategies were applied[14]. Looking at equation (9), Italy exhibits a negative surplus (SURP) and so the equilibrium is not achieved.

The lower presence of the state in the economy now, in comparison to past decades, modifies the duties of the public administration and leaves room for active incentive management. The public sector should not act in the economy by

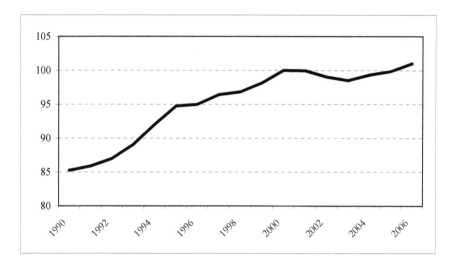

**Graph 3.1 Italy: Real GDP over total employment
           (yearly, productivity index)**
Source: ISTAT.

---

13   The reform of the Italian labor market (known as *Legge Biagi*, after the name of a labor economist shot by the Red Brigades in March 2002) introduced flexibility and temporary jobs, which are the norm in the rest of the Western world, and many immigrants enjoyed the positive effects of these easier ways to enter the Italian job market. The unemployment rate of the country has steadily decreased over the last decade, and the black market has been substituted by flexible instruments. Moreover, the stabilization rate of workers, i.e. the migration from a temporary to a stable job position, is more than 60 percent. This data is not very different from those of other European or G-7 countries.

14   At the present public administrations show a strong interest in research on pricing and effects of derivatives to hedge the ageing population and health risks.

means of firms or banks, but should monitor their working practices and find ways to increase efficiency.

The macroeconomic risks refer to the structural conditions of production, to exogenous shocks, and to the delocalization attitude toward emerging countries. An economic slowdown or negative shock worsens the public finance equilibrium, and influences the credit rating. The hedging of these risks would be the way to stabilize public finance effectively.

Legal, social and administrative rigidities influence growth negatively via the inefficient allocation of resources and the disincentives to entrepreneurship. Investment decisions, when the economy depends on services and not on goods or industry, can be heavily influenced by these negative elements, worsening performance.

Other than spending and raising funds, the public sector is a special investor, since it has collective resources to manage. It also has special purposes to achieve, such as improving citizen welfare and ameliorating collective standards of living. In public economics, setting the optimal rules to achieve these goals has always meant dealing with the free riding and moral hazard problems. To avoid these phenomena, responsibility is linked to the resulting expenses through the democratic system, and the 'no taxation without representation' principle. This principle is commonly employed to address the correspondence between taxes to be paid and elected politicians who allocate these resources. However, it should also apply to the problem raised by the length of financial operations—the time horizon of expenses—which can be different from that of the political mandate length.

Political mandates in Western countries are long enough to see the first results of the administration, and the time horizon of revenues–expenses should be bounded by the electoral time horizon, in order to guarantee full responsibility. Instruments used by the government, and duration of expenses and revenues, should be clearly written in the Financial Statements, in order for the voters to have complete information. A twenty-year interest rate swap lasts longer than any Western elected administration, so such an instrument introduces a different risk: the *mandate length risk*, which is the risk that the next elected politicians will have to pay back expenses, which previous politicians have benefited from. Suppose there is a four-yearly elected governor who uses a twenty-year swap, and shifts the effects of the swap bought today onto the next five governors. If this behavior is not monitored, there is a clear incentive to shift costs to the future and anticipate future revenues (i.e. free riding). This can be more likely to happen if accounting rules are not transparent or if the public sector is not subject to a complete responsibility principle.

A concrete example is the upfront loan, which is a loan to the administration providing cash when it is tight, but its effects can last for years (i.e. repayments). Up-front loans have been widely used in the recent past and are explicitly limited in most countries.

Derivatives can be used by states to lower their borrowing costs, to hedge or to raise cash when it is tight (GASB 2006). A number of sovereign states use derivatives, and especially swaps, to hedge and manage debt and expenses, but almost none of them allow the details to be known by the public (taxpayers or voters). OECD (2007) maintains that the use of derivatives is helping public debt managers in their operations, and in supporting market development. However, several impediments, such as a weak legal environment, the illiquidity of underlying, or deficiencies in regulation, prevent it from being used more actively.

6. Sovereign debt crisis and credit derivatives

As testified by the OECD (2002 and 2007), there has been a sharp growth in the use of derivatives instruments in both mature and emerging market economies. What is missing in emerging countries, however, is the necessary legal environment to support these securities.

The recent sovereign debt crises experienced in Russia (1998) and Argentina (2002) have underlined the problems raised by the absence of an international bankruptcy rule, which would diminish moral hazard, and safeguard bond holders, who suffered huge losses in the international bonds markets. Derivatives, providing insurance against certain risks and helping in shifting risks, can be very useful in sovereign debt structuring and crisis management. Goderis and Wagner (2006) are the first to consider this issue from a theoretical point of view. Again, the complete lack of data on derivatives does not block theoretical analysis.

By using a very stylized but powerful approach, Goderis and Wagner (2006) show how the introduction of credit default swap attached to sovereign bonds could improve the bondholders' wealth in cases of crisis. The story is really simple, but has interesting implications from a fiscal policy point of view. The economy lives over 3 periods (0, 1 and 2); in period 0 the sovereign state issues the bond, and funds are used for a project whose return is in period 2. Repayments are due in periods 1 and 2. Suppose a crisis happens in period 1; the bondholder can accept or reject the debt restructuring program. In the case of rejection, the state is in default, and the project cannot be continued any longer, thus introducing further losses (private costs, such as lower domestic consumption). In the case of accepting the program, the project continues. The welfare of the economy is determined by two aspects: efficiency of crisis resolution (*ex post*) and the debtor's moral hazard in avoiding crisis (*ex ante*).

Goderis and Wagner's (2006) result can be briefly summarized as follows: the introduction of protection (i.e. credit default swaps) does not change the crisis resolution, but reduces the moral hazard. By considering costs for litigation, and various other (state-contingent) conditions, the authors conclude that credit derivatives are beneficial to sovereign debt financing, and can contribute to lower the overall cost of financing. This theoretical result is very useful when considering the role of derivatives in fiscal policy analysis, although it is not possible to verify its empirical robustness, since governments do not disclose any data on their OTC transactions.

What we know by observing the behavior of some highly indebted countries is that most of them engage in financial management procedures (OECD 2007). For example, the Italian treasury hedges the public debt issued in foreign currency or on foreign markets by means of foreign exchange swaps, and can amortize the debt by means of interest rates swaps. Over the last decade, the maturity of the Italian debt, whose stock reached 108.6 percent of GDP in 2007, changed from an average of 5 years to over 10 years. This was done by substituting short-term bills with long-term bonds, and by rescheduling debt maturity by means of (plain vanilla) swaps. As shown in the next paragraph, the experience of most countries is of an active use of foreign exchange and interest rate swaps, but not credit default. The fact that these contracts reduce moral hazard is important in the pursuit of stability.

7. Public accounting of derivatives

Public accounting rules are different from those applied to the private sector, but should be designed in order to provide a reliable picture. When a government enters the market to issue debt, it uses the instruments provided to all market participants to smooth risks, as do all other market players. Systemic risk cannot be diversified, or shifted, but it can be managed. Over recent years, many financial instruments, such as securitization[15], have been used to manage public debt.

Financial innovation influences modern fiscal policy in two different ways: first, it helps in tax saving by taxpayers, firms and households; secondly, financial innovation can be used by the state itself (centrally or locally) to lower the cost of debt, to improve cash and debt management, and reduce costs (OECD 2002).

Derivatives and/or securitization are the innovative instruments used by states. Securitization is a way to pool together credits and other financial assets (Assets Backed Security, ABS), sell them on the market to institutions which then utilize securitization to finance their business. Assets are generally held by a tax neutral vehicle (Special Purpose Vehicle, SPV), which issues debt to fund the purchase of these assets[16]. In 2007 this system was heavily criticized, since the subprime crisis spread out globally because of uncollateralized credit derivatives used as

---

15 For example, the Italian social security (INPS), facing the fact of an ageing population, uses securitization to manage present and future revenues.

16 This procedure has been adopted extensively thanks to the mechanism allowed by the international credit rating. International investment funds sold subprime credits incorporated in ABSs, but without the guarantee of the issuer (funded type). After the subprime crisis spread out in 2007, the credit system found out that what seemed to be liquid, thanks to collateralization, actually was not, and the fears of credit crunch increased, stoking up further turbulence.

a vehicle to sell risks, without describing the risks properly to the market. What effects the subprime crisis will have on government debt management and costs is hard to guess, but since government do not invest in ABSs, we can suppose, with some probability, that they will suffer few direct losses, and only small ones due to indirect effects (i.e. increasing interest rates caused by liquidity squeeze which increase the cost of short term Treasury Bills). The indirect effects of the subprime crisis (i.e. the increase in short-term rate and stress in the credit market) have certain negative effects on the cost of debts.

I have already discussed the effects on firms (financial and non-financial) in paragraph 2, but will now go into more depth on into their effects on high-income taxpayers. Derivatives strategies are useful for tax-timing options, that is, postponing revenues and realizing losses, in order to lower the total amount of revenues, and so lowering the taxes to be paid. This has been shown for US firms and high-net worth individuals (Zeng 2003 and 2004, and Salcedo 2003), and it can induce a loss in total revenues of the state (Oldani 2004, SEC 2000). Most countries have tried to eliminate such tax loopholes, and most individuals cannot use derivatives, since they are complex financial securities unavailable to unprofessional investors. The European tax system is highly fragmented, and the European Commission has asked for homogenous definitions of what to tax and by whom, but not yet on how much, leaving that to the freedom of countries. Each European country has a different tax system on financial revenues and this leaves room for tax arbitraging, since it is theoretically possible to save by moving from one country to another. By helping taxpayers to lower their burden, derivatives confirm their nature: they are tailored to customers' needs. This special feature is modified by the states that implement rules to stop this form of tax saving.

The benefit of the use of financial innovation by sovereign states is that it is an off-balance-sheet item. In addition, it can increase funds available to the public sector, given budget criteria like those settled for European countries in the Maastricht Treaty where the ratio between deficit and GDP should not exceed 3 percent and that between debt and GDP should converge toward 60 percent. These criteria do not explicitly consider derivatives and a number of countries have exploited this loophole to match the criteria and enter the euro[17]. Non-European countries are subject to an Article 4 check by the IMF, but at present the Fund has very limited tools to evaluate derivatives' use by governments or local public administrations.

Derivatives increase international transparency, since capital markets are under intense international scrutiny[18]. They are alternatives to privatization, which is not always the solution to use public resources efficiently diversify investments and,

---

17   It has been demonstrated that, in order to match the Maastricht criteria, Greece did not fully describe its exposure. Other countries, such as Italy, are suspected of this, but no proof has been found.

18   The exposure of many sovereign states is known in the financial community because of the exposure of their counterparties.

by inducing more discipline, better manage debt. The clearness and disclosure of the strategy is very important for the market to believe in a sovereign state's financial management strategy.

The public sector has special accounting rules, and each year is subject to electoral control; the budget law is a crucial moment in democracy, since its composition is the expression of the political economy of the government. The public sector compiles the income statements, but the asset and liabilities analysis is very different from private accounting rules. It is not possible to quantify the amount of assets held by a state; just think of the Coliseum or the Grand Canyon! Similarly, the exact amount of liabilities is difficult to quantify. For example, the social security debt is inter-generational and depends on the growth of population and its ageing. The outstanding public debt, issued domestically or abroad, is a part of liabilities, but it is measured, monitored and managed.

Accounting rules for the public sector apply basically to the income statement and the public debt measurement. Certain maneuvers, such as privatizations, are computed as a way to diminish outstanding public debt because of their "capital" nature. Other maneuvers, either on revenues or costs, are computed in the income statement.

Results on derivatives investments, being losses or gains on financial instruments to manage public debt, are computed in the income statement, while the notional amount is not reported (for private firms and banks these are reported in the balance sheet).

The Governmental Accounting Standard Board (GASB 2006) is developing an international project to put derivatives in the financial statement of countries. The project is based on fair value accounting and asks for a certain degree of transparency. In particular, the details to be provided are the types of derivatives and the reasons why they have been purchased, the most significant terms, how the fair value has changed over the period, the net cash flow and the risks to which the derivative exposes the government. In particular, the risks specified are:

- the termination risk (the risk that the transaction might end before expected);
- the credit risk (the risk that the counterpart changes its credit rating);
- the interest rate risk (the risk that a change in the interest rate affects the value of the derivative);
- the basis risk (the risk to loose cash flows because the index upon which the derivative is priced changes);
- the rollover risk (if the derivative ends before its termination date, the government might be exposed to the risk of not finding another contract-counterpart to hedge the original risk);
- the market access risk (the risk that the government would not be able to issue debt, or that it becomes more expensive) (GASB 2006, 3).

According to the GASB, the initial payment to the public administration of the up-front fee is accounted as a loan, and not as cash. In this way, no public administration with tight cash can exploit derivatives to raise funds and increase the burden of future debt.

The present situation of opaque markets and transactions can leave room for moral hazard-free riding of the public sector, and this can have relevant effects on future budget equilibrium. Without complete and transparent accounting rules, banks can be tempted to sell risky but lucrative *ad hoc* contracts to the public administration, such as up-fronts, to finance an electoral period, and the state can provide incomplete information to the market and the bank. The GASB project should be applied worldwide in order to be effective. The implementation of GASB project would probably push those countries not yet active in this market to enter. As shown in Table 3.1, the potential benefits can affect their credit rating and ultimately the cost of debt. For those countries that exhibit free-riding opportunities, the introduction of GASB rules will be very expensive, since it will push for a radical change of internal rules.

Without the necessary complete information, the principle of no taxation without representation can be violated. Suppose a small public administration writes a twenty-year swap contract on interest rates and there is no limit on up-front. Suppose market rates are at 2 percent level, the swap can be made in order to pay 1 percent for the first 5 years and the floating market rates +200 basis points on the remaining 15 years. If it is possible for the public administration to underwrite such a contract, it is possible to shift present costs (1 percent of interests given by the difference between 2 percent market rate and 1 percent set in the contract) to future budget years. However, the result in the income statement is a 1 percent saving in interest payments, while nothing emerges in the balance sheet (if the GASB project is not translated into an effective commitment). An external observer, who is not very likely to read this technical book, would infer that the public administration has been clever to save such an amount of money, and would not be able to see "the shift".

A recent survey on government debt management practices in Europe highlighted the progressive autonomy of debt managers from the treasury, and the lack of data on innovative instruments issuances, especially swaps, which are used to separate the issue of liquidity from the risk profile (Wolswijk and De Haan 2006). The survey shows that "the European debt managers use interest rate swaps, whereby the government receives the long-term interest rate from the counter-party and pays the short-term interest rate. This effectively reduces the duration of outstanding debt as the remaining maturity until the next interest rate fixing decreases" (Wolswijk and De Haan 2006, 261). The use of interest rate swaps contributes to reducing financing costs as "it enables debt management agencies to continue concentrating on issuing in the favorite ten years bond segment, while at the same time reaping the cost advantages of short-term interest rates. Assuming an upward sloping yield curve, this reduces financing costs" (*ibid.*). A very limited number of debt managers publish cost savings from the use of swaps. In France, where the debt is managed by an autonomous body, swaps were introduced in 2002, and the estimated gain has been 0.5 percent of interest payments. The Dutch public-debt manager has calculated that in the period 1999 to 2001, it has annually saved some 0.4 percent of interest payments. As shown by Piga (2001), the use of interest rate swaps induce some risks, while contributing to save costs.

The ban on structured instruments or complex derivatives introduced in Italy and other European countries in 2003, and confirmed in the GASB project, is not enough, since it does not completely eliminate the moral hazard, which clearly emerges given present accounting asymmetries and limits[19]. It is not acceptable to live with this inefficiency, since taxpayers will finally pay the 200 basis points difference. There are various different solutions, which depend on the institutional rules and organization. The first step for all states worldwide should be to fully apply GASB rules on derivatives, and exotic and complex instruments, as an integral part of public debt management and monitoring. This could introduce a greater transparency, diminish (unsustainable) moral hazard and eliminate free riding.

8. Derivatives as a debt management instrument

Derivatives, like other financial securities, are used to manage the outstanding debt and its costs (interests and risks); they modify the structure of existing debt, by changing the risks profile and maturity. It is important to make clear that any sovereign state has a collection of risks already attached to its economy, for example, the risks implied in the ageing population, the financial risk related to securitization and foreign currency bonds issuance, or that related to health-care expenses. These risks should be managed, as they are the long-term sources of expenses and debt. The decision to adopt innovative tools should consider that the financial risk adds, in non-linear fashion, to these other risks.

In reducing its costs through the use of innovation, especially interest rate and currency swaps, the risks effectively undertaken by the state need to be carefully considered. Credit, liquidity and market risks are related to the use of derivatives, but are absent for the state, which does not engage in derivatives financing. The decision to underwrite such contracts should be carefully considered. The authorities should have people with the expertise to manage these special products and related effects, which are sometimes non linear. In any case, a relevant amount of resources needs to be invested. Different forms of mismanagement have caused many of the crashes of firms and banks, for instance those of Barings, LTCM, and the Orange County. The model risk (i.e. adverse effects due to a substantial change in the basic hypothesis of the model for risk) can have (unexpected) effects on financial equilibrium, and then alter the inter-temporal financial stability.

---

19 Moreover, the ban is similar to the traffic light, but we know that roundabouts work better with innovations.

The counterparties of sovereign states in OTC transactions are usually financial institutions interested in managing the global exposure of these portfolios. The procedure by which an OTC transaction is set up usually starts with the choice of the type of risk and contracts that can be underwritten (given particular limits on exotic or structural products). Then an official auction takes place for the settlement of contractual obligations (fees, and other costs), after the best OTC contracts have been chosen by the treasury (or the authorized underwriter). The contract might or might not be checked by a third party, depending on national regulation, and it then becomes effective. The risks associated with the transaction are priced, and sold at the market price. There may or may not be counterparties of the financial institutions, but this does not affect the contractual obligation. It is impossible to say, without comprehensive data, whether this is a zero sum game.

It is possible to give a rough evaluation of the benefit of derivatives by considering the spread of the Credit Default Swap (CDS) price on the financing costs of governments. This figure would, however, be very imprecise, since governments usually hedge only a portion of their outstanding debt (and then costs), based on their credit rating, foreign-currency risk management, or the necessity of shortening or lengthening the maturity of the outstanding debt. The sole official numbers that are known come from those autonomous bodies that manage public debt in France and Holland, and are presented in the next paragraph.

The general question of whether derivatives markets are deep enough to hedge such (enormous) debt cannot be unequivocally answered, since we do not know how much of world public debt is effectively hedged through them. However, an intuitive indirect answer can be provided by considering that OTC derivatives involve, measured at notional value, far more resources than world GDP. Sovereign debt is only, in a very few cases, bigger than a country's GDP, and then OTC derivatives should be on average bigger than the debt they could hedge. A practical proof of the size of the derivatives market is that if the LTCM[20] had been forced to deliver all the sovereign bonds underlying its derivatives portfolio, the entire UK debt would not have been sufficient to cover.

Before describing the actual experience of countries, it is relevant to clarify the juridical ability of public administrations, especially at local level, to underwrite such financial contracts. The British experience is remarkable in this respect. In 1989, a court ruled that the Hammersmith and Fulham Local Authority was unable to underwrite swaps contracts. This decision has been extended to all British local administrations, and more than 130 of them have been hit by the decision. The consequence of the ban was a massive problem for the 75 banks involved for an estimated amount of £750 million. The issue of legal capacity translated into legal risk for banks, and since then the British fiscal system seems to have been immune from "such toxic materials".

Examples of countries actively using financial innovation to manage debt and deficit (locally and centrally) are known, although with very few details.

---

20   See Chapter 1 for details about LTCM.

These can be briefly summarized based on a very rough geographical distinction: North America states, European countries (Austria, Denmark, Greece, Italy), and developing countries (Brazil, Hungary, India, Israel).

Table 3.3 Derivatives use by US states

State	Year	Notional Amount	Instrument	Purpose
Broward County (Fla)	2006	$166.2 mn	Swap Options	Debt Restructuring
California	2004	$600 mn	IR swaps	Debt Management and Infrastructure Financing
Louisiana	2008	$100–400 mn	Swaps	Debt Restructuring
Massachusetts	2001	$1.3 bn	IR swaps	Interest Rate Hedging
Miami Dade	2006	$300 mn	Swaps	Debt Restructuring
New Jersey	2004–2006	$3 bn	Swaps	Infrastructure Financing
New York	2005–2006	$2 bn	IR swaps	Interest Rate Hedging
New York	1999–2004	$5 bn	IR swaps	Interest Rate Hedging
Texas-Houston	2004	$200 mn	Swaps	Debt Management
Texas-Houston	2004	$1.53 bn	Securitization	Future Tax revenue

Source: The Bond Buyer (various issues)

North American states enjoy a high degree of fiscal autonomy, since the US is a federation. States can set their own tax rates, but are limited in running up large deficits. For this reason, they issue securities, such as municipal bonds, for certain specific public projects. Some of these states are bigger than European countries, so the dimension and frequency of their financing operations is huge. Over the last few years, interest rate hedging, debt management and infrastructure financing explain most operations. The latter, is particularly difficult to evaluate over future budget years since changes in rates can affect the cost of financing, rendering other issuances necessary. Disclosure of information about these operations is minimal, and very fragmented. Data reported here come from the newspapers and not from

Table 3.4 Derivatives use by states

Country	Year	Notional Amount	Debt/GDP percent	Purpose
Brazil	2002	$170 bn	54.5	$Swap
Hungary	2001	$150 mn	53.4	Securitization
India	1999	$10 bn	63	IR swap
Israel	2000	$200 mn	91	IR and currency swap
Austria	2001–2002	€13 bn	66.56	IR swap
Austria	2001–2002	€15 bn	67.3	Currency swap
Denmark	2001	120.5DKK bn	47.77	Swap
Italy	1999–2001	€6.5 bn	110	Securitization
Greece	2002	€3.745 bn	104.73	Securitization
Europe	2002	€145 bn	62.9	Securitization

Source: OECD, 2002; on debt/GDP: Thomson Financial Datastream.

any state press releases. Moreover, only a few specialized newspapers report such information. Historical data about past activities in derivatives is not available, rendering a comprehensive multi-period analysis impossible.

Brazil was hit by external shock in 2001. The currency depreciated by 40 percent in 9 months, FDI lowered and inflation increased. Derivatives have been used to manage this adverse shock and instruments have been US dollar futures, interest rate futures, interest and exchange rates swaps, and forwards, for a total $US170 billion (on 30 December 2001). Monetary policy intervened to enhance liquidity in the market and increase overnight target rates. The monetary and fiscal authorities worked together to manage foreign-exchange-denominated debt and sustain the exchange rate, issuing dollar-indexed bonds and supplying hedge to the market.

Hungary, as a country wishing to join the EMU has to strictly control monetary and real variables. Its outstanding public debt reached the value of €30 billion, which is small compared to other European countries, and securitization has been chosen as a debt and risk management technique. A marginal role is given to these innovative instruments, since market risks can be negatively influenced.

India had 63.7 percent debt over GDP ratio in 2001 and used financial innovation extensively to manage its costs. In March 2002, there were US$10 billion of derivatives transactions outstanding. The types of derivatives allowed are swaps and FRAs, written on interest and exchange rates and in various forms (caps, collars). The massive use of these instruments has grown dramatically over the 1990s and 2000s because of increasing public and trade deficits and internationalization of financial trading and management. Derivatives are used to manage risks and increase liquidity of markets, attracting investors and providing shorter dates on markets.

Israel had debt over GDP ratio of 96 percent in 2001, 26 percent of which was foreign denominated, and has settled on a single debt management strategy to enhance risk management, build an infrastructure for advanced pricing capability, and to find an optimal benchmark for liabilities portfolio. Derivatives are used "strategically in restructuring the liabilities portfolio vis-à-vis the benchmark" (OECD 2002). Instruments used are swaps, collars and swap-options; derivatives are chosen basically on risk–cost measures (efficient frontier) and to reshape the portfolio according to the benchmark.

Since 1981, **Austria** has used derivatives such as swaps, for long-term management, and FRAs, for short term management, on interest and exchange rates. The Austrian Federal Financing Agency is external and in charge of raising funds and restructuring the portfolio; particular attention is paid to credit risk and liquidity management.

Denmark uses derivatives extensively for debt management. Its instruments are basically swaps: currency, interest rates, structured, liability, asset and portfolio. In 2001, the total principal amount outstanding was 121 billion Danish krone (equivalent to €16 billion). The aim of this extensive use is to lower "long-term borrowing costs, while taking into account risks associated with the debt" (OECD 2002). Strict rating requirements support derivatives purchases together with a tendency toward plain vanilla-style contracts.

Greece has used securitization as a debt management instrument and has securitized credits coming from the lottery, air traffic, and revenue from the EU. The amount of securitized assets, €3,745 million, is, however, much lower than that of other European countries (OECD 2002).

Italy, with its 108 percent debt over GDP ratio in 2007, is one of the most sensitive countries to debt management problems. Securitization is one of the instruments used to hedge public debt and it has been applied to the National Institute of Social Security (INPS), and to public real estate. Credits have been securitized and performances with respect to target values were different in the two cases. Credits of the INPS are financial assets that can be traded on the market, domestically and abroad, without much difficulty. The securitization of INPS was successful and raises funds of up to €9 billion (OECD 2002). On the other hand, Italian public real estate has an incredible burden of rules, limits and privileges. The process of inventory alone took five years, and at the present moment securitization is under way, but is mainly raising funds domestically.

8.1 Implications of derivatives' use by highly indebted states

The use of derivatives by the public sector has certain cost saving effects, and brings benefits to national and international financial markets, increasing liquidity and the efficiency of public debt and deficit management.

However, financial innovation might directly increase existing risks (market, credit, liquidity and counterparty) over a pre-determined time length, and then could act in the opposite direction to that of financial stability. OTC derivatives can indirectly introduce different forms of risk due to the opacity of trading, low transparency of settlements systems, and scarce accounting. Moreover, the interaction between central and local public authorities using financial innovation can alter the financial equilibrium and modify the allocation process of resources, since risks do not add linearly. In 2007, these fears materialized with respect to the private sector.

A public sector characterized by a heavy burden of outstanding debt should take into consideration the binding budget constraints, and the risks embedded in its economy (ageing and health, or the probability of natural disasters) when managing its debt. A heavily indebted country should exhibit a low risk-loving attitude in financial markets, since it already has a certain number of risks to manage. The use of financial innovation for debt and cash management has certain positive effects[21], but it can have adverse effects in cases of shocks or wrong parameter settings, giving rise to a modified cost–return of the portfolio.

A distinction between high- and low-indebted countries is necessary, before proceeding with a more analytical approach. I have used the European criteria of debt over GDP, that is, whether it is smaller or larger than 60 percent.

Financial innovation is a powerful tool for debt management and it creates positive savings. However, high-indebted European countries (such as Italy and Greece) manage the combination of risks–costs and returns–costs savings from the use of financial innovation in order to match the Maastricht criteria, and only as a second step consider the other goals of public policy[22]. Highly indebted countries, in the presence of decreasing returns, and in turn shrinking demand for their bonds, look for cost-saving instruments, and because of their small amount of disclosure, derivatives are seen to be particularly attractive. These countries manage the flow of interest payments, and in this way try to diminish the stock of debt, after matching the deficit over GDP criteria. Derivatives are used to match budget constraints, but thanks to their opacity they can also be used to circumvent rules.

In the presence of developed financial markets and international credibility, derivatives can help in the pursuit of targets, but, on the other hand, the moral hazard or free riding of public administrations should be revealed.

European countries have multiple limits on their balance sheet as they have to satisfy a yearly budget deficit ($G_t - T_t$), contribute to not increasing outstanding debt (B_{t-1}) and act on the cost of debt ($r_t B_{t-1}$). More formally:

$$B_t = B_{t-1} + r_t B_{t-1} + (G_t - T_t) \qquad (9)$$

---

21   For instance, it is possible for the government to act on the preferred ten-year maturity, instead of the short-term portion of the yield curve.

22   This is also the main criticism of the rigid Maastricht budget criteria, which adjust automatically to figures, but do not consider different environments and the globalized world.

The dynamic behavior of European countries debt and deficit should be such that[23]:

$$\lim_{t \to n} \frac{B_t}{Y_t} \leq 60\% \tag{10}$$

$$\frac{(G_t - T_t)}{Y_t} \leq 3\% \forall t \tag{11}$$

An active use of derivatives can be considered as a tool to control the cost of debt, to hedge outstanding debt and to manage deficits, that is, increasing revenues and decreasing expenses (similarly to privatization) (Piga 2001, OECD 2002 and 2007).

An active use of derivatives for hedging and speculation can be an indirect source of financial instability and in a stylized macro model it can influence the investment–saving relationship of the public sector. The I–S relationship is dependent on the sensitivity of investments and savings, measured by the slope of the IS curve. Sensitivity influences the elasticity of the curve with respect to income, a part of which is made by investment, the interest rate and the price of investment (and savings). Financial innovation, whose use is based on expectations, by influencing the ability of the state to borrow on the market and inducing new risks through leverage effects, might increase the instability of the I–S relationship (its slope can change if adverse shocks take place). This effect is thought to be of particular relevance if the country is highly indebted; if the country is not highly indebted, this issue becomes irrelevant.

Derivatives can have indirect effects on the liquidity risk of the state, since they can be used to lower the burden of taxes paid by financial and non-financial firms and households. At a macroeconomic level, the tax-timing option can influence the relationship between investment and savings, the effect of which is an increase in volatility (i.e. the investment–saving puzzle, Kim 1999) and a change in risk attitude[24]. The final effect could be an increase in the resources at the disposal of the private sector, and a time-varying risk preference.

The tax-timing options of taxpayers (firms and households) can enhance the liquidity risks for the state. At a macroeconomic level, the tax-timing option can influence the relationship between investments and savings, since the private sector could have more resources at their disposal and exhibit higher risk-loving behavior, affecting the IS curve slope.

A very active use of derivatives by private and public sectors can become a source of "real" instability. The slope of the IS curve could become unstable as a

---

23 These rules are stated in the Amsterdam and Maastricht treaties.
24 BIS Quarterly Review (2003). This very important analysis will be further developed in Chapter 4.

result. The instability of the IS curve can be detected in the excessive volatility of financial markets, following a crisis or turbulence, which lowers the investment attitude by depressing consumer and business confidence, and translates into an economic slowdown.

A comprehensive analysis of monetary aspects has been sponsored by the Guido Carli Association over recent years[25]. The fiscal analysis is constrained by the absence of data, which on the one hand prevents us from knowing how much corporations and high net-worth individuals exploit derivatives or other innovative products in order to save taxes[26], and on the other hand, does not describe the effective exposure of sovereign states and local administrations. By improving the accounting rules for the private and public sectors, it is possible to eliminate such inefficiencies, and reduce the associated losses.

8.2 The modified IS-LM model

I have modified the IS-LM model to consider financial innovation explicitly as a tool of fiscal policy, not taking into consideration the effects of the tax-timing option, but only the active use of derivatives by the government[27]. This analysis basically considers the impact of derivatives on interest rates and, as a static approach, it has certain limits, which should be overcome in the near future. The first limit to keep in mind is that the complexity of derivatives, and of financial markets, is not entirely captured by the small number of equations and variables employed in this model. The Blanchard (1981) extended version of the traditional IS-LM considers the role of expectations, asset prices, and their interaction with output. This model is flexible enough to look at fiscal policy behavior, considering monetary policy as given and not dependent on fiscal policy, and at the portfolio approach[28].

The rational expectations hypothesis of the Blanchard model is coherent with the use financial innovations by authorities (as by other investors) since it is not in conflict with the increasing completeness of financial market following the decrease in inefficiencies due to the introduction of derivatives, as underlined by many authors (see for examples Savona 2003, von Hagen and Fender 1999).

I consider as given, the separation between the two policy authorities and do not alter any characteristic of monetary policy with respect to the Blanchard original model. I am conscious that financial innovation also alters the financial market's behavior (i.e. LM curve), and this should be directly modeled taking into consideration recent criticism of models using the LM curve (Romer 2000).

---

25   See the study group on derivatives at www.associazioneguidocarli.org.

26   Fiscal rules are designed in order to avoid the abuse of tax-saving operations, but the creativity of financial managers, as an expression of animal spirits, has no limit in this respect.

27   A previous version of the study can be found in Oldani and Savona (2005).

28   See also Blanchard and Fischer (1989) for extensions of the basic model.

The introduction of financial innovation into fiscal policy changes the specification of the model, and consequently its main implications. The distinction between short- and long-term adjustment is presented and discussed. An active use of financial innovation is particularly interesting for those countries characterized by high deficit and debt, whether domestic or foreign currency denominated because short- and long-terms effects can differ. Financial innovation (derivatives, securitization) can be particularly useful for cash management, cost reducing and hedging.

National spending (d) is given by:

$$d = aq + \beta y + g;$$
$$a > 0;$$
$$0 < \beta \leq 1 \qquad (12)$$

where q is the asset market, y is income, and g is the fiscal policy index. Fiscal policy uses financial innovation to hedge and, on the basis of expectations on future interest rates level, fixes the amount of interest to be paid on bonds net of fees, in between a certain corridor of rates. In this model, prices are fixed. The final impact will depend on the extent that these expectations are realized, that is, whether futures and options match spot prices.

The index of fiscal policy in our modified framework, g^*, is the debt–deficit level target, contrary to Blanchard model, where it was considered as a full employment deficit target. Decreasing debt and deficit targets is equal to a restrictive fiscal policy, and this comes with a lowering of public expenditure, decreasing national spending. To introduce financial innovation we need to consider expectations (Blanchard and Fischer 1989, 532). We can introduce them by assuming that the no arbitrage condition between long- and short-term bonds considers risk premium (χ).

$$R - \frac{\dot{R}}{R} = r + \chi \qquad (13)$$

where R is the real long-term interest rate, and r is the real short-term interest rate. This relationship can be considered as a term structure of the model, together with the no arbitrage condition between shares and bonds.

$$\frac{\dot{q}^*}{q} + \frac{\alpha_0 + \alpha_1 y}{q} = r \qquad (14)$$

Expectations are the most important ingredient in a portfolio composed of bonds, money and financial innovation. The dynamic evolution of debt and expenditure needs to be further clarified in order to consider the case of highly indebted countries. These countries usually look for an investment strategy, having some pre-determined expectations of future interest rates, and choose a corridor of rates, which is compatible with deficit and debt evolution ($r^* \leq r \leq r^{**}$). The dynamic of debt and deficit in each period of time is given by:

$$B_t = I_t + B_{t-1} + DEF_t; \quad DEF_t = G_t - T_t = G_t - tY_t; \quad I_t = rB_{t-1} \tag{15}$$

This relationship simplifies to:

$$G_t = B_t - (1+r)B_{t-1} + tY_t \tag{16}$$

where the public spending is dependent on debt (past and present) and is a function of income[29]. European countries and other federations of state (e.g. US, Australia) have budget conditions, which state that deficit and debt should converge to pre-determined levels, in order not to induce asymmetric shocks in the union or federation. With respect to the EU, the sensitivity of highly indebted member countries to interest rate variations is increasing, since it represents a (conspicuous) part of their overall spending[30]. Then the elasticity of public spending to interest rate (ψ) for these countries is higher than that to income (η), as exit from the union is not an acceptable solution[31].

We can synthesize this sensitivity of fiscal policy over interest rate and income, depending on debt outstanding, as:

$$g^* = \eta r + \psi y$$
$$\eta > \psi \tag{17}$$

I hypothesize that the sensitivity of fiscal policy, represented by the IS curve, to income (ψ), in between the pre-determined interest rates' corridor, high (r^{**}) and low (r^*) compatible with the desired hedging strategy, is very low or even constant, since the target costs of debt ($r_t B_{t-1}$) and deficit are matched through the use of financial innovation[32]. In efficient markets, derivatives in portfolio are priced in the corridor in order to manage the cost of debt, while outside the corridor the leverage effects multiply the exposure, which can worsen the credit rating and the prospective flow of interests payments. Derivatives can be used to control future interest payments and expenditure (G_t), as shown in the survey of

---

29   A further simplification would be to consider tax revenues T as a lump sum, and not as proportional to national income.

30   The Maastricht and Amsterdam treaties state that fiscal policy should act in order for the debt to converge to 60 percent of GDP, but many countries have an outstanding debt which is far bigger than that.

31   This comes straight with the pro-cyclicality argument of the Maastricht and Amsterdam criteria, as explained by Savona and Viviani (2003).

32   For example, using swaps or forward contracts to lock the costs in terms of interest or exchange rate.

countries' experiences described earlier. I suppose that derivatives are used only for hedging, and not speculation or fund raising (contrary to the US experience). Within the corridor, the cost of debt is stabilized, but income is not the primary target of policy action. As with the unholy trinity of monetary policy in the case of pegged or fixed exchange rates, portfolio and debt management limits the ability of the authority to achieve another target[33].

If the goal of debt dominates over the output, then within the corridor the sensitivity of fiscal policy to interest rates (η) is greater than that to income (ψ). Financial innovation is used to fix the cost of debt (or deficit), ηr, on the basis of some expectations on interest rates (which constitutes the portfolio strategy), and the target of income (or unemployment if you prefer) becomes a secondary policy target. We have to underline that this trade-off between output and debt–deficit targets of fiscal policy is true in the short run, since the long-run equilibrium of the model cannot be influenced by the financial innovation, which bets on short-term rates, is based on expectations, and is dependent on the sustainability of debt. Derivatives are used to fix the interests payments, as testified in the survey of countries by the OECD. Derivatives, contrary to the US practice, are employed for hedging purposes and not fund raising or speculation.

If outstanding public debt is not high, the two elasticities become relevant for fiscal policy, and income plays an explicit role in fiscal policy. This could be the case for those European countries that do not have a high outstanding debt or run a high deficit, such as Finland and Ireland, and which can then target output.

Starting from public spending (d) we can state that it is a function of income (y) in the short run, of fiscal policy index (g^*), and of stock market value (q), where the debt is managed. The short-term model can be rearranged as:

$$d = aq + g* + \beta y \qquad \text{IS curve}$$

$$a > 0 \quad 0 < \beta \leq 1$$

$$\text{Iff} \quad r^* \leq r \leq r^{**} \qquad \text{Interest rate corridor}$$

$$r = cy - h(m - p) \qquad \text{LM curve}$$

$$\frac{\dot{q}^*}{q} + \frac{\alpha_0 + \alpha_1 y}{q} = r \qquad \text{No-arbitrage condition}$$

$$r + \chi = R - \frac{\dot{R}}{R} \qquad \text{Term structure} \tag{18}$$

33   The ingredients of the unholy trinity for fiscal policy are high outstanding debt–deficit, which has to be lowered because of targets, an autonomous monetary policy, setting the interest rate, and a growth or unemployment target. The third target is not achievable by the fiscal authority given the other two.

The fiscal policy index ($g*$) is very sensitive to interest rates, so that if the equilibrium lies $r* \leq r \leq r**$ (expectations of the state about interest rates are satisfied in the market) the dynamic of debt and deficit is under control, and financial innovation contributes to lower the cost of debt and public spending.

Short-term interest rates are set through the interaction between the LM curve, the no-arbitrage condition and the term structure, so that the market sets interest rates, and the fiscal authority has not much power to influence them. Since interest rates represent the cost of debt, financial innovation is used to fix cost of debt, for example by fixing the floating rates of a portion of outstanding[34] debt. In this way, the floating rate payment is minimized, on the basis of the expected path of interest rates[35] (R) and a certain risk premium (χ). Fiscal policy uses derivatives to control $g*$ in the IS curve.

Figure 3.1 represents the stylized IS-LM model for a country running high debt and deficit, and having specific interest rate expectations. Within the corridor of expected rates, $r* \leq r \leq r**$, the equilibrium between the IS, the LM and the market is such that all targets are satisfied: fiscal policy reaches the desired levels of debt and deficit, monetary policy controls money (or prices), the market sets the interest rate and income is in equilibrium. The equilibrium in the corridor is such that debt and deficit are under control. The LM curve does not move.

The area labeled as 1 is characterized by high debt–deficit and high interest rates, so that public spending is not under control and derivatives used for hedging are "out of the money" (being out of the preferred corridor of rates). Area 3 is a low debt–deficit equilibrium with low income and low interest rates; derivatives are again "out of the money". In areas 2 and 4 the LM curve moves and can look for goals opposite to those of fiscal policy, leading to a coordination failure.

Outside the corridor of rates ($r \prec r*; r \succ r**$), the IS curve reaches an equilibrium which is associated with either higher or lower debt–deficit (areas 1 or 3), if the LM curve is not moving.

Financial innovation in the presence of constant risk aversion, χ, and no exogenous shock, can be effective to manage short-term costs of debt–deficit. Fixed price simplifies the story, reaching the desired equilibrium.

A shock can change expectations about long-term rates (R), and also affect the risk aversion (χ), given that the no-arbitrage condition is binding (eq. 14); the resulting equilibrium can lie outside the corridor, and the system is that described by Blanchard, but with an uncontrolled debt–deficit dynamic.

The long-run solution of the model[36] can be found by hypothesizing that income equals spending ($y=d$), fiscal policy controls $\bar{g}*$, the market expects r,

---

34   How large this portion is, is a question that could be answered only with detailed data.

35   This strategy is consistent with an increasing yield curve, where future expected rates should be greater the short-term rates.

36   Given by imposing and solve for y, q and r, given exogenous variables.

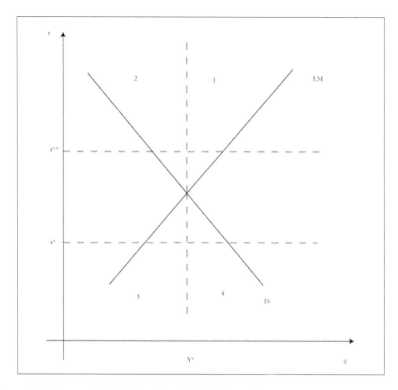

Figure 3.1 The modified Blanchard IS-LM model
Source: Blanchard 1981.

and monetary policy controls $\overline{m}$; prices are fixed ($\overline{p}$) and we can compute risk aversion (χ). The system solves finally as:

$$y = \frac{a}{b}q + \frac{1}{b}\overline{g}*$$
$$q = \frac{\pi}{r} = \frac{\alpha_0 + \alpha_1 y}{cy - h(\overline{m} - \overline{p})}$$
$$R - \chi = cy - h(\overline{m} - \overline{p}) \tag{19}$$

   The long-run solution is such that output depends on fiscal policy and the stock market; the stock market is the ratio between steady state profit and the interest rate[37]. The two curves exhibit the traditional shape but come from modified hypothesis and behavior.

---

   37   Blanchard (1981, 134).

My first conclusion is to underline the very positive role of financial innovation in matching short-term targets of debt–deficit ($\overline{g}*$), given autonomous monetary policy ($\overline{m}$), financial markets setting r, fixed prices ($\overline{p}$), but losing control over output target (y) by fiscal authority (i.e. sensitivity to income is low if outstanding debt is high).

The target of debt and deficit can be achieved in the short run by means of derivatives and securitization; in the long run, risk premium and exogenous shock make the game much more difficult to play since the equilibrium is set by the interaction of market and policies. Moreover, the risk attached to the mandate length (i.e. the mandate is shorter than the contract undersigned by the mandatory) and moral hazard due to the opaqueness of accounting rules can render the equilibrium unstable.

The importance of this theoretic result is indirectly confirmed by looking at the poor performance of highly indebted European countries (Germany, Italy and Belgium) in terms of low growth and higher than average inflation. They have been compelled to pay too much attention to debt management, in order to meet Maastricht criteria, but loosened control over economic performance and inflation, which in fact performs better in Spain and Ireland, which benefit from a lower burden of debt.

Over the last decade, OTC derivatives transactions have increased at incredible rates, together with countries' debt, but we can only identify a weak correlation on the basis of the poor quality data available with respect to counterparties.

From the sellers' side, there is an increasing interest in the products designed for public administrations, and leading investments banks and financial boutiques devote a large amount of effort to this niche.

8.3 Shocks and the effectiveness of the policy

Considering fixed-price levels, if a shock occurs and changes the risk aversion of the public sector, χ, the term structure and the equilibrium rate change, influencing the slope of the curves first, and then the final equilibrium of the system. If risk aversion increases, so that the public sector accepts less risk (and lower returns) the short-term rate, r, falls, influencing capital market value. If the rate falls below the lowest level accepted by the public sector ($r \leq r*$), the IS becomes elastic with respect to market interest rates, since derivatives become "out of the money".

If a shock occurs which lowers expectations of stock market value ($q*$), the final effect is the same as that described above.

Another shock can be considered a change in $g*$, for example in a climate of elections. If the target of fiscal policy changes, for instance increasing, so that a lower debt–deficit target is aimed at, the effect is that of a restrictive fiscal policy, moving to the lower bound of rates ($r \rightarrow r*$). This can be managed using more financial innovation, thus decreasing the risk aversion accepted by the public sector.

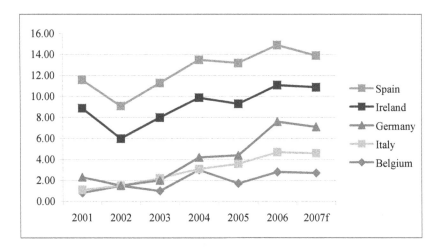

Graph 3.2 Performance of European countries (real GDP, yearly, percent)
Source: EuroStat. f: forecast.

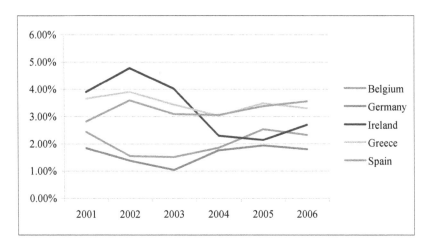

Graph 3.3 CPI index, growth (yearly, percent)
Source: EuroStat.

If a shock to financial markets changes expected long-term interest rates, the term structure changes, and rational expectations incorporate this in short-term rates and the capital market value increases. If the interest rate falls above the highest accepted by fiscal authority, $r \succ r^{**}$, derivatives become "out of the money" and the final equilibrium is expansionary on output, but "out of the money" for debt management.

Generally speaking, unless an un-anticipated shock occurs to the economy, derivatives are good instruments for reaching desired target levels of debt and deficit, lowering the sensitivity over income level. If a shock occurs, derivatives can exacerbate its effects, and alter the financial stability of the public sector by changing its liquidity risk and leading to an equilibrium with a highly undesirable deficit.

An expansionary monetary policy, moving the LM curve up to the right, can have different effects depending on whether the final equilibrium is inside or outside the corridor of rates ($r^* \leq r \leq r^{**}$). The best solution would be to get a level of rate inside the corridor, so that monetary and fiscal targets are reached at the same time. If the uncooperative monetary policy maneuver leads to fix the rate outside the corridor, $r \succ r^{**}$, the fiscal policy is in conflict with the monetary policy and market expectations over r influence the equilibrium.

My second conclusion is that fiscal policy can be considered as completely effective in its target of debt and deficit, without disturbing real spending and income, if the interest rate set by the interaction with the market is at the desired level. In this way, expectations are satisfied and no conflict between monetary and fiscal policy and the market arises. The focus then has to be put on the correct level of the rate expected by fiscal policy, that would be coherent with the market and monetary authority. The burden of risk implied in the use of financial innovation has to be properly considered, since this can modify the financial stability of the public sector.

In most surveys of countries using derivatives to manage cash and debt, Brazil is shown to be paying attention to this interaction (OECD 2002). Brazil shows a low risk-loving attitude, and a high degree of monetary and fiscal policy coordination, so that the market supports the investment and the hedging strategy. After the Argentine crisis, Brazil was not negatively influenced, contrary to what happened in the recent past, and its stock exchange is now one of the best performing of emerging countries. Data shown with respect to North American states (e.g. Texas, California) and municipalities seems to show an aggressive use of derivatives. Italy has shown fragmented behavior that is difficult to interpret, since, centrally and locally, there is a scarcity of information and little coordination; risk loving is likely to be low since the national burden of debt is very high, but free riding may, in all probability, take place.

8.4 A special tool to manage the real cost of debt: Inflation-linked bonds and derivatives

Over the first decade of 2000, very low nominal interest rates (between 2 and 3 percent) in Europe have contributed positively to reducing the cost of public debt, but have posed a demand problem, since the inflation rate lay around 2 percent for most of the decade, and consequently pre-tax real returns were null for Treasury Bonds. Risk-adverse investors might be willing to accept some risk together with a positive return, but usually reject null returns. For highly indebted countries, like

Italy, the problem is one of attracting risk-adverse investors, such as households, and assuring them a positive return. Inflation can become a parameter to issue bonds, in order to provide a certain real return to holder.

The UK government issued its first index-linked gilt in 1981, becoming the first G7 country to issue inflation-protected or "real" bonds. Since then, the governments of several other countries have begun to issue real bonds, including New Zealand (1983), Australia (1985), Canada (1991), Sweden (1994), United States (1997), Greece (1997), France (1998), Italy (2003) and Japan (2004). France, Italy and Greece actively use inflation-linked bonds as a mean to finance public spending, introducing the price risk into the group of risks already present in fiscal policy management (such as ageing population, and other welfare expenses). The most active countries, according to data available on market values of gilts, are the US, the UK and France.

For most government inflation-protected bonds, the reference price index is a domestic measure of consumer prices (CPI or similar). This index is chosen on the basis of the domestic price structure, and does not usually include energy prices (which have pushed the inflation rate well above 3 percent over recent years).

Table 3.5 The Gilt market (International inflation-indexed government bond markets)

Country	Market value ($US billion)	Number of indexed bonds	Longest maturity	Weighted average real yield (percent)
Australia	8	3	2020	2.51
Canada	36	5	2041	2.08
France	200	11	2040	2.00
Germany	23	2	2016	1.83
Greece	18	2	2030	2.38
Italy	95	6	2035	2.17
Japan	68	13	2017	1.02
Sweden	39	6	2028	1.67
UK	312	14	2055	1.18
USA	488	23	2032	1.67

Note: 1. Bonds of less than 1 year to maturity or with a market value of less than $100 million are excluded from these statistics.
Source: The United Kingdom Debt Management Office, December 2007.

An important feature concerns whether, in the event of deflation over the life of the bond, investors receive the nominal principal back in full (a par floor), or whether the nominal principal is reduced in line with the negative increase in the index (preserving its real value). Deflation is a temptation for fiscal policy, and inflation-linked bonds should be designed in order to avoid it. Most inflation-linked bonds are hedged by means of inflation-linked derivatives.

Inflation-linked derivatives (Deacon et al. 2004) were introduced in OTC markets more than ten years ago, are mostly OTC contracts, traded by leading investments banks, and in the last couple of years have become very liquid and available in most trading platforms. Inflation-linked derivatives are an essential tool for bringing together a diverse pool of issuers and investors, and lead to an enhanced and more efficient underlying, and create additional opportunities that bonds alone cannot reach (Mirfendereski 2004).

Investors in the inflation-linked derivatives market are inflation receivers (like commodity producers) and inflation payers (like consumers or governments issuing inflation-linked bonds). In the first group, we can find also pension funds, insurance companies, asset managers, corporations and hedge funds. In the second, there are those investors whose income is linked to inflation, such as regulated utilities (future income increases linked to inflation), or corporations worried about inflation going too low (e.g. retailers), or property-related businesses (e.g. housing associations).

The most common products traded in the inflation-linked derivatives market are various types of swap. Generally, one side of the trade is dependent on a defined price index, and the other is dependent on a standard fixed or floating stream of cash-lows. The benchmark product for inter-dealer trading is the zero-coupon swap; it allows a compounded inflation index to be traded against a fixed rate. It is then similar to the break-even rate in the bond market.

The most common indices traded with derivatives are those used by the bond markets: Euro Harmonized Inflation Index excluding tobacco, French CPI excluding tobacco, UK all-item RPI, or US Urban CPI NSA. The standard markets are becoming more and more liquid. Because of its simple structure, the zero-coupon product is the benchmark used to monitor the market level. Barclays Capital offers live prices in zero-coupon inflation swaps through the Bloomberg platform. Prices are updated continuously and provide an accurate monitor of what has been considered as an opaque market. Narrow bid–offer spreads reflect the increasing commoditization of the market.

The monthly turnover of inflation swaps reached €8 billion in the first quarter of 2004, according to the Bank of England data. This fast growing liquidity confirms the change in the attitude of markets towards these products. After some years of low inflation rates in Europe and the US, even deflation in Japan, increasing oil prices pose some doubts about price stability in the near future. By increasing the liquidity in inflation-linked derivatives transactions, it will be easier in the future to hedge inflation-linked bonds, whose issuance is limited at the present.

The pricing of these contracts is analogous to that of exchange rate derivatives, considering the consumer price index as the exchange rate; the easiest way to price such a (zero-coupon) contract is to consider a no-arbitrage condition, with $t<T$, and impose that the nominal price of a real zero-coupon bond equals the nominal price of the contract paying one unit of the CPI index at the bond maturity (Mercurio 2004).

9. Italy: Public debt, federalism and derivatives

The financial structure of the Italian public administration changed after the modification of the Constitution, Title V, which allowed all local public administrations to manage their expenses, revenues and funds. Local public authorities receive a part of national income tax on households and firms, contributing to increase the fiscal pressure on taxpayers. Cities and municipalities have introduced new taxes on real estate, and regions have introduced a tax on firms' revenues. The budget law of the government for 2001 introduced the freedom for all public authorities to manage debt and debt-related instruments. Before 2001, however, some public administrations had used derivatives (swaps) due to the hole in regulation, that is, the absence of an explicit prohibition. Following this normative freedom, local public administrations have actively started to manage their (increasing) financial exposure by means of innovative tools. The need to finance an increasing quantity of expenses, mainly related to education and the health system, has fuelled the issuance of bonds in the financial market, which enjoys the same credit rating as the Italian republic (A+). Since 2001, all public administrations and the treasury have started actively using OTC derivatives to hedge the flow of interest payments related to their debt, and in some cases have also raised funds[38]. Between 2001 and 2006, public administrations were compelled to manage their deficits by means of hedging strategies, that is, against adverse interest rate movements, and restructure and fine tune outstanding debt.

The problem of restructuring existing derivatives underwritten before the 2003 ban on structured products, has been solved by stating that the relative costs cannot be shifted to future budget years (when derivatives effectively expire). Risks should be borne (and paid) by those who raise them. This has contributed to worsen the financial conditions of those public administrations that were actively using derivatives before 2003.

In the budget law for 2007, new principles, of great importance for the financial stability of Italian local administrations, were introduced: first the up-front is permitted only in cases of restructuring outstanding debt, and should not exceed 1 percent of its nominal value; and second, the fees paid to the

---

38   The Italian Senate has investigated twice, in 2005 and 2007, the effects of derivatives' use by local administrations, but no final position has been taken.

financial intermediaries for any financing operation are limited to 4 percent of the nominal value[39].

The Ministry decides which types of derivatives can be traded by public authorities, and these are: plain vanilla interest rate swap, interest rate cap, interest rate collar, and forward rate agreements (FRAs). All derivatives should be plain vanilla style, that is, no derivatives on derivatives, and no exotic or structural instruments linked to any principal. In particular, knock-in swaps are forbidden (i.e. if the Euro Interbank Offered Rate (Euribor) reaches a pre-defined – usually high – level, the authority pays twice the Euribor to the counterpart). Positions are limited too, in particular long and short positions can be taken on swaps and FRAs, but only long positions on cap and collar are allowed. Moreover, the amount outstanding of derivatives, net of amortizing and exchange rate hedging, should not exceed that of debt. This aims at limiting the introduction of further risks. The *Corte dei Conti*[40], the administrative supervisor of Italian public accounting and practices, has stated that swaps can be used to manage the lower resources available from the centre to the periphery of the state. Specifically, the interest rate swap is designed to exchange interest rates paid on bonds issued on domestic and international markets. The regions of Tuscany and Sicily, the provinces of Varese and Pavia, the cities of La Spezia, Reggio Emilia, Udine and Venice have used swaps advised by JP Morgan Chase and other international banks. The Lazio region has established an office devoted to help local municipalities in the region to develop the best hedging and saving cost strategies. The public sector updates its knowledge and exploits new financing means and instruments, and their well-known advantages. In a speech at the Italian Senate in March 2004, the general director of the treasury, Domenico Siniscalco (2004a), explained the way the public sector used derivatives, and guaranteed that risks were properly addressed. Some local municipalities have been a little bit too aggressive in the past and maybe not very cautious, but sound monitoring and control have been guaranteed. This position was restated in 2007 by the Minister Padoa Schioppa, after the municipality of Taranto bankrupted[41].

Only the Minister of Economy, Siniscalco (2004b), has given some numerical information about the activity of local public authorities' (regions, cities, provinces and municipalities) use of derivatives and their purposes. Each year, in its financial report on regions, the *Corte dei Conti* collects data on their activity in the derivatives market.

---

39   Some professionals in the field maintain that this limit can be circumvented, since it does not specify whether it is the nominal fee or the final fee.

40   The *Corte dei Conti* is a bureaucratic court that looks after the formal completeness of contracts, but has no evaluation ability over their economic effects or any ability to fine malpractices.

41   A first estimate of gross exposure of Taranto reports a figure of €230 million. This data has not been confirmed by the Italian treasury.

Table 3.6 gives a picture of the derivatives activities of the Italian regions. In 2000, before the freedom was introduced, only a few regions engaged in swaps, and no one exhibited up-fronts. In 2003, after the freedom was allowed, and before the ban on structured products, almost all Italian regions engaged in an ever-increasing notional amount of swaps, and a considerable number of them raised funds using up-fronts. In 2006, up-fronts were eliminated, while the use of swaps has not diminished at all. In 2000, less than 13 percent of outstanding debt was swapped, while in 2006, the figure was around 41 percent. Most recent data provided by the *Corte dei Conti*[42] says that in 2007, 23 new interest rate swaps contracts were underwritten by Italian regions, for a notional amount of €5,398 million. The amount of debt covered by swaps, net of swap amortizing and exchange rates swaps, reached €10,421 million at the end of 2006, with an increase of €4,200 million with respect to the year 2005. The increase is due to the necessity to lengthen the maturity of outstanding debt, to restructure the outstanding debt following the restrictive monetary policy of the ECB after 2005, and to hedge newly issued debts. The exposure of small and medium public administrations (municipalities and counties) reflects riskier positions, due to the structure of contracts, which generated net positive cash flows in the first years, and negative ones afterwards.

The database of derivatives activity by all local authorities other than regions is not publicly accessible. In 2007, following a number of criticisms (Risk 2006), the treasury clarified that derivatives underwritten by all public administrations are not guaranteed as debt, since they are debt-related instruments. This apparently simple bureaucratic statement, coming after the bankruptcy of the city of Taranto, has changed the price of these securities, which are no longer guaranteed at 100 percent by the state, and has completely eliminated the ability of local administrators to raise cheap funds using innovative financial securities.

The bankruptcy of the city of Taranto is considered to be a scandal outside the country (Risk 2006) because of its (estimated) size, worth €230 million, and because of the related number of frauds and rule circumventions, which showed how free riding and moral hazard can materialize, and at what costs[43].

---

42   Corte dei Conti (2007), Relazione sulla gestione finanziaria delle Regioni 2005–2006 (Report on Financial Management of Regions, 2005–2006).

43   It is worth saying that the bankruptcy of the city of Taranto will be paid by Italian taxpayers.

Table 3.6 Italian regions' derivatives activity

Region	Year 2000			Year 2003			Year 2006		
	Outstanding debt	Swap*	Up front	Outstanding debt	Swap*	Up front	Outstanding debt	Swap*	Up front
Piedmont	4932,581,423	0	0	331,715,222.50	152,632,379.45	223,291.00	3,827,929,595	1,856,000,000	0
Lombardy	691,912,587	0	0	458,371,923.21	97,278,045.99	1,195,416.43	2,987,032,983	288,098,929**	0
Friuli Venezia Giulia				357,499,369.52	148,342,418.02	0			
Veneto	1,007,090,953	0	0	286,171,192.51	49,012,653.48	445,047.33	1,744,899,458	328,325,500	0
Liguria	273,654,839	88,200,000	0	173,803,197.25	81,450,799.54	0	726,887,577	97,136,888	0
E.Romagna	860,609,136	0	0	349,023,525.95	66,348,069.61	800,000.00	1,134,541,946	438,988,364	0
North	3,325,848,937	88,200,000	0	1,956,584,430.94	595,064,566.09	2,663,754.76	10,421,291,558	3,008,549,681	0
Tuscany	930,174,881	393,294,659	0	742,289,308.12	229,292,745.33	153,000.00	1,525,339,645	551,156,742	0
Umbria	313,429,615	0	0	33,623,267.04	33,791,163.27	574,000.00	334,761,535	253,138,502	0
Marche	737,558,211	0	0	176,470,759.53	39,274,213.89	519,935.71	943,178,758		
Lazio	1,508,000,000	800,000,000	0	177,307,230.68	176,836,220.70	1,971,496.56	3,607,260,877	1,269,794,638	0
Center	3,489,162,707	1,193,294,659	0	1,129,690,565.37	479,194,543.19	3,218,132.27	6,410,540,815	1,074,089,882	0
Abruzzo	262,922,542	129,114,000	0	280,636,879.38	134,163,691.18	2,226,427.74	1,058,071,181	804,425,095	0
Molise	110,465,132	0	0	40,044,999.73	12,290,025.80	250,000.00	274,073,984	257,817,575	0
Campania	1,202,473,772	0	0	136,754,837.98	33,902,521.29	450,000.00	4,237,928,892	2,714,707,311	0
Puglia	2,210,500,249	0	0	253,410,884.65	174,558,260.08	5,217,431.26	2,346,702,397	729,474,474	0
Basilicata	92,138,655	0	0	42,219,276.64	21,511,065.98	300,000.00	181,206,975	218,000,000***	
Calabria	614,900,000	0	0	154,272,361.40	128,317,634.48	2,786,077.63	626,391,327	614,046,040	0
South	4,493,400,350	129,114,000	0	907,339,240	881,168,763.33	11,229,936.63	8,724,375,256	5,338,470,495	0
Total	11,308,411,995	1,410,608,659	0	3,993,614,236.1	1,579,002,308.28	17,111,823.66	25,556,207,629	10,421,110,058	0

Note: * End of year value, net of swap amortizing and currency hedging. ** Underlying operations are guaranteed at 70 percent by the state. *** Swap refers to a mortgage paid by the state.
Source: Corte dei Conti, Relazione Generale sulle Regioni, 2001, 2004 and 2007.

The picture of derivatives' use by the entire public sector is not available, but it should be provided according to European savings protection principles. However, it is likely that a stronger statement by the Commission will be necessary in the coming years, when deficit is expected to worsen. The experience of the city of Taranto teaches us that the different length of the mandate and of contracts undersigned is not merely a theoretical issue, but, unfortunately, a concrete danger to financial stability. The dilemma is as old as the state itself: the incentive to cheat, be re-elected and then gain on an personal basis can overcome the costs attached to the worse scenario, paid by a multitude of individuals. Many other countries, industrialized and developing, engage in derivatives activity to hedge on domestic and international markets[44]. Plain vanilla swaps and options are widely used and back office procedures and control have been developed in order to manage related risks.

Public accounting rules and principles are completely different from those that apply to the financial system of private corporations; financial innovation can play the role of a very useful financial tool to hedge debt-related risks, but can also be employed because the opaque accounting rules cannot entirely describe the exposure. The Italian legal system, after the modification of the Constitution, introduced the ability for all to raise debt, but did not clarify at the beginning the responsibility related to the issuance of obligations. This has led financial intermediaries to attribute the credit rating of the Italian republic to all public administrations, including very small municipalities! This is not only a huge mistake, but it exacerbated the moral hazard previously described in more general terms.

Counterparties in derivatives contracts should have the same rating as the Italian Republic, in order to minimize the counterparty risk (i.e. at least A). Before the budget law for 2007, nothing was said about the *ex ante* control on derivatives contracts; this lack has been rectified and, for the contract to be valid (i.e. produce a legal obligation), the administration must send the contract to the Italian treasury for approval. However, nothing is said about the maximum time length the treasury has to reply to the request of authorization, and it is not clear whether the principle of "silence means approval", largely applied in the Italian public law to overcome the slowness of bureaucracy, is valid also for this type of authorization. Therefore, our doubts about the effective ability to disclose data and monitor expositions still remain[45].

The introduction of GASB rules on transparency will probably have severe effects on Italian public finance, but it is just history repeating itself. The only way for Italy to reverse the path of public debt was to join the euro; the only way to eliminate or reduce the dangers posed by excessive and irresponsible financial

---

44   See Tables 3.3 and 3.4 and OECD (2002) for further details.

45   According to the press, the city of Taranto engaged in a certain number of contracts that were never authorized by the treasury. The treasury has not confirmed this.

freedom given to local authorities was to adopt GASB principles, and be forced to eliminate part of the freedom.

The years to come will probably be characterized by worsening public financial conditions at the central level, since over the last few years no structural budget modifications have been approved, especially on current expenses. At local level, health-care expenses are under little budget control in a number of big regions and this will contribute to increase debt and taxes, and finally worsen the fiscal pressure on taxpayers. Following the British experience of the Hammersmith and Fulham local authorities, we believe that a way to lower the costs of the Taranto bankruptcy could be to rely on the lack of legal ability of the municipality (i.e. legal risk); this would be to the detriment of credibility of the Italian public system, which is already quite low, but would contribute by shifting part of the cost of bankruptcy to those intermediaries who sold expensive and aggressive contracts to Taranto, exploiting the lack of financial control and the free riding[46].

10. Derivatives: A great opportunity or a jungle?

The issue of financial management of the public sector is complex, and local characteristics can influence the evaluation and analysis of effects. The pursuit of stability and the no taxation without representation principle should light the way in rule setting, monitoring or control and in any policy analysis. The public sector is an incentive manager in modern globalised economic systems, and raises funds on financial markets from households, firms and foreign investors. By going on the market it is compelled to accept its rules, in terms of pricing, returns and transparency. At times, it can exploit its relative size and, thanks to different accounting principles, can be tempted to gain from its peculiar advantages. The issue of the risk attitude that a public administration should exhibit is of particular relevance for this analysis but has no clear answer, since it depends on the burden of other risks, on the business cycle (domestic and global) and on the state of the art.

The risk due to the different lengths (mandate and contracts undersigned) can modify the overall burden of debt and risks over different budget years, and present accounting rules do not eliminate this risk. The GASB project on derivatives introduces the fair value and directly addresses the opaqueness of accounting. Information to stakeholders needs to be implemented for risks to be effectively managed. Accounting is not transparent and incentives are not well designed. The market of OTC derivatives looks like a jungle for small to medium public administrations, unable to evaluate overall risks and exposures properly, while it is heaven for financial intermediaries, who earned amazing fees from local

---

46   A leading Italian news magazine investigated how banks sell these financial securities to small firms and the public sector, and it reported the existence of a number of operations which were not transparent nor satisfied the best business practices rules.

administrations[47]. The position I suggest for public administrations is similar to that for small private investors; namely, they should not be allowed to trade such complex securities, since it is not possible to ensure the full comprehension of effects and risks attached. Moreover, small and medium public administrations do not have the expertise necessary to evaluate the most complex effects and drawbacks of these OTC contracts and, in most cases, ask for advice directly from the seller, exacerbating the conflict of interests. The British choice of a complete ban might appear too strong, but, since it is impossible evaluate whether potential costs exceed gains, I consider the ban to be the most risk-reducing choice in the short and medium term.

The fiscal devolution process and the increasing duties left to local authorities, in the absence of clear rules, can create a hole where moral hazard and free riding proliferate. An efficient solution in the medium run would be to introduce, without delay, the fines and the full responsibility principles over costs, present and future (i.e. caused by certain administrative acts) and over revenues (efficient managers earn more than lazy ones), to ensure the elimination or at least severe reduction of moral hazard and free riding.

11. Conclusion

In this chapter I have discussed how derivatives can affect the public sector's financial stability with respect to different variables: revenues (taxes), expenses and debt.

Tax rules can create a gap between corporate and market values of income, and the value to be taxed. Narrative information on the difference between the three can be very important for the market to be able to evaluate the effective exposure and risk. The tax burden (of firms, financial and non financial, and of households) can be managed by means of derivatives. This management is basically a problem of international accounting standards and the domestic applications of these rules. The IAS 39 has filled the information and evaluation gap regarding derivatives. Once the accounting is transparent and represents the effective exposure, tax arbitraging becomes tax management. The US Security and Exchange Commission (SEC), the Security and Investment Board (SIB) and the Commodity Future Trading Commission (CFTC) have been studying how to regulate the OTC markets, to limit problems and tax avoidance, but in doing so they want to avoid the effect of "sand in the wheel" (i.e. they prefer principal-based regulation to rigid rules).

Public expenses, especially those related to debt repayments, can be positively influenced by financial innovation, if it helps to meet specific targets and reach the desired maturity.

---

47 Before the explicit limit imposed by the budget law for 2007, intermediaries could earn as much as a 4 percent fee.

Modern fiscal policy is no longer conceived as Keynesian deficit spending, but as active incentive management. Various constraints limit the working of public authorities, and change the dynamics of economic variables and growth. Over the last few years, a certain number of sovereign debt crises have decreased international confidence on the bonds market, also affecting the private sector. Special types of derivatives, such as credit derivatives, can be of great help in order to improve international bond issuance, but are of no help in cases of crisis, as we saw in 2007.

Derivatives can be very useful for hedging, but if they are used without confidence and knowledge, they can be dangerous, thanks to the leverage effect, as the Orange County and LTCM experiences teach us. A new stream of the literature, behavioral economics, is trying to explain the role and effects of various violations of the perfect markets hypothesis, and can be of help for further studies in this fascinating field. The illusion of being able to control outstanding debt and derivatives written on it, or bought to hedge, can induce governments to be more aggressive than necessary (i.e. overconfidence). This illusion would vanish once we realize that financial markets are far bigger than governments, and usually more powerful and faster in influencing investors' choices and sentiments.

Derivatives, and especially swaps, can be introduced in a stylized Blanchard IS-LM model in order to look at the interest rate effects on public sector portfolios. Interconnections between fiscal and monetary policies are taken into consideration, since they influence wealth and income distribution. The analysis is static and the general result is that highly indebted fiscal authorities should be very cautious in using risky securities, regardless of the type of instrument, since the sensitivity to interest rate movements is higher than that to income (the public debt objective is binding and dominates that on income), introducing financial instability into the IS curve.

The state is a special player in the bond market, given its relevant size, interacting with financial markets, managing public resources and raising funds. The recent GASB project to put derivatives into the financial statement of countries would address many of the problems previously discussed, such as the lack of transparency, the risk associated with the different lengths (of the mandate and of contracts undersigned), and the resulting moral hazard or free riding.

Today, only a few countries admit the use of derivatives (especially swaps) to hedge, but I am confident than many more are exploiting their well-known advantages. US states are quite aggressive, but bear the full consequences of their financial strategies; developing countries engage in derivatives with a fairly cautious approach, which is healthy for their stability. Some European countries have been accused of having exploited the opaque accounting of financial innovation to meet Maastricht and Amsterdam criteria.

The experience of Italy over recent years is very interesting, since benefits and risks are both evident. The government has allowed local public administrations to use derivatives, but the picture of their use is unclear and there seems to be space left for avoidance of rules. Central government can hedge outstanding public debt, but local public administrations (regions, municipal cities and the health care system) can also enter the derivatives market to manage expenses, revenues and debt. New risks can emerge in this context, and fiscal devolution (which increases the duties of local authorities) in the absence of clear rules and transparent markets, can temporarily create holes where moral hazard and free riding proliferate, as testified by the city of Taranto crash.

Chapter 4
The Theory of Investments and Derivatives: The Frontier of Economic Analysis

1. Introduction

In the preceding chapters, I concentrated on the fiscal, monetary and institutional analysis of derivatives. Fiscal and monetary analyses underline the effects on short-run interest rates (setting and variation), which is the price of money, and the return or cost on public debt. In this chapter, I look at other effects of derivatives on the interest rate, by considering the investment decision. Investment is the seed of capitalism; capital accumulation is influenced by the availability of information, of means of financing, and by the efficiency of trading. Derivatives are instruments that contribute to complete the market, increase investment opportunities, speed up the monetary transmission mechanism, and hedge risks. Hedging and risk management practices are strategic in the globalised financial system, and the ability to gauge information is of great importance for the investment decision. The investment decision is influenced by market expectations, and derivatives have proven to be able to gauge them. I shall then consider an industry characterized by a structural lack of investments: the energy and oil industry. In considering the role of investments in the macro-economy, I move my attention to the Tobin's Q approach, where the firm's evaluation of assets is the key variable and is market based. Since financial markets are intrinsically unstable and not very adherent to the perfect market hypothesis, I move from the Minsky approach and consider the stabilizing role that can be played by derivatives under certain circumstances.

The effects of derivatives in the macro-economy can be synthesized with a flows' chart (Figure 4.1), which has the interest rate as its key variable. The interest rate influences capital formation, since it is the price of capital and a benchmark for investments. In an economic system with imperfect competitive markets (i.e. oligopolistic) the mark-up is the mechanism through which corporate profits are reflected in prices. The price level influences growth and disposable income; then, these, in turn, affect the L_1 (money demand for transactions), and modify the L_1 by increasing the L_2 (substitution effect, see Chapter 2). The interest rate is also the return on public debt and influences the deficit, as clarified in Chapter 3.

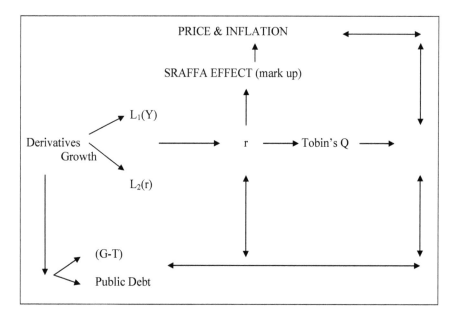

Figure 4.1 Flows' chart of derivatives effects
Source: Savona 2007.

2. The theory of investment

Investments can be considered as the voluntary reduction of consumption (of firm or state) in order to create a stock of capital over time. Investment is an inter-temporal choice and as such should be evaluated on a multi-period basis. The role of uncertainty and expectations are crucial here. Investment is a component of national accounting, in a demand and supply driven scheme. Using a simple notation, we can say that, in a closed economy with the government, the national income can be allocated between consumption (C), investment (I) and public spending (G).

$$Y=C+I+G(1) \tag{1}$$

The savings of an economy can be used to finance investments (I), to finance public deficit (G-T) given by the difference between expenditures (G) and revenues (T), and to finance the current account deficit, given by the difference between exports (EXP) and imports (IMP).

$$S=I+(G\text{-}T)+(EXP\text{-}IMP) \tag{2}$$

Financial relationships are of central importance, in mature capitalist systems, in determining economic dynamics. Hyman Minsky[1] summarizes his microeconomic theory of investments at firm-level decisions, with the lip diagram. A firm can partially finance investments with its own cash flow (*CF*), which is independent from market interest rates and has a quasi-fixed cost (*R*). The residual part of investments needs to be financed externally on the market, comparing the marginal cost of investment (P_I), and the expected present value of future cash flows from the new investments (P_K). The distance between *R* and P_I represents the lender's risk. This risk affects the debt and its cost; when firms become more risky, their lender's risk increases. The borrower's risk is subjective, and is the discount that the firm applies to the expected present value of the project that must be financed with the debt. Risk aversion, together with subjective beliefs, can affect the borrower's risk.

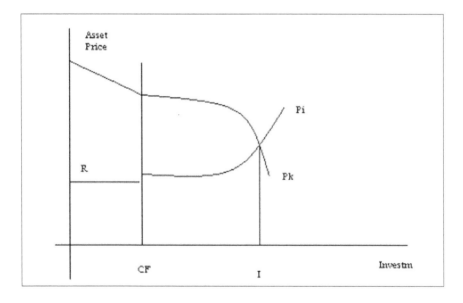

Figure 4.2 The Lip diagram
Source: Bellofiore and Ferri 2001.

---

1   The following discussion is taken from Bellofiore and Ferri (2001) *The Economic Legacy of Hyman Minsky*.

The P_K curve is steeper than the P_I curve, because the elasticity of investment with respect to external financing decreases more quickly as external debt increases, and is lower than that of internal financing (CF). A further complication of the investment's function is the effect of leverage:

$$I_t = (1 + \lambda_t)CF_{t-1} \qquad (3)$$

where the λ_t coefficient is time dependent, varies inversely with leverage and represents the debt-ratio multiple on retained earnings. The λ_t coefficient is affected by the business cycle (y_t), and can be expressed as:

$$\lambda_t = \lambda_0 + \lambda_1 / (1 + e^{x(t)})$$
$$x(t) = \lambda_3 - \lambda_4 [Debt_{t-1} / Equity_{t-1}] + \lambda_5 [y_{t-1} / y_{t-2}] \qquad (4)$$

A positive business cycle supports investments and allows firms to increase their debts, without affecting their lender's or borrower's risks; upper and lower limits should be imposed to λ_t in order for the model to provide a finite and stable solution. The expected cash flow from the new investment (P_k) is influenced by firm's judgment; different curves reflect different expectations and the equilibrium setting.

The link between savings and investments lies basically in financial markets, and investment is a way to reduce asymmetric information among players on markets, and to lower the risk premium (Rajan and Zingales 2003). The efficiency of financial markets contributes to improving the investment opportunities, decreasing the average risk premium[2]. Financial markets, by financing attractive investments in a competitive way, contribute to break the link between investments and collaterals, and reduce the need for real estate collaterals[3].

I believe that derivatives, by completing financial markets, should influence the investment decision[4] positively. This issue needs to be discussed along with the criticism often made against derivatives, that they are zero-sum game, and thus cannot represent any substantial innovation in the financial market and cannot contribute in any way to its completeness. The fact that derivatives are considered to be zero-sum games comes from the hypothesis of rational expectation in an arbitrage-free environment. This approach, consistent with complete and perfect financial markets, considers derivatives as replicates of underlying securities, and so if summed at expiration, they give "zero". However, financial markets are far from being complete and frictionless. As we will see, the proof of their incompleteness is that implied and realized volatilities never match. From this viewpoint, having

---

2   Graphically, it means that it lowers the variations in the price of assets.

3   This is another reason driving derivatives' growth and attractiveness.

4   Savona (2007) underlines the role of derivatives in the investment decision and growth; Fan et al. (2007) underline the possibility of lowering the cost of external financing, and then increasing investments, through the hedging strategies allowed by derivatives.

a set of securities that is liquid, flexible, and tailored to customers' needs can improve investment opportunities by widening the financing tools available. Fan et al. (2007) maintain that derivatives, by reducing costs of external financing, can positively influence the value of the firm.

Robert Shiller (2000) considers future contracts as a powerful tool to create new opportunities for investors. Futures are a very important class of innovation, and are designed to provide insurance on various risks related to commodities, securities and events. They also provide liquidity where it is substantially small or even absent, as in the catastrophe insurance market. Shiller, moving from the flexibility of futures, maintains that the hedging opportunities they provide should be available to all agents. He has a democratic viewpoint over the role of financial markets, and he is confident that the market can find the best way to allocate risks and resources. By completing financial markets, futures can provide investors with relevant means to finance new investment opportunities. Shiller also considers futures could hedge macro risks[5], and not only financial risks.

3. The problem of capital measurement

The debate over the centuries by economists on the definition of capital is large, but a single and commonly shared view has never been reached. Capital is the accumulation of investments and is the basis for economic development. Capitalism, whose root lies in the capital accumulation process, is the economic organization based on the market, competition, individualism and freedom. Varying amounts of these ingredients can change the effective working of the system, moving away from the efficient allocation of resources and moving toward oligarchy.

From an historical point of view, the interpretation and role of capital in the social organization has changed over the last two millennia. In particular, to accumulate capital it is necessary to have someone who provides funds; the lending activity corresponds to an interest rate accrued, and various justifications have been used in support of the credit activity. Moral justifications to lending have been taken further and religious or moral principles are useful in order to avoid dependency or blackmailing.

Economic justifications for the investment usually refer to the sacrifice of liquidity or consumption to finance capital formation. But the fundamental economic problem refers to the measurability of capital itself. The return on capital, the profit, should be known in advance in order for the entrepreneur to decide whether to invest or not. The profit should be compared to the rate of interest paid on borrowings. However, to know the profit you need the interest rate paid on debt and vice versa, introducing a disruptive circularity in the capital accumulation and investment decision.

---

5   For instance, inflation, growth, investment or unemployment risks.

John Maynard Keynes tried to overcome the circularity problem by considering only the short-run equilibrium, and looking at the influence of the marginal efficiency of capital[6] (as a proxy for profit) on the expected return on capital (as a proxy for the interest rate). The first influences the second on the market in the short run, breaking the circularity. Keynes stated that the equality between the marginal efficiency of capital and the interest rate determines the stock of capital. In a growing economy, the rate of accumulation of capital is equal to the rate of growth of the economy, and at equilibrium, no new investment takes place. In the *General Theory of Employment, Interest and Money* (Keynes 1936, Chapter 12), the stock exchange plays a special role, increasing the efficiency of transactions, and positively influencing the rate of current investments. The stock exchange can help in the flow of funds and the exchange of the ownership of firms.

Piero Sraffa (1960), not satisfied by his mentor's arguments (Keynes), argued that the interest rate setting is the result of the class struggle between bankers and entrepreneurs. If bankers are more powerful than entrepreneurs, the profit will follow after the interest rate is set. If bankers are less powerful, the opposite will take place. Looking at more recent macro-models, capital formation and its circularity are still unsolved problems[7].

A stable economic environment attracts a greater amount of investments, and virtuous financial markets should contribute to improve the matching price process and their overall efficiency. Derivatives have certain stabilizing effects, with respect to their underlying asset markets[8], and this property can be exploited for the investment decision. Investment is risky, but risk is better controlled if markets are working well and rules of the game are clear. The introduction and spread out of derivatives are signs of the increasing completeness of markets. This is true if derivatives are used for hedging purposes; if speculation emerges and overcomes the (stabilizing) hedging, the final effect could be an increase in financial fragility.

4. Macroeconomic derivatives: Hedging on future world performance

An evolution of financial innovation is that of macroeconomic derivatives, which allow for hedging macro-risks, such as inflation, unemployment and growth. Since growth drives and is driven by investments, complicating further the circularity problem, the link between the two should be clarified before proceeding.

---

6   The marginal efficiency of capital is the first derivative of the production function of output with respect to capital.

7   New Keynesian or classical models consider the equality between marginal efficiency of capital and the (market) interest rate, without any further theoretic clarification regarding the causal direction, to be an equilibrium condition.

8   Ang and Cheng (2005); Cohen (1999); Hung-Gay Leung (1993).

Expectations play a key role in capital formation. Jaimovich and Rebelo (2006) consider overconfidence and optimism of rational agents in the expectation formation in the real business cycle model. This modification of agents' preferences is useful when looking at the contribution of these biases to the business cycle's (unexplained) volatility. Although these violations of rationality seem to be strong, if applied to rational agents, the authors show that the impact of optimism is actually quite small. Overconfidence can amplify the agent's forecasting errors, influencing the volatility of the economy, but amplification leads to an error that is smaller than the one observed on real US data.

Based on the national accounts, we can say that investments (I) are part of the GDP, together with consumption (C), public spending (G) and net foreign trade (NX).

$$GDP_t = C_t + I_t + G_t + NX_t \tag{5}$$

Present capital (K) is the sum of past investments (I) over n periods:

$$K = \sum_{t=1}^{n} I_t \tag{6}$$

Investments can be financed through different channels:

$$S_t - I_t = (G_t - T_t) + NX_t \tag{7}$$

These are national saving (S), public primary surplus (G-T) or current account surplus (NX), and they can be fine tuned, according to contingent domestic and international situations. An additional channel is public debt (B), resulting from the deficit. An important channel for financing the difference between savings and investments is the financial account of the balance of payments[9].

An inflow of funds from abroad, which corresponds to a surplus of the financial account, needs international accountability, good and stable returns and, preferably, a reserve currency. These three characteristics are very hard to replicate in the world economy; as far as I know when writing, the US and, to a much smaller extent, Europe can rely on them in different ways. The United States over the 1990s and the first decade of 2000, has exhibited a negative saving rate, that is, high public spending together with tax cuts, and an increasing current account deficit (i.e. twin deficits). The US locomotive can sustain its growth with international credibility in its currency and attractive financial markets. In 2007, growth slowed down because of financial turmoil, but there is room left for hope of recovery in 2008–09.

Expectations on future performance of markets drive investment decisions, and influence institutions' policy making. The irrational exuberance on real estate or *dot*

---

9   See the details of the way derivatives are accounted in the balance of payments in Chapter 1.

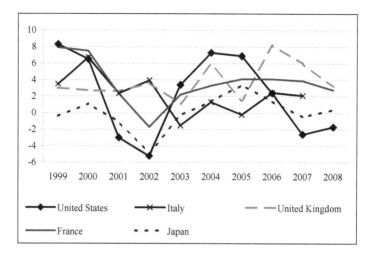

Graph 4.1 Gross fixed investments (yearly, percent)
Source: Thomson Financial Datastream.

com shares are (extreme) examples of self-fulfilling expectations of ever-increasing prices. The management of risks implicit in the future behavior of price, rate and quantities, is the main objective in derivatives, so macroeconomic derivatives are a special class of contracts. They bet on the future expected behavior of certain macroeconomic variables, such as income, consumption, inflation, unemployment and so on, as reflected in surveys and qualitative indices of business climates and confidence. Robert Shiller (2000) supports the necessity of financial contracts representing macroeconomic variables. This new securities market should fill the absence of efficient ways to allocate macro risk, and provides macro-insurance.

The behavior of real gross fixed investments in some G7 countries over the last eight years reflects the great amount of uncertainty embedded in the investment decision. The UK and the US exhibit high level of gross fixed investments, while Italy and Japan have a really negative trend. The better business cycle in the US and the UK can help explain a part of the investment decision, but not all, since other than the actual performance, the expected performance also plays a relevant role in the choices made by firms.

A pioneering study by Gurkaynak and Wolfers (2006) looks at the very first months of macroeconomic derivatives trading, to analyse the efficiency of these contracts, and the possibility of using the prices to capture "subjective beliefs", which are useful in the study of expectations and their formation. Macroeconomic derivatives are basically option contracts (call and put, digital and binary) whose payoffs depend on the path of some macro-indicators. These contracts are traded

OTC and their pricing is not yet completely established[10]. The data used by authors refers to a leading bank (Deutsche Bank). Their results show that "market-based measures of expectations (i.e. coming from derivatives) are similar to survey-based forecasts, although market-based measures predict more accurately responses to surprise in data". This evidence comes from panel estimates on non-farm payrolls, business confidence, retail sales and unemployment indices.

Option prices can be used to construct a risk-neutral probability density function for each data release. The market runs as a series of occasional auctions, in order to maximize liquidity[11]. The density forecast obtained from options is efficient, and this justifies the use of options standard deviation to measure the uncertainty about data release[12]. The fact that densities of economic derivatives prices are efficient means that the risk premium associated is not very large. The authors' results show that derivatives provide hedging against very high frequency movements. This is different from what Shiller wished, as he thought securities would be able to democratize risks and bring the risk-sharing opportunities of Wall Street to Wal-Mart (i.e. share macro-risks at the very micro-level).

Macro derivatives on investments, not yet investigated in the literature by market practitioners, if built and priced as efficiently as other macro-derivatives, could be a tool to hedge on future capital formation and then on economic performance.

5. Energy and derivatives[13]

According to most macroeconomic analyses of the global economy, the last decade of the 20th century exhibited a strong, negative trend in one strategic sector: energy. This trend is substantiated in a steady decrease in fixed investments, following a decade of structural change of the energy market. The collapse of the Russian Federation, and the change in the energy supply policy, modified the supply of energy and fuels in the world.

Following the change in the supply of energy, fossil fuels still play a strategic role, while other sources (like nuclear, and renewable) still play a very minor role in the energy production of industrialized countries. In most developing countries, they are completely absent. The demand of energy in the 21st century is moving

---

10   The pricing mechanism is corrected to be robust, and the market uses a series of auctions to maximize liquidity, instead of a continuous double auction.

11   Each transaction takes place a series of auctions at all intermediaries: Goldman Sachs, ICAP, Deutsche Bank.

12   Of course, the short timescale covered by the data might alter the robustness of these results.

13   For this section I gratefully thank the President, Prof Salvatore Zecchini, the Chief Economist, Ferdinando Zullo, and the Manager of the Trading Floor of the Italian Energy Stock Exchange, Giovanni Battista Aruta, for their very helpful discussions.

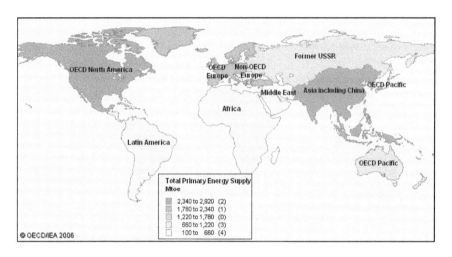

**Figure 4.3 World total primary energy supply
(million oil equivalent tons, 2006)**
Source: World Energy Outlook 2007.

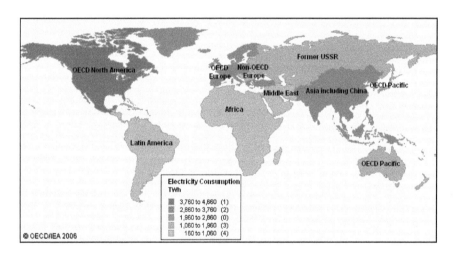

Figure 4.4 World electricity consumption (terawatts per hour, 2006)
Source: World Energy Outlook 2007.

from being G7-driven, to being driven by emerging countries (i.e. over 50 percent
of the increase is due to China and India).

The energy sector is dependent on the economic cycle, but the economic life
of most infrastructures is greater than a decade. Following the increase in the
oil price, which started in 2004 (see Graph 4.2), a push toward new investments

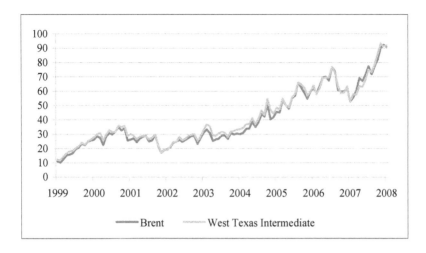

Graph 4.2 Crude oil monthly price (US$ per barrel)
Source: Thomson Financial Datastream.

should have been detected in world energy supply data. This push is completely absent, and this, after being a thorny problem difficult to solve can explain much of the excessive prices we observe[14] (and pay).

The reasons for the lack of investments depend on the geographical area: in the Russian Federation, after the 1998 crisis, state-owned energy corporations sold oil at very low prices to conquer market shares, but with no long-term plan of supply expansion; in the US, a number of tornados damaged the Gulf of Mexico oil and gas pipelines; Canada invested in technologies for the oil industry, but only contributed to a small extent to the supply increase. The Arabian producers, and other OPEC countries (like Venezuela or Mexico) are delaying important investments, to sustain high oil prices and profits.

The energy sector is worthy of attention because of its long history of lack of investments, and because derivatives have spread out at amazing rates in this industry. Finance, similarly to energy, has no physical presence, but has real-world consequences. Has there been any sign of potential stress in the energy sector too, following the stress in the financial market in 2007–2008. Ignorance kills people and destroys wealth.

The energy sector exhibits high excess returns and the financial system devotes to it a large share of its resources. In particular, most international banks build and sell securities to their customers to hedge energy-related risks; in most case they

---

14 See the World Energy Outlook of the International Energy Agency of the OECD (2006 and 2007), and the 2006 Report of the Italian Energy Stock Exchange (*Gestore del Mercato Elettrico*).

started *ad hoc* OTC trading platforms to ensure liquidity. The pricing of these contracts follows the rules of traditional derivatives corrected for their peculiarities, for example storage and transport costs, or environmental risks (Geman 2004). What concerns most researchers is the ability of derivatives prices to reflect future expected spot prices, and the liquidity of these contracts. Exchange-traded future prices on oil, traded since the 1980s, have proved to be very bad predictors of spot prices, but are liquid and marketable (Tabak 2003). Moreover, some variables, like the price of natural gas, follow the oil price, while in theory it should not, since it is a commodity with very different transport and storage costs, and is traded on different markets, following other rules and contractual standards. This fact diminishes the ability to price derivatives efficiently on many energy commodities, and on the other hand, increases the necessity of hedging tools for market participants.

The liquidity of the exchange-traded market is good for the oil market. On the hand, OTC transactions are not very liquid, since these contracts are quite young, not well established and linked to a sector which is structurally far from competitive.

Textbooks and trading manuals are rich in details for building pricing and hedging strategies, but do not even devote a line to the structural lack of investments in the industry, which defeats most efforts for efficiently pricing contracts with multi-annual maturity[15]. The lack of predictive ability of exchange-traded contracts

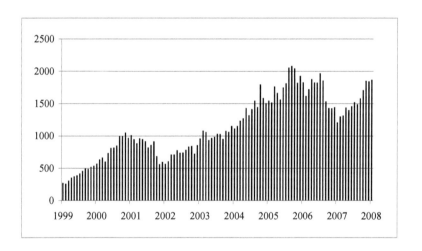

Graph 4.3 GSCI energy total return (monthly index)
Source: Thomson Financial Datastream.

---

15   The standard maturity for a natural gas supply contract is no less than ten years, but if investments are lacking, the ability efficiently to price contracts linked to an under-supplied sector vanishes.

is probably present in OTC transactions too; however, I do not have any empirical evidence to sustain my position[16].

There are basically two dangers in energy derivatives: mispricing and illiquidity. Mispricing changes the risk–return profile of portfolios, altering the effectiveness of hedging, or diminishing the gains from speculation. The lack of liquidity, similarly to what happened to the American mortgage industry, can have domino effects first in the industrial sector and then in the financial sector. Like credit derivatives, energy derivatives can be similar to hell: easy to enter and impossible to exit. The industry has a structurally high level of risk, and this pushes forward the demand for hedging tools. However, since most derivatives do not settle with the physical delivery, but with the financial compensation or roll-over, they are not very likely to cause an "energy crunch". If the structural lack of investments does not reverse, the hedging strategies will continue to be mispriced. This causes an inefficient management of energy related risks which do not help market players in their actual and perspective choices. However, an endogenous solution to the lack of investments is the technological improvements, which has positive effects on the supply.

6. The Tobin's q approach

Capital measurement is linked to the evaluation of investments. James Tobin tried to get over the circularity between the interest rate and profitability, and employed a market approach. Tobin's theory moves from the fact that there is always a distance between historical costs of investments, and the corresponding market value. This distance, expressed as a ratio, represents the effective value of the capital (q). The overall cost of production is an important factor in the valuation of assets. The market for business takes several forms, and the most important are those for corporate securities (Brainard and Tobin 1977). The embedded risk is one of the main features distinguishing the different forms of investment (bonds, securities, shares and so on). Since both market values and historical cost are affected by the interest rate (and its expectations), and derivatives affect this rate, then the link between derivatives and the q needs to be further clarified. This issue was first discussed in the literature by Savona (2007), who considers the role of derivatives with respect to real income, via the capital accumulation process, as specified in the Tobin's q approach.

According to the Tobin's q approach, new investments should be implemented if they are able to increase the value of the firm. However, the new investments can be in a different class of risk from that of existing investments, complicating the measurement of impact on the value of the firm.

---

16 The informative advantage of energy prices is very important; for example, the price of natural gas supplied by Russia is a government secret.

Macroeconomic models usually consider the riskless asset (and rate) as a baseline to evaluate alternative (risky) assets; moreover, the financial structure of a firm is non-neutral with respect to its valuation. A small tractable IS-LM model can be useful to explain the basic analysis, which will be developed further. The investment function can be expressed as:

$$\partial K / K = \varphi(q - \bar{q}) + g \tag{8}$$

where K is capital, $\bar{q}$ is the normal value of q, φ is a positive parameter, and g is the natural growth rate. Equilibrium occurs at $q = \bar{q}$; the IS locus in the (q, Y) space will have the usual positive slope $(\partial q / \partial Y \succ 0)$ and consumer wealth rises with q.

The LM locus can be constructed in the same (q, Y) space, but I will consider as given the inflation rate, the stock of debt, and the real quantities of high-powered money in order to draw one curve. The problem with the LM curve is that, under certain conditions on the relationship between income (Y) and the marginal efficiency of capital (R), its slope can be positive (and not negative, as the standard Hicksian interpretation supposes). Moreover, liquidity and credit conditions can influence the sensitivity of the LM curve to monetary policy maneuvers, influencing the slope of the curve (and not only shifting it up and down).

The existence of many q for a given firm makes it very difficult to use it as a single parameter of investments valuation, but its path can be a useful sign of the market sentiment.

Another important point to clarify is that taxes are non neutral for the q valuation, and this can influence the investment decision. Tax arbitrage and special incentives can artificially increase the rate of return on special investments.

A tax incentive for firms to set their headquarters in a geographical area is an example of this. For instance, Delaware and Nevada, because of their lack of domestic production, have tax savings options for newly established firms. Ireland in the EU has a corporate tax which is almost half that of other EU member states (such as Germany or Italy) in order to fill the production gap of the country. The tax rate paid on corporate income influences the savings rate on one side, and the investment decision on the other, since with more after-tax-income, higher investments can be supported. The tax saving can be considered as an increase in income, given equal interest rates (e.g. set in the monetary union by the central bank), shifting the equilibrium between the LM and IS curves to the right.

The effects of the tax savings on the IS-LM Tobin scheme are that the normal value of $\bar{q}$ is higher, with a higher growth rate of the economy (g), for a given value of government debt, money supply and inflation. Tobin observed the role of inflation on the q; in particular, anticipated inflation has no effect on q, but the nominal neutrality can fail in reality for various reasons. Unanticipated inflation can increase the valuation of future investments, but this type of shock is supposed not to occur frequently, so that the marginal q is not affected.

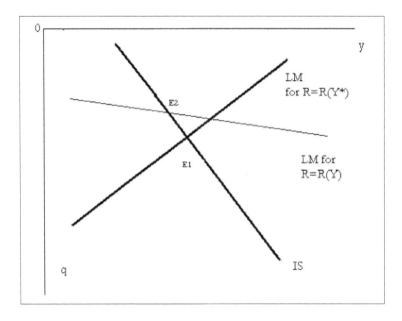

Figure 4.5 The Tobin and Brainard IS-LM
Source: Brainard and Tobin 1977.

7. Derivatives' *q*

The measures of derivatives in portfolio are the nominal (or notional) value, the margins–premiums paid or earned, or the net exposure. However, these are not satisfying measures for our purposes, that is, evaluating investments, because they provide very partial pictures. Recent projects are trying to provide narrative information on risks and management procedures related to derivatives, but at present these are at a very early stage[17].

Let's try to clarify the relevance of this point; the measure of the investor's exposure in the financial market is given by the number of securities (shares, bonds, etc.) multiplied by the market price. The same measure in derivatives markets, the nominal value, plays a different role: it is never exchanged in full between the parties and is a parameter to compute the effective payment due, which is usually lower than 10 percent of the notional value. The final exposure of the buyer–seller is computed as a net value, that is, credit minus debit, and is usually provided quarterly. As explained in Chapter 1, the trading activity between domestic investors is reported on a yearly basis in the national financial accounts and is measured at market value, while cross-border transactions are reported in

---

17   They come from the application of the IAS and SFAS standards, and from the credit rating requirements.

the balance of payments (financial account) on a net margin basis[18]. If we want to look at the global derivatives market (OTC and ET) we need data collected more frequently, which are not available at the present.

The capital valuation is strategic when the firm decides upon starting new investments. A very simplified approach is that of financial ratios (Return On Equity, ROE and Return On Investment, ROI). However, these ratios are computed on balance sheet figures, which can be influenced by accounting rules, and, more importantly from our viewpoint, they are not risk weighted. Once the firm chooses the ROI-ROE as the base for deciding whether to invest or not, it implicitly assumes that the old and the new investment have the same risk. A modern approach is that of risk-weighted measures, such as the Risk Adjusted Return on Capital (RAROC) (James 1996) where the investment decision is weighted with the risk in order to maintain a pre-defined leverage of the firm.

A key point in the investment decision and evaluation is the role of expectations. These influence the path of investment (i.e. business-cycle booms maintain over investments), and the speed of adjustment. Expectations enter the monetary policy setting and fiscal policy maneuvers[19]. Their contribution can be stabilizing or not, depending on the interactions with the business cycle, and the market sentiment. The investment decision is set in an uncertain environment, and subjective belief can modify the outcome of the decision.

The financial asset price reflects market expectations (i.e. forward looking), since it is the discounted expected value of the stream of future pay-offs. Thus, the discount rate is the key variable. Derivatives prices incorporate a number of other relevant characteristics (ECB 2000) and the expected future volatility computed from option prices provides a measure of the uncertainty that the market attaches to future developments.

The market sentiment can be further specified as being risk aversion (how much investors dislike uncertainty), risk appetite (the willingness to bear risk) and risk premium (the difference between the price of risk and the risk of a given asset) (Gai and Vause 2006). Risk aversion varies with investors, while risk appetite varies over time for each investor. Gai and Vause (2006) find that a plausible measure of risk appetite is the inverse of the price of risk. This measure is based on the variation in the ratio of risk neutral to subjective probabilities, derived from the S&P 500 option price. This measure responds to major financial events, and has some advantages (i.e. it uses the entire set of information available from risk neutral and subjective probability distribution).

Option contracts can be used to extract investors' attitudes toward risks (BIS Quarterly Review 2003); the risk attitude changes over time and the level of investors' effective risk aversion changes with financial market dynamics.

---

18   It is computed by the national central bank while the BIS collects data, consolidates them by sector operators and publishes them in its Quarterly Review.

19   See the models presented in chapters two and three and the role of expectations.

Derivatives are able to incorporate expectations and market sentiments. Considering their role in the investment decision clarifies their (stabilizing) contribution toward growth and development. Their negative potential impact (i.e. excessive volatility, unexpected losses, and so on) is not different from those of other securities in cases of mismanagement, herding or exogenous shocks.

Tobin's q can be used as a signal of market sentiment, starting from a given security, which, if representative, can provide good signals of market expectations. I move away from Tobin's q in order to extract the signal from future prices; in this way we acknowledge the importance of the approach and adapt it to the globalized financial markets. The problems previously explained regarding the lack of uniqueness of the q ratio are still valid, but I am more interested in the path, and in filling the gap of knowledge.

Derivatives prices depend on underlying assets and we base on their efficient pricing the other way round: as substitutes to underlying. The q ratio can then be computed not by means of the distance between the historical and the market value, but as the distance between the derivative and the underlying[20], that is, a measure of financial market efficiency. Considering that derivatives prices, referring to the same underlying, differ based on the expiration dates or the distance to expiration, we can take into consideration the time-varying difference. What is the most appropriate measure of value? Not the price or the notional value. My candidate is the implied volatility. The reasons for this choice are that the implied volatility is a parameter used in pricing, that it does not change across expiration dates (i.e. no jumps or zeros), that it is usually computed as a continuous series, and it is used for the portfolio evaluation.

I define the "q derivatives based" in two alternative ways, maintaining the rationale of Tobin's q (i.e. the distance between different evaluations of the same asset) but stressing that Tobin never considered derivatives in his analysis:

1. the ratio between the risk of investing in the underlying and in the derivative (chosen with the cheapest deliverable strategy[21]); *Replication q*, i.e. the ratio between the historical and the implied volatilities;
2. the inter-temporal risk ratio (*Time q*), i.e. the ratio between different implied volatilities, at different moments of time. They can be computed using different option prices, and expirations.

The first measure represents how markets price expectations. Usually, historical and implied volatilities match on average, but at high frequency[22] they can be very different because of rumors which mostly affect spot transactions. If the historical and implied volatilities differ by a large amount, their ratio will be far from its

---

20   I am not assuming the perfect market hypothesis.
21   See Hull (2002) for details.
22   For example, tick or intra-day data.

mean value[23]. This can mean that the market expectations are changing or that they are misaligned[24].

The second measure is the distance between expectations measured in different moments of time and can be useful to gauge market instability. If the distance between implied volatilities is high, because expectations differ, this ratio will be far from its average mean value. This can be read as a further proof (after the first measure) for firms that expectations are changing, and this ultimately affects the investment decision (i.e. it changes the price of risk).

7.1 DJX & VIX q

Operators can use options as predictors of future prices (profits) in order to maintain their investment decisions. This is true if, and only if, the pricing mechanism is efficient and both variables are affected by the same shocks in the same direction[25]. Options prices are efficient predictors of future prices, and exploiting these properties the other way round, firms can look at the ratio between implied and historical volatilities to gauge market sentiment (i.e. to see if risk is changing) and then choose how better to price future investments[26]. Pricing an investment means that it is in a similar class of risk of the old investment, from which the firm takes the price (return or cost). This is a very restrictive hypothesis, and if market sentiment (or risk) changes, the old investment cannot be of help in the evaluation process.

The *Time q* is the distance between expectations measured in different moments of time. However, the distance between moments of time can be taken in different ways, and given that we can have various implied measures of volatility, computed from in, out or at-the-money prices, and with different maturities, a unique *Time q* cannot be defined. Instead, I will focus on the *Replication q*.

As an exercise, I took the two most representative stock indices, the S&P 500 and the Dow Jones Industrial Average (DJIA); they are very liquid, and representative indices of the US financial market. The DJIA is maintained by *The Wall Street Journal,* is composed of 30 main stocks of industrial US firms, which are selected based on their liquidity, sustained growth and strong reputation. The S&P 500 is a relevant stock index, and its constituents do not change very frequently. The S&P 500 should exhibit a lower variability than the DJIA.

---

23   If implied and historical volatilities were measured in the same scale, their ratio would be above or below one, but they are not, so I have used the mean as a benchmark value.

24   For example, the misalignment can be due to exogenous shocks, which affect only one of the two.

25   Then the distance between the two would be close to their average value.

26   In particular, if the price of risk is changing, the evaluation of new investments would be much more cautious.

Over the period taken for the analysis (10/03/1997 to 15/07/2005) the DJIA has very high daily variance and standard deviation, its mean is above 9,500; the kurtosis and asymmetry measures describe a platokurtic function, right-skewed[27].

Table 4.1 Descriptive statistics of DJIA (1997–2005)

St. Dev.	1010.5836
Var.	1021279.3
Mean	9777.1728
Asymmetry	-0.5490036
Kurtosis	-0.8119615

Source: Thomson Financial Datastream.

The daily implied volatility of the put and call contracts (DJX) written on the DJIA Index[28] over the same period of the index has a mean value (around 20), which is similar for put and call, and exhibits reasonably small variance and standard deviation. The kurtosis, which is greater than zero, refers to leptokurtic distributions; the symmetry describes two left-skewed functions[29].

Table 4.2 Descriptive statistics of DJX (1997–2005)

Put		Call	
St. Dev.	6.0294668	St. Dev.	5.8374805
Var.	36.354469	Var.	34.076178
Mean	20.667707	Mean	20.493657
Asymm.	0.7585562	Asymm.	0.8215853
Kurtosis	0.6540244	Kurtosis	0.9083857

Source: Thomson Financial Datastream.

The daily series of the computed percentage change in the implied volatility on call and put options written on the Dow Jones Industrial Index (DJX) has some

---

27   The right-skewed can be compared to other non-normal distributions, whose shape reflects the overconfidence of investors (i.e. consider increases as being more probable than reductions).

28   Data on implied volatilities come from Bloomberg and have been computed with their algorithm. Other data come from Thomson Financial Datastream.

29   As with the interpretation of the underlying index, investors may reflect their irrationality in the options' implied volatility, the left-skewed function, which considers lower volatility as more probable than high volatility.

clear peaks (i.e. daily change above or very close to 4 percent or -4 percent); these peaks can be associated with exogenous shocks affecting market expectations. The first peak corresponds to the mini-crash experienced in October 1997; the second is the Lewinsky effect (08/1998), when, for the first time in the US history, a President was asked to report to the Grand Jury; the third is the dot com crash (02/2000) and the fourth is the downgrading of General Motors bonds to junk level, which negatively affected market sentiment over the general economic climate (07/2005). The daily historical volatility of the Dow Jones Industrial Index (DJINDUS) varies between 0 and 0.023. Its peaks can be identified on the same dates as those mentioned above.

The ratio between historical and implied volatilities (put) (*Replication q*) has a mean value of 0.00045; it has very high daily variability, which reflects that of

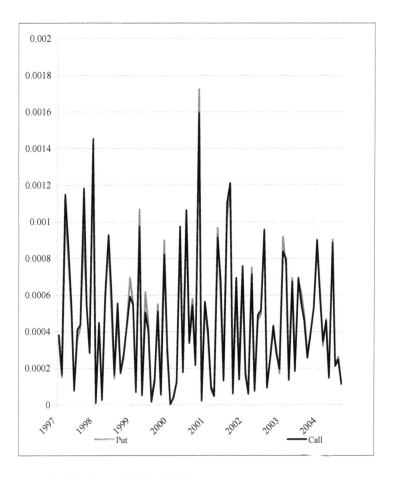

Graph 4.4 *Replication q* **(DJIA, DJX)**
Source: Thomson Financial Datastream.

the two variables, and exhibits peaks in the above-mentioned dates[30]. *Replication q* referred to the call contracts shows a similar pattern. Using this index on a daily basis is, however, a heroic hypothesis, since firms evaluate new investments on a less frequent basis. The monthly and quarterly ratios between historical and implied volatilities have a smaller variability and similar shapes. Moving to lower frequencies, the kurtosis changes, since the position of tails can be modified.

Table 4.3 Descriptive statistics of *Replication q* (DJIA, DJX)

	Put	Call
St. Dev.	0.0003544	0.0003575
Var.	1.256E-07	1.278E-07
Mean	0.0004549	0.0004599
Asymmetry	0.9300039	0.8650688
Kurtosis	0.8193296	0.3430096

Source: Thomson Financial Datastream.

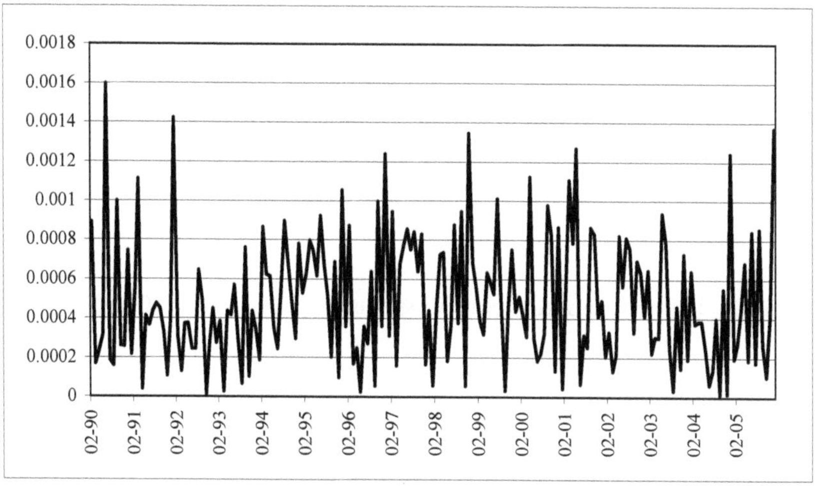

Graph 4.5 *Replication q* (S&P500, VIX)
Source: Thomson Financial Datastream.

---

30   The peak in the ratio confirms that in a period of market turbulence, the pricing mechanism is not efficient, and expectations affect volatility.

The S&P 500 monthly series has a very high variance and mean. The main peaks of the period are the same as those described above. Over the period under consideration, the stock exchange experienced a bubble (1998–2000), and a burst (after 2001). Between 2001 and 2006 the stock exchange recovered to a large extent.

Table 4.4 Descriptive statistics of S&P 500 (monthly, Jan 1990 to Dec 2005)

Standard Deviation	594.3492239
Variance	353251
Mean	1043
Asymmetry	-1.702701905

Source: Thomson Financial Datastream.

Table 4.5 Descriptive statistics of S&P 500 historical volatility (monthly, Jan 1990 to Dec 2005)

Standard Deviation	0.009176121
Variance	8.42012E-05
Mean	0.009806774
Asymmetry	1.848360695
Kurtosis	4.514144165

Source: Thomson Financial Datastream.

Table 4.6 Descriptive statistics of VIX (monthly, Jan 1990 to Dec 2005)

Standard Deviation	4.2032
Variance	17.6667
Mean	15.5000
Asymmetry	0.0000
Kurtosis	-3.9067

Source: Thomson Financial Datastream and Bloomberg.

**Table 4.7 Descriptive statistics of *Replication q* (S&P 500, VIX)
(monthly, Jan 1990 to Dec 2005)**

Standard Deviation	0.000380
Variance	0.000000
Mean	0.000492
Asymmetry	0.927334
Kurtosis	0.000035

Source: Thomson Financial Datastream and Bloomberg.

The exercises with the DJIA index and its implied volatility (DJX), and that with the S&P 500 and VIX, are functional in order to look at how the *Replication q* behaves with respect to different stock indexes, but over the same time period (i.e. in the presence of the same shocks) and how it can be employed in the investment decisions of firms.

The statistics on the *Replication q* are very similar; but original indexes are quite different. The DJIA is more variable and its constituents change on a very frequent base, while the S&P 500 refers to a very large number of stocks (500 instead of 30 of the Dow), and its constituents are not revised that frequently.

In our examples, the monthly mean of the *Replication q* is close for the two series, although measured over a different time span, and around 0.0004. By observing a value which is above or below this value, we can infer that the replication is not working, and we should investigate the reason. It could be due to shocks which influence only one of the two variables (e.g. rumors on spot transactions), or it could be due to a change in the price of risk (i.e. expectations). Once we have checked whether there is any shock taking place, we can say whether the options price (i.e. future expected price) can be considered in the investment decision[31]. The firms consider the future expected cash flows of the existing investments to price the new investments, but this is fundamentally wrong when the *Replication q* is different from its average value, since options are not predicting efficiently. On the other hand, if there is a shock occurring, the distance can be explained by it, and the future expected price can be corrected as a result in order to price investments.

---

31 If expectations are changing, options prices are not good predictors of future spot prices.

8. Minsky and derivatives[32]

Hyman Minsky (1977) introduced the Financial Instability Hypothesis (FIH) as an alternative interpretation to the Keynesian Theory, in which he considers instability to be endogenous. The key to the theory is the capital development of the economy, rather than the allocation of given resources to alternative uses. Capital development is accompanied by exchanges of present for future money. In the capitalist economy, the past, present and future are linked not only by capital assets and the labor force, but also by financial relations. The level of profits becomes the key determinant of the system behavior. In a simplified economy, aggregate profits in each period equal aggregate investments. In a slightly more complex system, aggregate profits equal aggregate investments plus the government deficit. So, the FIH is a theory of debt impact on the economic system, and banks are profit-seeking businesses (not simply intermediaries of resources)[33].

Three distinct income–debt relations can be identified for economic units; these are hedge, speculative and Ponzi finance. Hedges fulfil their payments by their cash flows; governments and corporations with floating debt and banks are hedges. Speculators finance their payments, but cannot repay the principal and need to roll over their liabilities. Ponzi units are unable to pay their obligations (interest and the principal), and need either to borrow or to sell assets; by doing this they tend to lower their overall margin of safety.

According to the Minskian interpretation of the model, if hedge finance dominates in the economy, it is more likely to reach a stable equilibrium; if Ponzi and speculative units dominate, the likelihood that the economy deviates from equilibrium increases. The economy has financing regimes, some of which bring stability and others that are unstable. Over periods of prosperity, the economy moves from financial relations bringing stability to those bringing instability. This means that after periods of prosperity, the financial structure tends to move toward Ponzi and speculative structures. If inflationary pressures arise, because of exogenous or endogenous events, speculative units become Ponzi, and Ponzi units can even default. The evolution process, from being robust to fragile, is endogenous[34]. The FIH is a system which does not need any exogenous shock to generate a business cycle, since the cycle is the result of the internal dynamics and of the existing regulation and interventions. The government has a duty to stabilize the economy, but it can fail.

---

32 For this section I am indebted to Phillip Arestis.
33 Notation used is that of Charles (2004).
34 This is probably the main difference from all other macro-financial models, which always introduce instability caused by exogenous source or shock.

8.1 A stylized Minskian financial instability hypothesis

Let us consider a closed economy, where price levels and the interest rate are constant and workers do not save ($C_w = W$). There is no issue of new shares (fixed supply), D is debt, r is the (constant) interest rate, P is the flow of profits, and the propensity to save on profits is $0 < s_f < 1$. The capitalist propensity to save on dividends and interest received is s_c.

We modify the saving function, in order to introduce financial innovation, by means of the possibility given to investors of using financial innovation for hedging purposes. The saving function can then be expressed as:

$$S = s_f[\Pi + (\theta - r)D] + s_c\left[(1 - s_f)(\Pi - rD) + rD\right] \tag{9}$$

The savings (S) by firms depends on the propensity to save on profits (s_f), profits (Π), debt (D), the propensity to save on dividends and interest received (s_c) and two parameters: r and θ. The hedging parameter we introduce, θ, is supposed to be constant $0 \prec \theta \prec 1$; and if it approaches zero it means there is no hedging, while with a bigger parameter a greater propensity to hedge is present. Derivatives enter the saving function through the firms' savings. Unlike other interpretations of the Minskian model, I consider derivatives by means of their hedging ability, which is universally recognized as their most important characteristic. In this way, I consider only the stabilizing effects of derivatives, due to hedge units. Firms, governments and financial operators use derivatives to hedge, and only if they are risk lovers, to speculate.

With a constant propensity to hedge (θ) the solution to the Minskian model is that shown by Charles (2004), since the new parameter (the hedging parameter, θ) enters the equilibrium condition but does not enter the final equations. The non-linear form of the model is still unsolved; the introduction of a new parameter introduces further conditions for non-negative debt, but the representation by Charles (2004) is still valid.

The debt dynamic is given by:

$$\dot{D} = I - s_f[P + (\theta - r)D] \tag{10}$$

I is the investment, which is financed either by new issued debt ($\dot{D}$) or by retained earnings. The equilibrium condition on the goods markets, which is the net cash flow, is given by:

$$s_f[\pi + (\theta - r)d] = s_f \frac{g - s_c rd}{s_F} \tag{11}$$

where $\pi = P/K$ is the profit rate, $g = I/K$ is the rate accumulation; $d = D/K$ is the debt to capital ratio, $0 < s_f < 1$ and $1 > s_F = s_f + s_c(1 - s_f) > s_f$, $s_c > 0$. The rate of accumulation evolves according to the law:

$$\dot{g} = \delta(g^d - g) \tag{12}$$

This is the difference between the desired and the effective levels. The desired level depends on the net profits, $g^d = \gamma s_f[\pi + (\theta - r)d] + b$, where γ is a positive coefficient, which links the net cash flow to the investment decision, and b is a positive parameter.

The non-linear system of differential equations described above has no closed-form solution, but the phase diagram helps to explain their behavior.

Following Charles (2004), the isoclines[35] are:

$$d(\dot{g} = 0) = \left[(\gamma s_f - s_F)g + bs_F\right]/\gamma s_f s_c r$$
$$d(\dot{d} = 0) = (s_F - s_f)g/(s_F g - s_f s_c r) \tag{13}$$

which describe the system's behavior after some predefined values are given to the parameters (e.g. values of r compatible with a non-negative debt). I form no special hypothesis about the relationship between the parameters (γ, s_f, s_c, s_F, r), except the

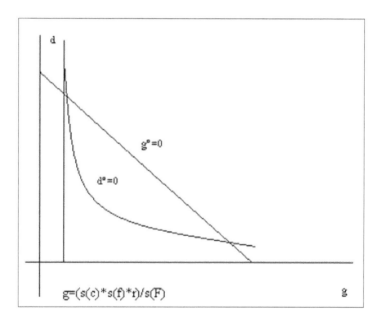

Figure 4.6 Isoclines of the Minskian model of accumulation of debt
Source: Charles 2004.

---

35   Since the system is non-linear, isoclines can be useful tools to describe its dynamic; they are computed imposing the differential term to zero, then obtaining the slope of the curves, but not their exact positions. We can have a rough idea of the behavior of the curves, but not of the points of equilibrium.

one expressed in the functions. The phase diagram describes the behavior of this non-linear system between g and d.

The difference from Charles' (2004) elegant analysis of the FIH is the introduction of the hedging parameter, θ, which enters the equilibrium condition. If the hedging coefficient increases ($\theta \to 1$) the shape of the curve changes, depending on the value of the (new) equilibrium condition (13)[36]. In particular, if θ increases, the left-hand side of equation (11) increases, inducing either an increase in the numerator of the right-hand side, or a decrease in the denominator, or a combination of the two. The variation of θ can correspond to a variation in one or more of the other four parameters and/or two variables.

8.2 Derivatives: Bringing (in)stability

Innovation plays a special part in the process of growth of the capitalist economy; it contributes to push forward growth, profits and investments endogenously, in period of tranquility and stability. If volatility increases and the economy is hit by a shock (e.g. due to inflation) financial innovation can contribute to amplify the negative effects, like the "evaporation" of the Ponzi units, and highly leveraged and off-balance-sheet items can increase the final exposure, fuelled by the volatility[37]. Comprehensive regulation and control are still necessary for the innovation not to be a source of danger for the capitalist economy. In the recent past, the lack of control on corporate governance practices, failures in risk management procedures and valuations, and on the internal control of companies, exacerbated the negative effects of the stock exchange slowdown, moving the US economy from being stable and growing to being unstable and subject to recession.

The prevailing literature has referred to derivatives as securities, which contribute to complete financial markets thanks to their microeconomic properties[38]. Since the markets are efficient and agents are rational, the availability of hedging securities completes the investment opportunities, and ameliorates the allocation process.

At a macroeconomic level their contribution has not been fully investigated since their role, stabilizing or not, is not taken for granted. On the basis of neo-classical macro-models, financial markets are complete, and derivatives, being replicates of the underlying assets, are zero-sum games and thus add nothing new in terms of risk or wealth to the financial and real sectors. So, derivatives are

---

36   The equilibrium depends on five parameters (r, θ, s_c, s_f, γ) and two variables (d, g).

37   Ponzi units are very likely to apply financial strategies, which, in case of initial loss, double all the positions betting on a subsequent gain. This type of strategy is explained by the overconfidence that characterizes (irrational) investors, and has been detected in a number of cases (e.g. Barings Bank and the Orange County).

38   See the *Journal of Derivatives*, the *Journal of Futures* Markets, Ang and Cheng (2005); Cohen (1999); Hung-Gay Leung (1993).

stabilizing securities, similar to others, except in case of shock. In NK models, the introduction of complex financial markets (and government) gives rise to enormous algebraic problems, lowering the intelligibility of results and policy implications[39]. By considering a simplified approach[40], we can fairly say that derivatives can be meaningfully added to NK models, and their contribution is not toward instability, when markets are tranquil.

In case of shock or turbulence, as testified in the subprime mortgage crisis of 2007, the leverage effect which characterizes derivatives can exacerbate losses, fuelling the volatility of financial markets, and they can then amplify instability.

Provided that derivatives play a role in the macro-economy, either from a monetary point of view[41] or from a fiscal policy point of view[42], their introduction into standard Keynesian and Neo-classical models gave initial theoretical results that need further discussion and implementation, which I hope will be supported by empirical evidence. The Minskian model can be useful in this respect, because debt, public or corporate, banks and financial markets play a role in pushing the economy away or toward a stable equilibrium. The turmoil of financial markets observed in 2000 and 2006, when equities and bonds experienced high volatility, decreasing trends of prices and low returns, did not hit derivatives, which on the contrary have grown in dimension and liquidity. The turmoil of 2007, which originated in the subprime mortgage sector, has spread out the world economy, due to credit derivatives contracts. Financial instability finally hit the real economy, and forecasts of growth for 2008 are not very encouraging.

The next step is to imagine how much of this activity is reflected in the hedging coefficient, θ; inefficient financial markets provide very poor opportunities for hedging ($\theta=0$), while perfect financial markets can provide good, but not full hedging[43]. The creation of a derivatives market is, according to the literature, a sign of increasing efficiency of financial markets. Using our notation, it means that financial systems with derivatives are characterized by a better hedging parameter.

Another feature is the stability of hedging activity. Exchange-traded derivatives have been steadily increasing over the last two decades and are becoming more efficient and attractive, even for medium and small-size (non-professional) investors. The investment in these securities has also finally entered the balance sheets of banks and firms. Over-the-counter derivatives transactions are quite

---

39   See Benigno and Woodford (2003) on high-order solutions to NK model.

40   See chapters two and three for a reduced-form NK model, where derivatives affect the saving–investment relationship, or the Taylor rule.

41   See Savona (2002), Violi (2000), Vrolijk (1997), Banca d'Italia (1995, a and b) among others.

42   See Oldani and Savona (2005), Piga (2001), OECD (2002) and Chapter 3.

43   Having full hedging ($\theta=1$) means that no matter what the risk of the investment, an insurance is always provided on the capital, but this gives rise to adverse effects.

opaque, but, up to the present, only a very small number of failures have been reported in this type of business.

With these stylized elements, I argue that the variability of θ should not be too different from the one recorded in the stock exchange, in the absence of adverse shocks. As stated by Paul Volcker (1993), derivatives "by their own nature do not introduce risks of a fundamental different kind than those already present. Systemic risks are not aggravated". Of course, they can hide the existing risk, complicate the transmission of impulses and shocks, and render the regulation and monitoring inappropriate and ineffective, weakening Volcker's position.

To conclude, the presence of sophisticated financial instruments ameliorates the hedging ability of agents in a stylized Minskian model where financial instability is not ruled out. The virtues of derivatives work when they are used to hedge, if the system endogenously reaches a stable equilibrium. If the system becomes unstable, derivatives can contribute to increase instability, similarly to what happens with other securities.

8.3 The measure of (in)stability

An important part of the analysis of (in)stability is its measurement. In traditional textbooks, instability reflects high variation in prices (or quantities). However, standard deviation and correlation are not always stable through time. As observed by Page (2004) using a multivariate outlier methodology, by partitioning historical returns into those associated with normal periods and those associated with periods of market turbulence, which refer to unexpected instability, it is possible for investors to estimate risk parameters over the two distinct regimes.

Derivatives are efficient instruments due to their good pricing mechanism, which rules out arbitrage. Their volatility is comparable to that of underlying financial securities, testified to by an enormous literature, which has verified this property on a market and instrument basis. A market-based measure of instability is the implied volatility of options. We should underline that the implied volatility is estimated from past prices, and this can affect its reliability if the pricing mechanism is not efficient (e.g. in the energy industry).

I doubt the aggregation of the virtues of derivatives, widely employed in many macroeconomic analyses[44]. I cannot affirm that these markets are completely efficient, since there is a distance between the historical and the volatility implied in options prices, and this inefficiency fuels my doubt over the validity of aggregation of single virtues.

---

44 The aggregation principle is applied in many macro-models where financial markets are generally considered as complete, with maximum liquidity and where the virtues of a single security are considered to be valid for all.

9. Conclusion

Capital accumulation is a theme which economic theory has not succeeded in converging to a single position, as it has with other issues. The investment decision at the basis of capital accumulation is fuelled by the voluntary reduction of consumption, or by external financial opportunities. The link between investments and savings lies in the financial market and then its stability ultimately influences the investment decision. The investment decision is heavily influenced by market expectations. I investigated how derivatives, able to gauge them, could be employed to assess the degree of instability which affects the valuation of new investments, and to ameliorate the hedging ability of agents in a stylized Minskian model. Instability can be directly perceived by looking at volatilities (historical and implied) of prices; the distance between historical and implied volatilities can be considered as a measure of changes of expectations, similarly to the Tobin's Q where the distance between market and historical cost signals the incentive to invest. In my empirical investigation, the monthly mean of the ratio between implied and historical volatilities is similar for the S&P 500 and the DJIA indices, although measured over different time spans. A value of the ratio different from its average (or any other benchmark value), has to be investigated since it can be due to a shock which influences only one of the two variables (e.g. rumors on spot markets which do not reflect in the options market) or it can be caused by a change in the price of risk (i.e. expectations) which alters the reliability of options prices and volatility.

In the preceding chapter, I analysed the role of derivatives with respect to the interest rate, which is the price of money, the return (and cost) of the public debt, and the price of investments. The circularity between the interest rate and profitability is still unsolved, but by looking at the flows' chart (Figure 4.1) I have tried to clarify small pieces of the complex relationships in the economy. Financial markets are not perfect, and this dramatically changes the way the analysis can be put forward. Profitable opportunities arise often because of asymmetries, inefficiencies and regulatory failures. The evolution of financial markets and the availability of new securities contribute to breaking the link between investments and collaterals, improving market efficiency. Derivatives have stabilizing effects, and this feature can be exploited in the investment decision by the firm that can rely on the implied volatility of options to gauge market expectations, and so evaluate the new investment.

However, if markets are unstable, or collateralization is not transparent, or the monitoring system fails, the virtues of derivatives (and other securities) suddenly evaporate and are of no help for the firm's investment decision.

The Minskian Financial Instability Hypothesis (FIH) is a very interesting model for underlining the stabilizing role of financial instruments in the process of capital accumulation. Risk plays a relevant part in the preferences setting of lenders and borrowers, and derivatives can be introduced in this framework as hedging instruments to further underline that, in period of tranquil market, they pose no special risk. The measure of new instability they bring to financial markets can be thought of as the Replication Q. Macroeconomic derivatives are spreading out the market, and are written on inflation or business climate expectations, but in the near future I hope that derivatives on investments will be priced and traded, satisfying the needs of firms for tools to evaluate the investment decision.

To conclude, it would be important to investigate the empirical effects on the capital accumulation process, including considering different theories and approaches. This first piece of research would have tremendous value for the economic analysis of financial markets and their impact on capital accumulation and growth.

Summary

Financial innovation is the endogenous engine for the development of financial market and it is fuelled by imperfections and the animal spirits of market players. Innovation temporarily exploits market inefficiencies, circumvents regulation and gives rise to extra profits for innovators. Derivatives are a very interesting example of innovation, although their trading dates back to ancient Mesopotamia. Nowadays, derivatives can be split into exchange-traded (ET) and over-the-counter (OTC) derivatives, the latter covering two thirds of world trade.

The poor disclosure of data on OTC is the thread running through the book', since the lack of knowledge limits analysis and has negative effects on empirical investigations. Deregulation is the main driving force of the present financial market, and refers to securities such as derivatives, but also to operators such as hedge funds. The temptation to heavily regulate innovative phenomena is a common feature of the economic evolution, and a number of steps have recently been taken further. The improved accounting rules and better statistics should help to depict the situation of the market, while the GASB project to improve states' disclosure of innovative instruments deserves the outmost support.

The effective burden of risk that derivatives add to the world financial system is an open question that needs to be answered. Those relying on the perfect market hypothesis consider derivatives as zero-sum games that bring no new risk and therefore do not alter stability. The turmoil of 2007, linked to the credit derivatives market, cast doubts on this belief. Warren Buffet, knowing to a certain extent the irrationality which permeates financial operators, believes that they do bring risk. I think that derivatives can hide the existing risk, and the application of rules to improve market transparency cannot be delayed any further. Examples of derivatives bankruptcies are under intense scrutiny, but our age, the age of turbulence, should not become the age of crashes.

Financial globalization is a very challenging process. Institutional reform should be addressed first, in order to cope better with the changing environment. The reform of the International Monetary Fund should come with a new structure of international financial monitoring and rule setting. The structure of the new financial governance should not be inspired by rigid regulation, but by principles-based rules, where agents pursue their targets (usually profits) and shoulder the entire responsibility for their decisions, whether positive or negative. The goal of promoting stability can be more effectively pursued by the Fund if it can ensure proper market and risk management procedures, including effective surveillance of financial risks, which are very likely to cause crisis and turbulence in the near future. The fund should focus on fiscal transparency and ordered fiscal conditions, which contribute to creating ordered market conditions. Its role would probably be carried out better if it improved disclosure and accounting and cooperated to a greater extent with other financial institutions in charge of stability, such as the BIS.

Monetary analysis of financial derivatives is probably one of the few fields where the literature has admitted the disruptive role of derivatives. The transmission mechanism of impulses changed after the spread of derivatives; credit derivatives increased the availability of credit-related instruments, for investors, affecting the ability of the central bank to influence the credit channel. This modification materialized in 2007 with the subprime crisis and related tensions in the credit markets, which forced the European Central Bank to inject liquidity and the Federal Reserve Bank to cut interest rates. Derivatives can be of great help in managing the exchange rate, but are useless in cases of a speculative attack on a currency. Derivatives influence the monetary aggregates, through portfolio substitution and replication, and force the monetary authority to update its tool box. Derivatives have been proven to influence the expectations setting, and monetary policy maneuvers. The interest rate channel is heavily affected, since with the innovative instruments at their disposal, the response of banks' lending rates to monetary actions is relatively small. However, liquid and relevant derivatives can be employed in the monetary rule to address market instability explicitly, and the first empirical results are encouraging. Moreover, derivatives can be taken into consideration in the traditional demand for money equation to gauge financial market contributions to the demand. Monetary policy is an expectations management exercise, and this feature can be modeled in the context of neo-Keynesian economics.

Probably the most challenging field in the study of derivatives is that of its effects on fiscal policy. Derivatives can be used by taxpayers to manage the burden of taxes (tax timing), as testified by the Security and Exchange Commission (2000), but they can be used also as tools of public debt management, and, in a very limited number of cases, for fund raising. The set of rules for public resource management should be updated following the evolution of financial markets and the economy. The availability of new tools modifies the behavior of authorities and the effectiveness of prudential regulation. The state accepts market rules when it issues debt, and it can exploit the associated advantages, similarly to private market players, and circumvent regulation. Moral hazard is a common feature in financial markets, but when it involves sovereign states its dimension becomes considerable, and then it needs to be addressed directly. As well as moral hazard, free riding is a behavior commonly detected in public financial economics, and rules should be designed in order to avoid both of them. The possibility for the public sector to enter these types of transactions, especially OTCs, for various purposes, in the absence of any accounting duty, strongly influences the choice and risks involved. The bankrupt of the Italian city of Taranto showed that the mandate length risk, i.e. the risk that the next elected politicians will have to pay back expenses, which previous politicians have benefited from, is not a theoretical issue. A number of risks work actively in fiscal policy implementation, and exogenous forces and shocks modify the path of relevant risk. The accounting rules for the public sector provide very poor descriptions of their use of financial innovation, at the central or local level, and this is a clear danger, first for taxpayers, and then for market players.

The use of swaps for interest and exchange rates management by a certain number of countries underlines the hedging ability these securities provide; in some cases they are even used to raise funds, through the up-front. According to most debt managers' surveys, swaps are basically perceived as risk management contracts, and not as tools to fine tune cash. The case of some highly indebted countries is remarkable; debt management, instead of growth stimulus, becomes the first target, and in the presence of a autonomous monetary policy setting the interest rate, the equilibrium can lead to an uncontrolled debt–deficit dynamic. The experience of Italy is of particular interest, since it is a highly indebted country. It changed the structure of the public sector and introduced a higher degree of federalism, but the resulting freedom has not been properly limited. The first free rider, the city of Taranto, has already been bankrupted. The project by the GASB to put derivatives in the financial statement of countries deserves our outmost support, since it will dramatically increase transparency, enhance best business practice and ameliorate the stability of the financial market. The technicalities and complexity which are embedded in this type of securities (especially OTC) needs special skills to be managed, and, like households and unprofessional investors, small public administrations should not be left free to operate them. Financial markets are far bigger than sovereign states, and the debt of public administration can be hedged, but the burden of risk should not be aggravated.

The price of money and that of the public debt, the interest rate, is also the price or return of investments, which are the seeds of capitalism. Investments influence the level of production, and later, profit. The industry which is suffering from a structural lack of investments, reflected in incredibly high prices, is the energy sector. Because of this structural lack, there is room for speculation and arbitrage, and this is reflected in exchange-traded futures being bad predictors of spot prices. Energy derivatives attract an ever-increasing amount of resources, and are a very challenging field of study, especially for practitioners, who can earn amazing fees.

The decision to invest is an economic choice, which is influenced by the actual price of capital and by the expected return on new investment. The latter is the most relevant unknown variable, and depends on the risk of the investments and on the expectations of the market, which influences the discount factor. Expectations can be extrapolated from derivatives prices, and employed in the investment decision. Macroeconomic derivatives attached to inflation and expectations of growth are already traded and priced, following Schiller's idea of democratization of risks. The development of derivatives on investments would contribute to ameliorating macro-hedging. As with Tobin's Q approach, which looks at the distance between the market valuation and historical cost, derivatives can be plugged into the evaluation, on the basis of their matching-price ability. By considering the distance between the underlying and the derivatives, we do not need to refer to prices. Since the measure of the value is not unequivocally defined in the literature, we can refer to exchange-traded options and look at the distance between the historical and the implied volatilities. The fact that implied and historical volatility should match is denied in most data sets, fueling the idea that the distance can provide a signal of market expectations. I investigated this distance on the basis of very marketable options, written in US stock indices (DJIA and S&P500) over the period 1997 to 2005, and confirmed the existence of the distance. Among the macro-models, I chose one where instability is endogenous and equilibrium is not unequivocally defined, nor automatically reached. This approach, by Hyman Minsky, is the Financial Instability Hypothesis (FIH). I modified the FIH and introduced the hedging ability of derivatives into the saving function of firms. The hedging parameter is considered to be constant and the equilibrium conditions are not negatively affected by them.

The reality of the financial market, especially after the subprime crisis, is one of increased turbulence, opaque trading and asymmetric rules and monitoring. Instability can be guaranteed for transparent markets where players know the rules, and violations are punished. However, if rules are not homogenous, and an exogenous shock hits the stability, the financial system deviates from equilibrium and the stabilizing role of derivatives is wiped out. Moreover, the leverage effect, which characterizes uncollateralized OTC transactions, exacerbates the evaporation of hedging and the squeeze of liquidity.

Challenges in Governing Global Derivatives

We live in an age of turbulence in the international financial system, as crystallized in Alan Greenspan's memoirs, characterized by deregulation, large un-qualification, where agents are pushed by their animal spirits, searching for profits. The turbulence is fuelled by the absence of compensation of risks, which leads to excessive risk taking, undermining stability. This has to be eliminated as soon as possible. The interest rate is the key to open the doors of the macroeconomic analysis of derivatives. The interest rate represents the price of money, the instrument of the central bank, the price of public debt, and the price of investments[1]. These four are influenced by derivatives in different ways. First, they affect the demand for money, in particular altering the speculative motive. They contribute to make the job of the central bank harder, since the possibility of influencing the interest rate and the entire yield curve is diminished when financial markets are complete and less dependent on the central bank's money or liquidity. Derivatives can be used by taxpayers to smooth tax payments, and on the other hand, can be actively employed to manage public debt, or even raise funds. Because of their ability to embody market expectations, they can be employed in the investment decision by firms.

The global market of derivatives is a powerful resource for improvement, but can boomerang and multiply its most negative drawbacks, since a substantial share of the global derivatives activity is traded OTC, and is characterized by a high degree of opaqueness.

The spread of derivatives modifies the transmission mechanism of impulses, via the interest rate, and allows it to speed up. This has speeded up the processes that lead to a crisis in the presence of excessive risk-taking behavior. The tendency toward deregulation has to be carefully revised, since it proved to be unable to guarantee stability in the presence of asymmetric rules on accounting reporting and statistical disclosure. In more detail, at present, regulation is stronger on traditional market players (banks and financial institutions or funds) while it is weak on innovative players (such as hedge and sovereign wealth funds) and governments. The resulting imbalances cannot be compensated by imposing the regulation of the former on the latter, since innovation needs different treatment and moves faster; such rules would be revealed as ineffectual, especially with respect to governments. The revision of the international financial structure should start from the principles that inspire the new financial structure: flexibility, rather

---

1   In the Keynesian interpretation, the interest rate to be paid on debt is compared to the efficiency of capital, which is the return on investments.

than rigid rules. A deeper disclosure of transactions, especially those OTC, is vital for the soundness and strength of the market. The second step is statistical disclosure, which is the key to reading and interpreting the size, path and risks undertaken in the financial system.

Financial globalization under asymmetric rules can exacerbate the deviations from the perfect market hypothesis, and for this reason it has to be governed and managed. The monetary nature of exchange-traded derivatives justifies a more comprehensive management, especially with respect to risks associated or hidden by them. The optimistic position by Paul Volcker, and the quite pessimistic one by Warren Buffett, are two interpretations of the same world, but Buffet doesn't give any credence to the perfect market hypothesis and interprets the (dis)equilibrium as a result. The violation of rationality and market completeness reaches its zenith in sovereign states' management of debts, which should be placed first in the agenda of the new IMF acting in the new financial structure. The second important wave to look at, after deregulation, is the risk and hazard created in the financial system under small un-collateralization. Securitization is an established financial practice of our world, but the lack of collaterals for some portions of the market (e.g. OTC derivatives) creates holes for hazard, which are neither sustainable nor efficient. The Minskian theory of financial instability is just one possible interpretation, but this issue deserves more attention and academic effort.

The lack of compensation of risks and the resulting hazard need to be addressed as soon as possible. An alternative to excessive deregulation is not to regulate strongly, but to specify and locate responsibilities. In this way, crises like the one generated in the subprime mortgage sector are not solved by eliminating this market *niche*, which involves a non-negligible amount of resources, and gives access to homeownership to millions of Americans. Instead, those institutions involved in the securitization of those credits, that is, credit-rating agencies, financial intermediaries, originators and banks who failed to honor the confidence of investors, should be held responsible. This reform of the financial structure is not cheap, but the resulting benefits should overcome the global costs. Such an environment would help restore market confidence, lower the volatility and improve soundness and global strength.

The macroeconomic analysis of derivatives (and other innovative financial securities) is limited by the lack of availability of data, other than the rough statistics on counterparts, effective volumes and turnover, making any further policy inference weak. International and domestic institutions should rely on more effective principles to improve disclosure on balance of payments, balance sheets of the public sector and private investors, and high-frequency market data. The design of principles is more economically efficient than relying on rigid rules, which sooner or later, will be circumvented. The assessment of risks cannot be properly implemented in the absence of this information, and the crisis of rating agencies, following the subprime mortgage turbulence, is just a proof of the costs of this global inefficiency. After this radical change has taken place, it would be possible to draw further policy implications, especially on the effectiveness of monetary maneuvers on the interest rate, which is heavily affected by financial innovation, and on the effective burden of risks of those states involved in swaps and other contracts. In this new system, risks will be borne by those who create them and costs or prices will be risk-adjusted. As a result, the pricing of assets and liabilities in certain sectors affected by structural rigidities (such as the energy sector) will improve. This reform of the international financial structure is not easily translated into practice and represents a real challenge to policy makers, but its positive effects would be long lasting and succeed in governing global derivatives.

References

ANG, J., CHENG, Y., *Financial Innovation and Market Efficiency: The Case of Single Stock Futures*, Journal of Applied Finance, Spring-Summer, 38–51 (2005).

ANGELONI, I., MASSA, M., Mercati derivati e politica monetaria, in *Moneta e Finanza*, G. Vaciago, 259–272 (Bologna: Il Mulino, 1998).

ASNESS, C., KRAIL, R., LIEW, J., *Do Hedge Funds Hedge?*, Journal of Portfolio Management, 28(1), 6–19 (2000).

AUGIAS, C., I segreti di Londra (Milano: Mondadori, 2003).

AVELLANEDA, M., LAURENCE, P., *Quantitative Modelling of Derivatives Securities* (London: Chapman & Hall RC, 2000).

BAGELLA, M., OLDANI, C., *The Death of M3 and Derivatives*, paper presented at the XV Tor Vergata Conference on "Money, Banking and Finance" (December 2006).

BANCA D'ITALIA, *Lo sviluppo dei prodotti derivati nella realtà italiana. Aspetti di mercato, prudenziali e gestionali*, Tematiche Istituzionali (Rome: 1995a).

BANCA D'ITALIA, *Problemi di politica monetaria sollevati dallo sviluppo dei mercati dei derivati*, Bollettino Economico 24, February (Rome: 1995b).

BANK FOR INTERNATIONAL SETTLEMENTS, *New Development in Clearing and Settlement Arrangements of OTC Derivatives*, Committee on Payment and Settlement System (Basle, 2007).

BANK FOR INTERNATIONAL SETTLEMENTS, *Triennial Central Bank Survey of Foreign Exchange and Derivatives Market Activity (2001–2004)* (Basle, 2005).

BANK FOR INTERNATIONAL SETTLEMENTS, *Quarterly Review* (Basle, 2002, 2003, 2004, 2005, 2006, 2007).

BARBERIS, N., THALER, R., *A Survey of Behavioural Finance*, NBER Working Paper No. 9222 (Cambridge, MA, 2001).

BARNETT, W.A., *Which Road Leads to Stable Money Demand?*, The Economic Journal 107, July, 1171–1185 (1997).

BARRO, R.J., GORDON, D., *A Positive Theory of Monetary Policy in a Natural Rate Model*, Journal of Political Economy 91, 589–610 (1983).

BARTRAM, S.M., FEHLE, F., *Competition Without Fungibility: Evidence from Alternative Market Structures for Derivatives*, Journal of Banking & Finance, 31(3), 659–678 (2007).

BASLE COMMITTEE ON BANKING SUPERVISION, *Sound Practices for Banks' Interaction with Highly Leveraged Institutions* (Basle, 1999).

BELLOFIORE, R., FERRI, P., *The Economic Legacy of Hyman Minsky* (Cheltenham, UK: Edward Elgar, 2001).

BENIGNO, P., WOODFORD, M., *Optimal Monetary and Fiscal Policy: A Linear Quadratic Approach*, NBER Working Papers No. 9905, National Bureau of Economic Research (2003).

BERNANKE, B., *Hedge Funds and Systemic Risk*, Speech at the Federal Reserve Bank of Atlanta's 2006, Financial Markets Conference, May 16 (Sea Island: Georgia, 2006).

BERNANKE, B., *The SubPrime Mortgage Market*, Speech at the Federal Reserve Bank of Chicago's 43rd Annual Conference on Bank Structure and Competition, May 7 (Chicago: Illinois, 2007).

BLACK, K., *Managing a Hedge Fund: A Complete Guide to Trading, Business Strategies, Risk Management and Regulations* (New York: McGraw-Hill, 2004).

BLACK, F., SCHOLES, M., *The Pricing of Options and Corporate Liabilities,* The Journal of Political Economy, 81, 637–654 (1979).

BLANCHARD, O.J., Output, the Stock Market, and Interest Rate, American Economic Review, 71(1), 132–143 (1981).

BLANCHARD, O.J., FISHER, S., Lectures on Macroeconomics (Cambridge: MA, The MIT Press, 1989).

BLEJER, M.I., SCHUMACHER, L.B., *Central Banks Use of Derivatives and Other Contingent Liabilities: Analytical Issues and Policy Implications*, IMF Working Paper No. 00/66 (Washington, 2000).

BRAINARD, W.C., TOBIN, J., *Assets Markets and the Cost of Capital*, Cowles Foundation Paper No. 440 (1977).

BRYAN, D., RAFFERTY, M., *Capitalism with Derivatives* (New York: Palgrave Macmillan, 2006).

BUFFET, W., *Shareholders Letter*, various issues, Omaha (Nebraska).

CABALLERO, R.J., *The Macroeconomic of Asset Shortages*, European Central Bank conference paper on "The Role of Money: Money and Monetary Policy in the Twenty-first Century", November (Frankfurt am Main, 2006).

CABALLERO, R.J., KRISHNAMURTHY, A., *Inflation Targets and Sudden Stops*, in "The Inflation Targeting Debate", B. Bernanke and M. Woodford eds. (Chicago: Chicago Press, 2005).

CARARE, A., TCHAIDZE, R., *The Use and Abuse of Taylor Rules. How Precisely Can We Estimate Them?*, IMF Working Paper No. 148, July (2005).

CARLIN, W., SOSKICE, D., *The 3-Equation New Keynesian Model: A Graphical Exposition*, CEPR Discussion Papers No. 4588 (2004).

CESARANO, F., *Financial Innovation and Demand for Money: Some Empirical Evidence*, Applied Economics, 22(10), 1437–42, October (1990).

CHARLES, S.A., *Note on Some Minskyan Models of Financial Instability*, Working Paper No. 13, University of Paris 8, March (2004).

COFFEE, J., *The Role and Impact of Credit Rating Agencies on the Subprime Credit Markets*, testimony before the Senate Banking Committee (Washington 26 September, 2007).

COHEN, B., *Derivatives, Volatility and Price Disco*very, International Finance, 2(2), 167–202 (1999).

COMMODITY FUTURE TRADING COMMISSION, *OTC Derivatives Oversight, Statement of the SEC, the CFTC and SIB* (Washington DC, 2000).

CONRAD, J., *The Effect of Option Introduction*, The Journal of Finance, XLIV(2), June, 487–98 (1998).

CORNAGGIA, F., VILLA, N., *ItaliaOggi Sette*, 25 April (2005).

CORTE DEI CONTI, *Relazione sulla gestione finanziaria delle Regioni 2005–2006* (Report on Financial Management of Regions, 2005–2006) (Rome, 2007).

CORTE DEI CONTI, *Relazione sulla gestione finanziaria delle Regioni 2004–2005* (Report on Financial Management of Regions, 2004–2005) (Rome, 2006).

CORTE DEI CONTI, *Relazione sulla gestione finanziaria delle Regioni 2003–2004* (Report on Financial Management of Regions, 2003–2004) (Rome, 2005).

DAREHNDORF, R., POLITO, R., *Dopo la democrazia* (Milan: Laterza, 2003).

DE SANTIS, R., *Current Account Imbalances and the Role of the Exchange Rate: The Case of the US Economy*, Associazione Guido Carli, mimeo (Rome, 2007).

DEACON, M., DERRY, A., MIRFENDERESKI, D., *Inflation-Indexed Securities: Bonds, Swaps, and Other Derivatives*, 2nd edition (New York: Wiley Finance, 2004).

DERMAN, E., *Model Risk*, Goldman Sachs Quantitative Strategy Research Notes, April (1996).

DRIFFILL, J., ROTONDI, Z., SAVONA, P., ZAZZARA, C., *Monetary Policy and Financial Stability: What Role for the Futures Market?*, Journal of Financial Stability, 2(1), 95–112 (2006).

DUNNE, T., HELLIAR, C., POWER, D., *Digging Deep Into Derivatives: Accounting for Derivatives: How the Accounting Standards Stack Up*, Balance Sheet, 11(3), 23–28 (2003).

ELGER, T., JONES, B.E., NILSSON, B., *Forecasting with Monetary Aggregates: Recent Evidences for the United States*, Journal of Economics and Business, 58(5–6), 428–446 (2006).

ERISK, *NatWest Case Study*, October (2001).

ESTRELLA, A., *Financial Innovation and the Money Transmission Mechanism*, Working Paper, Federal Reserve Bank of New York (New York 2001).

EUROPEAN CENTRAL BANK, *Managing Foreign Exchange Reserves*, International Relations Committee Task Force, Occasional Paper No. 43 (2006).

EUROPEAN CENTRAL BANK, *The Role of Money: Money and Monetary Policy in the Twenty-first Century*, Frankfurt am Main, 9–10 November (2006).

EUROPEAN CENTRAL BANK, *The Information Content of Interest Rates and Their Derivatives in Monetary Policy*, Monthly Bulletin, 37–56, May (2000).

FALKSTEIN, E., *Value-at-Risk and Derivatives Risk*, Derivatives Quarterly, 4(1), Fall (1997).

FAN, Y., MENSAH, M.O., NGUYEN, H.V., *Derivative Instruments and Their Use for Hedging by U.S. Non-Financial Firms: A Review of Theories and Empirical Evidence*, Journal of Applied Business and Economics, 7(2), 35–57 (2007).

FAZIO, A., *Base monetaria, credito e depositi bancari*, Quaderno di ricerca Ente per gli Studi monetari, bancari e finanziari Luigi Einaudi 2 (Rome 1968).

FEDERAL RESERVE BANK, *Statistical Release: Discontinuance of M3* (9 March 2006).

FEDERAL RESERVE BANK, *US Cross Border Derivatives Data: A User's Guide*, Monthly Bulletin, May, pp. A1–A16 (2007).

FERGUSON, R.W. Jr, *Thoughts on Financial Stability and Central Banking*, Conference on Modern Financial Institutions, Financial Markets, and Systemic Risk, Federal Reserve Bank of Atlanta (Atlanta: Georgia, 17 April 2006).

FERGUSON, R.W. Jr, *The Role of Central Banks in Fostering Efficiency and Stability in the Global Financial System*, Speech at the National Bank of Belgium Conference on Efficiency and Stability in an Evolving Financial System (Brussels: Belgium, 17 May 2004).

FINANCIAL SERVICES AUTHORITY, *Principles Based Regulation: The EU Context*, Speech by John Tiner, Chief Executive, APCIMS Annual Conference Hotel Arts (Barcelona, 13 October 2006).

FITCH RATINGS, *Hedge Accounting and Derivatives: Study for Corporate*, Roger W. Merritt (10 January 2005).

FONDAZIONE U. LA MALFA, *Rapporto sull'Unione Monetaria Europea (2002)*, Enzo Grilli, Giorgio La Malfa, Leonardo Melosi, Laura Ilaria Neri, Chiara Oldani, Mauro Piermarini and Paolo Savona (Rome, 2002).

FRANCE PUBLIC DEBT MANAGEMET OFFICE, *Inflation-Linked Bonds*, http://www.aft.gouv.fr/article_774.html?id_article=774.

FRATIANNI, M., SAVONA, P., *The International Monetary Base and the Eurodollar Market*, in K. Brunner (ed.), Konstanz-Symposium I on Monetary Theory and Monetary Policy, Kredit und Kapital, 347–409, March (1973).

FREITAG, A., KIRTON, J., SALLY, R., SAVONA, P. (eds) (forthcoming), *Securing the Global Economy* (Aldershot: Ashgate).

FRIEDMAN, M., SCHWARTZ, A., *Monetary History of the United States, 1867–1960* (Princeton: Princeton University Press, 1963).

FUKUYAMA, F., *Our Post-Human Future* (New York: Farrar, Straus and Giroux, 2002).

GAI, P., VAUSE, N., *Measuring Investors' Risk Appetite*, International Journal of Central Banking, 2(1), 167–188, March (2006).

GALÌ, J., GERTLER, M., *Macroeconomic Modeling for Monetary Policy Evaluation*, NBER Working Paper No. 13524, October (2007).

GARBER, J., *Derivatives in International Capital Flows*, NBER Working Paper No. 6623 (1998).

GEMAN, H., *Commodities and Commodity Derivatives: Modelling and Pricing for Agriculturals, Metals and Energy* (New York: Wiley, 2004)

GESTORE DEL MERCATO ELETTRICO, *Rapporto sul 2006* (Report on 2006), June (Rome, 2007).

GLENNON, D., LANE, J., *Financial Innovation, New Assets and the Behaviour of Money Demand*, Journal of Banking and Finance, 20, 207–225 (1996).

GODERIS, B., WAGNER, W., *Credit Derivatives and Sovereign Debt Crises*, Working Paper, October (Cambridge: University of Cambridge, 2006).

GORTON, G., ROSEN, A., *Banks and derivatives,* NBER Working Paper No. 5100, April (1996).

GOVERNMENT ACCOUNTING STANDARD BOARD-GASB, *Preliminary Views on the Government Accounting Standard Board*, Plain Language Supplement: Accounting and Reporting Financial Derivatives (28 April 2006).

GOVERNMENT ACCOUNTING STANDARD BOARD-GASB, *Proposes to Put Derivatives Into the Financial Statement*, May (2007).

GRAMLICH, E., *Subprime Mortgage Lending: Benefits, Costs, and Challenges*, Speech at the Financial Services Roundtable Annual Housing Policy Meeting (Illinois: Chicago, 21 May 2004).

GREENSPAN, A., *Over-the-counter derivatives*, Testimony of Chairman of Federal Reserve Before the Committee on Agriculture, Nutrition and Forestry, United States Senate (10 February 2000).

GREENSPAN, A., *The revolution in information technology*, Speech before the Boston College Conference on the New Economy (Boston, MA, 6 March 2000).

GREENSPAN, A., *Reflections on central banking*, Federal Reserve Bank of Kansas City (Jackson Hole, Wyoming, 26 August 2005).

GROUP OF THIRTY, *Derivatives: Practices and Principles* (July 1993).

GUAY, W., *The Impact of Derivatives on Firm Risk: An Empirical Examination of New Derivative Users*, Journal of Accounting and Economics, 26, 319–51 (1999).

GUAY, W., KOTHARI, S.P., *How Much do Firms Hedge with Derivatives?*, The Journal of Financial Economics, 70, 423–461 (2003).

GURKAYNAK, R., WOLFERS, J., *Macroeconomic Derivatives: An Initial Analysis of Market Based Macro Forecasts, Uncertainty and Risk*, NBER Working Paper No. 11929 (2006).

HAGEN, J. von, FENDER, I., *Central Bank Policy in a More Perfect Financial System*, Open Economies Review, 9(1), 493–532 (1998).

HAMILTON, J.D., *Time Series Analysis* (Princeton: Princeton University Press, 1994).

HERBST, A.F., MABERLY, E.D., *The Informational Role of End-of-the-Day Returns On Stock Index Futures*, Journal of Futures Markets, 12(5), 595–602 (1992).

HERRERA, H., SCHROTH, E., *Profitable Innovation Without Patent Protection: the Case of Derivatives*, Working Paper, Berkley Centre, Stern NYU (2002).

HIRTLE, B., *Derivatives, Portfolio Composition and Bank Holding Company Interest Rate Risk Exposure*, Working Paper No. 43, Wharton School Financial Institution Centre (1996).

HOLMSTROM, B., TIROLE, J., *Modelling Aggregate Liquidity*, The American Economic Review, 86(2), Papers and Proceedings of the 108th Annual Meeting of the American Economic Association San Francisco, CA, January 5–7, 187–191 (May, 1996).

HULL, J., *Options, Futures and Other Derivatives*, 5th edition (Prentice Hall, 2002).

HUNG-GAY, F., LEUNG, W. K., *The Pricing Relationship of Eurodollar Futures and Eurodollar Deposit Rates*, Journal of Futures Markets, 13(2), 115–126 (1993).

INTERNATIONAL ENERGY AGENCY, *World Energy Outlook* (Paris, 2007).

INTERNATIONAL ENERGY AGENCY, *World Energy Outlook* (Paris, 2006).

INTERNATIONAL MONETARY FUND, *Global Financial Stability Report*, April (Washington, 2006).

INTERNATIONAL MONETARY FUND, *World Economic Outlook*, September (Washington, 2006).

INTERNATIONAL MONETARY FUND, *The International Monetary Fund in the New Millennium* (Washington, 2005).

INTERNATIONAL MONETARY FUND, *Global Financial Stability Report market Developments and Issues*, April (Washington, 2004).

INTERNATIONAL MONETARY FUND, *Balance of Payment Manual 5* (Washington DC, 1996).

INTERNATIONAL SWAPS AND DERIVATIVES ASSOCIATION (ISDA) http://www.isda.org.

IRELAND, P., *Endogenous Financial Innovation and the Demand for Money,* Journal of Money, Credit and Banking, 27(1), 107–123, February (1995).

JAIMOVICH, N., REBELO, S., *Behavioural Theories of the Business Cycle*, NBER Working Paper No. 12570 (Cambridge, MA: 2006).

JAMES, C., *RAROC Based Capital Budgeting and Performance Evaluation: A Case Study of Bank Capital Allocation*, Wharton School, Financial Institutions Centre, Working Paper No. 40 (1996).

JORION, P., *Risk-management Lessons from the Long Term Capital Management*, Working Paper, University of California (1999).

JORION, P., *Orange County Case: Using Value at Risk to Control Financial Risk* University of California (2005).

KEARNEY, A.K., LOMBRA, R.E., *Stock Market Volatility, the News and Monetary Policy*, Journal of Economics and Finance, 28(2), 252–259 (2004).

KEYNES, J.M., *The Treaty of Peace* (London: Norton, 1931).

KEYNES, J.M., *The General Theory of Employment, Interest and Money* (London: Norton, 1936).

KIM, S.H., *The Investment Saving Correlation Puzzle Is Still a Puzzle*, Working Paper, Brandeis University (1999).

KPMG, *Complessità nell'applicazione dello IAS 39 ai bilanci bancari*, Corporate Statement by Mario Corti (2005).

KRUGMAN, P., *Catastrophe Foretold*, New York Times (26 October 2007).

KRUGMAN, P., *Currencies and Crisis* (Cambridge, MA: The MIT Press, 1992).

LANCASTER, K., *Modern Consumer Theory* (USA: Edward Elgar, 1971 and 1991).

LIPUMA, E., LEE, B., *Financial Derivatives and the Globalization of Risks*, Public Planet Books, Duke University (2004).

MARGRABE, W., *Option Pricing Models and Stochastic Methods in Finance: 1900–1990*, in Modern Risk Management, RISK Books (2003).

MARTHINSEN, J., *Risk Takers: Uses and Abuses of Financial Derivatives* (Boston, MA: Pearson, 2003).

MARTHINSEN, J., *Comment on Financial Derivatives and the Globalization of Risks*, by E. LiPuma and B. Lee, in American Journal of Economics and Sociology, April (2006).

MERCURIO, F., *Pricing of Inflation-Linked Derivatives, Product and Business Development Group*, Banca IMI (2004).

MINSKY, H.P., *The Financial Instability Hypothesis: An Interpretation of Keynes and Alternative to Standard Theory*, Challenge, March-April, 20–27 (1977).

MIRFENDERESKI, D., *The European Inflation-Indexed Derivatives, in Inflation-Indexed Securities: Bonds, Swaps, and Other Derivatives*, 2nd edition (New York: Wiley Finance, 2004).

MULVEY, J., *Inflation Derivatives Offer New Options for Beating Risk*, Finance Magazine.com. (2005), http://www.finance-magazine.com/supplements/trea sury2005/display_article.php?article_id=5129.

NAKAMURA, H., SHIRATSUKA, S., *Extracting Market Expectations from Option Prices: Case Studies in Japanese Options Markets*, Federal Reserve Bank of Chicago Working Paper No. 1 (Chicago: 1999).

NEW PALGRAVE DICTIONARY OF ECONOMICS AND FINANCE, Palgrave Macmillan, UK.

NICOLÒ, A., PELIZZON, L., *Credit Derivates, Capital Requirements and Opaque OTC Markets*, Cà Foscari University of Venice, Working Paper No. 58 (Venice, 2006).

NORTH, D., *Institutions, Institutional Change and Economics Performance* (Cambridge, UK: Cambridge University Press, 1990).

OECD, *XII Workshop on Government Securities Markets and Public Debt Management in Emerging Markets*, Ministero dell'Economia e delle Finanze (Roma, 2002).

OECD, *Use of Derivatives for Debt Management and Domestic Market Development*, 9th OECD-WB-IMF Bond Market Forum, 22 May (2007).

OLDANI, C., *The Taylor Rule and Financial Derivatives: The Case of Options*, in Advances in Monetary Policy and Macroeconomics, P. Arestis and G. Zezza (eds), February (Macmillan, 2007).

OLDANI, C., *I derivati finanziari: dalla Bibbia alla Enron*, F.Angeli (ed.) (Milan: 2004).

OLDANI, C., SAVONA, P., *Derivatives, Fiscal Policy and Financial Stability*, The ICFAI Journal of Derivatives 3, July (2005).

PAGE, S., *Innovations in Risk*, Canadian Investment Review, Winter, 17(4), R25–R25 (2004).

PAWLEY, M., *Financial Innovation and Monetary Policy* (London: Routledge, 1993).

PELANDA, C., SAVONA, P., *Sovranità e ricchezza* (Milano: Sperling and Kupfer, 2002).

PIGA, G., *Derivatives and Public Debt Management*, ISMA center and Council of Foreign Relations (London, 2001).

PRESIDENT'S WORKING GROUP ON FINANCIAL MARKETS, *Over The Counter Derivatives Markets and the Commodity Exchange Act* (Washington DC, 15 February 2000).

PRESIDENT'S WORKING GROUP ON FINANCIAL MARKETS, *Hedge Funds, Leverage and the Lessons of Long-Term Capital Management* (Washington DC, 28 April 1999).

RAJAN, R.G., ZINGALES, L., *Saving Capitalism from Capitalists* (Crown Business, USA, 2003).

RISK, *The Italian Clampdown*, 19(5) (22 May 2006).

RISK ITALIA, *Corporate derivative: Poste smarrite*, July (2004).

ROMER, D., *Keynesian Macroeconomics without the LM Curve*, Journal of Economic Perspectives, 14(2), 149–169 (2000).

SALCEDO, Y., *A Time for Trade, a Time for Taxes*, Futures, 62–64, April (2003).

SAVONA, P., *Introductory Remarks on "Money, Derivatives, Innovation and Growth"*, Fondazione Cesifin Alberto Predieri (Foligno, September 2007).

SAVONA, P., *La finanza dei derivati*, Enciclopedia del Novecento, Istituto Treccani (Roma, 2003).

SAVONA, P., *On Some Unresolved Problems of Monetary Theory and Policy*, in M. Fratianni, P. Savona, J.J. Kirton (ed.), Governing Global Finance (Aldershot: Ashgate), 177–184 (2002).

SAVONA, P., MACCARIO, A., OLDANI, C., *On Monetary Analysis of Derivatives*, Open Economies Review, 11(1), 149–176 (2000).

SAVONA, P., VIVIANI, C., *The Impact of the Stability and Growth Pact on Real Economic Growth: Automatic Mechanisms or Policy Discretion?*, Review of Economic Conditions in Italy 56, 263–279, May-August (2003).

SCHLEIFER, A., *Inefficient Markets: An Introduction to Behavioral Finance* (Oxford, UK: Oxford University Press, 2000).

SFA (2000), *SFA Disciplines NatWest and Two Individuals* (18 May, 2003).

SECURITY AND EXCHANGE COMMISSION, *OTC Derivatives Oversight, Statement of the SEC, the CFTC and SIB* (Washington DC, 2000).

SECURITY AND INVESTMENT BOARD, *OTC Derivatives Oversight, Statement of the SEC, the CFTC and SIB* (Washington DC, 2000).

SELLON, G.H. Jr, *The Changing U.S. Financial System: Some Implications for the Monetary Transmission Mechanism*, Economic Review of the Federal Reserve Bank of Kansas City, 1, 5–35 (2002).

SHILLER, R.J., *Macro Markets* (Oxford: Oxford University Press, 1993).

SHILLER, R.J., *Irrational Exuberance* (Princeton: Princeton University Press, 2000).

SHIN, H.S., *Derivatives Accounting and Risk Management* (London: Risk Books, 2004).

SIKLOS, P.L., WOHAR, M.E., *Estimating Taylor-Type Rules: An Unbalanced Regression?*, Advances in Econometrics, 20(2), 239–276 (2008).

SINISCALCO, D., *Effetti e tecniche di controllo dei flussi di finanza pubblica in ordine all'andamento del debito con particolare riferimento alla componente non statale*, Audizione alla Commissione Programmazione Economica e Bilancio, Senato della Repubblica (Roma, 24 Marzo 2004a).

SINISCALCO, D., *Effetti e tecniche di controllo dei flussi di finanza pubblica in ordine all'andamento del debito con particolare riferimento alla componente non statale*, Audizione alla Commissione Programmazione Economica e Bilancio, Senato della Repubblica (Roma, 24 Luglio 2004b).

SODERLIND, P., SVENSSON, L., *New Techniques to Extract Market Expectations for Financial Instruments*, CEPR Discussion Paper No. 1556 (1997).

SOROS, G., *On Globalization*, Public Affairs (2002).

SPYROU, S., *Unobservable Information and Behavioural Patterns in Futures Markets: The Case for Brent Crude, Gold and Robusta Coffee Contracts*, Derivatives Use, Trading & Regulation, 12(1–2) (2006).

SRAFFA, P., *Produzione di Merci a Mezzo di Merci* (Torino: Einaudi, 1960).

STIGLER, G.J., *The Theory of Economic Regulation*, Bell Journal of Economics, The RAND Corporation, 2(1), 3–21, Spring (1971).

STIGLITZ, J.E., *Globalization and Its Discontents* (London: Norton, 2002).

STOCK, J.H., WATSON, M.W., *Forecasting Output and Inflation: The Role of Asset Prices*, Journal of Economic Literature, 41(3), 788–829 (2003).

SWAN, E.J., *Building the Global Market: A 4,000-year History of Derivatives* (London: Kluwer Law International, 1999).

TABAK, B.M., *On the Information Content of Oil Future Prices*, Brazilian Journal of Applied Economics, January-March 7(1), 111–31 (2003).

TARASHEV, N., TSATSARONIS, K., KARAMPATOS, D., *Investors' Attitude Toward Risk: What Can We Learn from Options?*, BIS Quarterly Review, June (2003).

TAYLOR, J.B., *Discretion versus Policy Rules in Practice*, Carnegie-Rochester conference series on public policy 39, 195–214 (1993).

THALER, R., *Advances in Behavioural Finance* (New York: Russell Sage Foundation, 1993).

TINER, J., *Principles Based Regulation: The EU Context*, speech at the APCIMS annual conference (Barcelona, 13 October, 2006).

TUCKER, A., *Risk Uncertainty and Monetary Policy Regime*, Bank of England Quarterly Bulletin, Spring, 84–96 (2004).

TRIANA, P., *Smiling at Black-Scholes*, Garp Risk Review, November/December 2006.

TRICHET, J.C., *Money's Vital Role in Monetary Policy*, Financial Times (8 November 2006).

UPPER, C., *Derivatives Activity and Monetary Policy*, BIS Quarterly Review (September 2006).

VAHAMAA, S., *Option Implied Asymmetries in Bond Market Expectations Around Monetary Policy Actions of the ECB*, Journal of Economics and Business, 57(1), 23–38 (2005).

VIOLI, R., *Mercati derivati, controllo monetario e stabilità finanziaria* (Bologna: Il Mulino, 2000).

VOLCKER, P., *Report on Practices and Principles*, Group of Thirty (1993).

VROLIJK, C., *Implications of Derivatives for Monetary Policy*, IMF Working Paper No. 121 (Washington DC, 1997).

WALSH, C., *Monetary Theory and Policy* (Cambridge, US: The MIT Press, 1998).

WARREN, A.C. Jr., *US Income Taxation of New Financial Products*, Journal of Public Economics, 88, 899–923 (2004).

WOLSWIJK, G., DE HAAN, J., *Government Debt Management in Europe: Recent Changes in Debt Managers Strategies*, Public finance and management, 6(2), 244–277 (2006).

WOODFORD, M., *Interest and Prices, Foundation of a Theory of Monetary Policy* (Princeton: Princeton University Press, 2003).

WOODFORD, M., *How Important is Money in the Conduct of Monetary Policy?*, ECB conference paper on "The role of money: money and monetary policy in the twenty-first century" (Frankfurt am Main, November 2006).

YIUMAN, T., *Price discovery and volatility spill-overs in the DJIA index and futures markets*, The Journal of Futures Markets, 19(8), 911–930 (1999).

ZENG, T., *Tax planning using derivatives instruments and firm market valuation under clean market valuation*, PhD dissertation Queen's University 2001, Doctoral Research in Taxation, Journal of the American Taxation Association, Spring, 25(1), 142–3 (2003).

ZENG, T., *Tax Timing Options: Firms Use Derivatives to Save Taxes*, mimeo, Wilfried Laurier University (2004).

ZHANG, I.X., *Economic Consequences of the Sarbanes-Oxley Act of 2002*, Working Paper, Stern NYU, February (2005).

Index

Global Finance Series

Full series list

For Product Safety Concerns and Information please contact our EU
representative GPSR@taylorandfrancis.com
Taylor & Francis Verlag GmbH, Kaufingerstraße 24, 80331 München, Germany

www.ingramcontent.com/pod-product-compliance
Ingram Content Group UK Ltd.
Pitfield, Milton Keynes, MK11 3LW, UK
UKHW021120180425
457613UK00005B/158